21世纪高职高专商务英语规划教材

实用商务英语综合教程（第一册）

（学生用书）

主　　编　肖安法　赵芝英

副主编　袁　萍　唐志华

编　　者　肖安法　赵芝英　袁　萍

唐志华　沈　剑　吕园园

熊　杰

东南大学出版社

·南京·

图书在版编目(CIP)数据

实用商务英语综合教程.第一册/肖安法,赵芝英主编.
南京.东南大学出版社,2008.2
学生用书
ISBN 978-7-5641-1115-1

Ⅰ.实… Ⅱ.①肖… ②赵… Ⅲ.商务—英语—
教材 Ⅳ.H31

中国版本图书馆 CIP 数据核字(2008)第 010381 号

实用商务英语综合教程第一册(学生用书)

出版发行　东南大学出版社　　出版人 江 汉
社　　址　南京市四牌楼 2 号(邮编:210096)
电　　话　(025)83795801(发行部)/83790510(传真)
　　　　　　83374334(邮购)/57711295(发行部传真)

经　　销　全国各地新华书店
印　　刷　南京京新印刷厂
开　　本　700mm×1000mm　1/16
印　　张　14.5
字　　数　285 千字
版　　次　2008 年 2 月第 1 版第 1 次印刷
书　　号　ISBN 978-7-5641-1115-1/H·135
印　　数　1—3000 册
定　　价　20.00 元

总　　序

　　21 世纪是全球经济一体化的时代,给人们带来了更多的机遇与挑战。随着国际经贸方法的更加灵活多样,对外商务联系与交往的日趋频繁以及中国经济融入世界经济的进程越来越快,努力培养和造就一大批具有国际视野、精通经贸业务、熟练掌握外语、能积极有效地参与国际竞争与合作的高素质商务人才已成为非常紧迫的时代课题。

　　高职高专教育是高层次的职业技术教育,是高等教育的一个重要组成部分。如何改革高职高专的商务英语教育机制,加强这一层次的商务英语学科建设、课程体系建设,特别是教材建设,对人才培养具有十分重要的现实意义。为此,东南大学出版社和江苏省几十所高职高专院校联合推出了一整套全新的高职高专商务英语系列教材。该套教材基于继承传统、重在创新的编写理念,以高职高专商务英语基本课程建设为依据,紧紧围绕国际商务的各种主题与实际的业务内容,广泛取材于当代国内外商务活动,材料新颖,内容充实,语言规范,信息量大,体现了知识性、实用性、系统性和技能性的有机结合,从而使学习者既学习国际经贸知识,又掌握当代流行的国际商务英语,注重培养学习者运用商务英语知识与技能从事国际商务工作的实际应用能力。

　　本套系列教材共分三个系列。第一系列为商务英语基础课程教材,包括《实用商务英语综合教程》(1-4 册)、《实用商务英语阅读教程》(1-2 册)、《实用商务英语听说教程》(1-3 册)、《实用商务英语口语教程》(1-2 册)、《实用商务英语函电》、《实用商务英语写作教程》、《实用商务英语谈判与实务》、《实用进出口单证与实务》、《实用国际贸易与实务》、《高职高专实用英语语法》等。今后还将陆续推出第二、三系列教材:商务英语专业核心课程教材和商务英语文化课程教材等。各套教材自成体系,同时又形成一个有机的整体。

　　本套系列教材的编写者都是多年来从事国际商务英语教学和工作的专家、学者和优秀的一线教师,有丰富的教学与实践经验,保证了教材的编写质量,具有一定的指导性与权威性。

　　本套教材的编写一直得到各院校、东南大学出版社的关心和支持,我们在此特致以衷心的感谢。

总主编　程同春教授

2006 年 8 月

21 世纪高职高专商务英语规划教材编委会成员单位

（排名不分先后）

无锡商业职业技术学院	徐州建筑职业技术学院
无锡城市职业技术学院	南京信息职业技术学院
无锡科技职业技术学院	南京理工大学高等职业技术学院
无锡工艺职业技术学院	南京工业职业技术学院
江阴职业技术学院	江苏海事职业技术学院
苏州农业职业技术学院	江苏经贸职业技术学院
苏州托普信息职业技术学院	应天职业技术学院
苏州工业园区职业技术学院	钟山职业技术学院
苏州职业大学	连云港师范专科学校
苏州经贸职业技术学院	连云港职业技术学院
苏州工业职业技术学院	常州纺织职业技术学院
扬州环境资源职业技术学院	常州机电职业技术学院
扬州职业大学	常州轻工职业技术学院
扬州教育学院	南通纺织职业技术学院
扬州工业职业技术学院	南通航运职业技术学院
徐州工业职业技术学院	东南大学出版社

前 言

　　随着经济一体化和市场规范化的步伐加快,全球化进程越来越明显,英语作为国际贸易语言变得越来越重要,既具有专业知识又能熟练运用英语的复合型人才更加受到欢迎。为了适应高职高专教育教学改革的需要,培养大批既具有良好的英语语言能力又熟悉商务知识和商务操作的应用型高技能人才,我们组织编写了《实用商务英语综合教程》。本教材可供高职高专商务英语专业和国际贸易专业教学使用,也可供具有一定英语水平的从事外贸、商务等活动的人员培训及自学使用。

　　《实用商务英语综合教程》编写的基本出发点是把语言能力的培养和商务知识及技能的学习很好的结合。本教程的特点是基础性、实用性、科学性和新颖性等因素的和谐融合。基础性是指教程巩固并拓展学生中学阶段的英语知识和能力,打好语言基础;实用性是指教程紧扣高职高专学生的职业方向;科学性是指吸收先进的教学理念和方法,符合语言学习规律,利用现代信息技术手段,在内容和形式上力求合理呈现,有利于教师使用,有利于学生学习;新颖性是指材料新颖,选取最新的国际商务英语文章,涉及国际商务的基本理论知识、概念,国际上重大的政治、经贸动态、区域经济、外经贸事业在中国的发展,中国的经济改革,传统意义上的国际贸易,多边经贸组织,经济贸易的基本理论,市场经济的运作规律,现代企业的经营管理,国际经贸活动的基本概念与程序,有关的经贸法规、伦理和文化知识等。

　　《实用商务英语综合教程》共计为四册,一学期学习一册,两学年连续使用,各册相互之间为递进关系。本书为第一册,共八个单元和两个测试卷。每单元以模块结构作为呈现方式,具体模块如下:

　　Learning Objectives(教学目标),包括课文涉及的话题,主题性词汇,语法要点等。

　　Pre-reading Activities(阅读前活动),在课文 A 前面有此练习,练

习形式为 Listening Comprehension(听力练习)和 Questions for Discussion(讨论题)。两者都与单元话题有关，目的是启发学生和提高学生的学习兴趣。

Text(课文)，课文有 **Text A** 和 **Text B** 两篇。课文选材应选自国外书刊，内容新颖，话题与商务英语话题有关。课文配有使用英语和中文解释的 Words & Expressions(生词与短语)，并适当做派生词，帮助学生扩充词汇。还有 Notes(注释)，对课文来源、背景知识、专有名词、有关术语和商务知识以及艰深语句等作出解释等。

Word Study, Vocabulary Building and Word Formation(词汇学习、词汇扩展与构词法介绍)，目的是让学习者对词语的用法举一反三，掌握词汇学习的有效方法，增强自学能力，熟悉更多的商务英语词汇和构词法，以便有效快速地扩大词汇量。

Post-reading Activities(阅读后活动)，课文 A 后有 4 项练习，其形式为：1. 阅读理解，由浅入深，反映课文概貌，有助于学生理解课文；2. 选词填空，全部为课文中出现过的词和短语，进一步帮助学生加深对课文的理解；3. 大意归纳，再次检验和强化学生对课文的理解；4. 翻译练习，巩固课文 A 所学的词汇和句型。课文 B 后练习形式为：1. 正误判断，检查学生对课文的理解；2. 选词填空，巩固课文中出现过的词和短语；3. 听写，为可文 B 的大意，既练习听力理解又帮助课文理解。

Exercises(单元独立练习)，其形式为：Structures(句法结构)，Vocabulary(词汇)，Translation(句子翻译)，Cloze(完形填空)，Reading Comprehension(短文阅读)，Writing(写作)，Presentation(Speaking)(口头发言)，Enjoy Your Time(快乐时光)等。练习形式多样，对语言基本功进行深入、系统的训练，从听、说、读、写、译及文化等方面提高学习者的能力。

教材后附录 Vocabulary, Useful Expressions 和 Word Study，便于学习者查找。

本册教材由肖安法和赵芝英担任主编，袁萍、唐志华担任副主编，编者有沈剑、吕园园和熊杰。肖安法负责制定编写大纲。第 1 单元编写、附录编写和统稿工作，赵芝英负责第 6 单元编写和统稿工作，袁萍负责第 2 单元、第 5 单元和测试试卷 1 的编写，唐志华负责第 4 单元编写，沈剑负责第 7 单元和测试试卷 2 的编写，吕园园负责第 8 单元和测试试卷 2 的编写，熊杰负责第 3 单元编写。

本册教材教师用书分别由各单元编写者编写。在教学过程中，教师不必拘泥于教师用书，可以有选择地加以利用。我们主张采用折衷主义的教学方法，在充分发挥教师主导作用的同时，提倡学生自主学习，教师在备课时应针对每个单元甚至整本教材和单元之间的衔接通盘考虑，采用交互式教学方式，如 pair work，team work，group discussion，presentation，debate 等，或采用基于任务的方式进行教学。

建议每两周(8－12 课时)完成一个单元的教学，在听、说、读、写、译、文化等方面全面提高学生的语言能力和商务知识。本教材配有多媒体光盘和录音磁带。

在本教材编写过程中,我们得到了东南大学出版社的很多支持和帮助,在此,我们致以衷心的感谢。

由于编者水平有限,书中不妥之处在所难免,敬请广大读者批评指正。

编者

2006 年 8 月

目录

Contents

Unit 1

The Nature of International Business

Learning Objectives

In this unit you will ◆ understand the nature of international business;

◆ know the reason of learning international business;

◆ and review the grammar item: subject-predicate concord(主谓一致).

Pre-reading Activities

New Words: personnel   manufacturing   finance   diverse   entertaining   marketing

Ⅰ. **Listen to the following short passage twice and fill in the blanks with the words you've heard.**

English language ___1___ are important in today's global environment. A personnel or training ___2___ would send their employees on Business English courses which can impact directly on the performance of their ___3___, their personnel team, and their success. An ___4___ may take a Business English course helping improve his or her own job performance and help build a successful future ___5___.

The business world—manufacturing, ___6___, finance, and services—is very diverse. However, job functions within different organizations are often very ___7___. A good Business English course takes ___8___ of these similarities, helps you tailor them for your particular professional needs, changes your "everyday" English into language

_9_ for business situations, and builds your confidence _10_ you use business English.

Ⅱ. **Which topics are you interested in? Choose from the list below, discuss with your classmates and tell why.**

Travel ☐   Entertaining ☐   Sales and marketing ☐

International trade ☐   Recent business news ☐

Text A

International Business

International business consists of transactions that are planned and carried out across national borders to satisfy the objectives of individuals and organizations. These transactions take on various forms. Primary types of international business are export-import trade and direct foreign investment. The latter is carried out in varied forms, including wholly owned branch companies and joint ventures. Examples of such transactions include buying raw materials or inputs in one country and shipping them to another for retail sale, building a plant in a foreign country or making use of lower labor costs there, or borrowing money from a bank in one country to finance operations in another.

International business is important and necessary because economic isolationism has become impossible. Failure to become a part of the world market causes the declining economic influence of a nation and a falling standard of living for its citizens. Successful participation in international business, however, holds the promise of improved quality of life and a better society, even leading, some believe, to a more peaceful world.

International business differs from domestic business to a great extent for the following reasons. The countries involved may use different currencies, forcing at least one party to change its currency to another. The law systems may also be different, and the parties involved have to adjust their behavior to obey the local law. The different legal systems may create major headaches for international managers. For example: U. S. law promotes equal employment opportunities for women, while Saudi Arabian law discourages the employment of women when they will have to interact with adult males to whom they are not related. The cultures may differ. For example, U. S. businesspeople prefer to start meetings on time and to get down to specific things quickly, but Latin American businesspeople are less concerned about a quick action and more concerned with learning more about the people with whom they are doing business. Different countries may have different resources. One country may be rich in natural resources but poor in skilled labor, while another may enjoy a productive, well-trained work force but lack natural resources.

International business offers companies new markets. Since the 1950s, the growth of international trade and investment has been much larger than the growth of domestic economies. Today's technology continues to increase the reach and the easiness of doing international business, pointing to even larger growth potential in the future. A combination of domestic and international business, therefore, presents more opportunities for expansion, growth, and income than does domestic business alone. International business causes the flow of ideas, services, and money across the world. As a result, innovations can be developed and spread more rapidly, human capital can be used better, and financing can take place more quickly. International business also offers consumers new choices. It offers a wider variety of products, both in terms of quantity and quality, and does so at reduced prices through international competition. International business helps the change of factors of production—except land—and provides challenging employment opportunities to individuals with professional and business skills. Therefore, both as an opportunity and a challenge, international business is very important to countries, companies, and individuals.

In most cases the basic skills and knowledge needed to be successful are much similar whether one is doing business domestically or internationally. For instance, the need for marketing managers to analyze the wants and desires of target audiences is the same regardless of whether the managers are engaged in international business or purely domestic business. But although international and domestic business are similar to some degree, there is little doubt that the complexity of skills and knowledge needed for success is far greater for international business. International business people must be knowledgeable about cultural, legal, political, and social differences among countries. They must choose the countries in which to sell their goods and from which to buy inputs.

Words & Expressions

1. transaction /træn'zækʃən/ n. a single business deal, esp. a sale or purchase
   生意;交易
2. border /bɔːdə/ n. the dividing line between two countries; the land near the

line 边界(线)

3. objective/əb'dʒektiv/*n.* an object to be won; purpose of a plan 目标

4. resource/ri'sɔːs/*n.* things owned and useful; possessions [常用复数]资源；财力；物力

5. primary/'praiməri/*a.* chief; main 主要的

6. investment/in'vestmənt/*n.* the act or action of investing 投资

7. joint venture/dʒɔint'ventʃə/*n.* a partnership formed often to share risk or expertise 合资企业

8. retail/riː'teil/*n.* the sale of goods to the general public 零售 *a.* selling to the public 零售的 c. f. wholesale 批发

9. finance *n.* /'fainæns, fi'næns/*v.* to provide or arrange means of payment 提供资金；金融支持 *n.* the management of money matters 金融；财政

10. isolationism/ˌaisə'leiʃənizəm/*n.* [贬] 孤立主义 isolate *v.* isolation *n.*

11. participation/pɑːˌtisi'peiʃn/*n.* the act of taking part or have a share in an activity or event 参与；参加 participate *v.*

12. inputs/'inputs/*n.* factors of production put into a business [复数] 投入(物) c. f. outputs 产出

13. domestic/də'mestik/*adj.* of the home; of one's own country；家庭的；国内的

14. currency/'kʌrənsi/*n.* any kind of money that is in general use as a medium of exchange, esp. circulating paper money 货币

15. adjust/ə'dʒʌst/*v.* to change to make suitable for a particular job or a new condition 调整；调节

16. promote/prə'məut/*v.* help to happen, increase, or spread 促进；提升；推销 promotion *n.*

17. Saudi Arabia/'sɑ'udiəreibjə/*n.* 沙特阿拉伯

18. lack/læk/*v.* to be without; not have 缺乏

19. potential/pə'tenʃəl/*n.* possibility for developing or being developed 潜力 *adj.* 有潜力的

20. combination/ˌkɔmbi'neiʃən/*n.* the act or state of combining or being combined 联合；结合 combine *v.*

21. expansion/iks'pænʃən/*n.* the action of expanding; the state of being expanded 扩张；扩大 expand *v.*

22. innovation/ˌinəu'veiʃən/*n.* the introduction of something new; a new idea, method, or invention 发明；创新

23. quantity/'kwɔntiti/*n.* a measurable property of something; an amount or number 数量

24. variety/və'raiəti/*n.* a group containing different sorts of the same thing or people 种种

25. factor/'fæktə/*n.* any of the forces, conditions or influences that helps to bring about a result 因素

26. analyze/'ænəlaiz/*v.* to examine carefully in order to find out about 分析 analysis *n.*

27. target audience/'tɑːgit'ɔːdjəns/*n.* 目标受众

28. complexity/kəm'pleksiti/*n.* (an example of) the state of being complex 复杂

29. carry out/'kæriaut/to fulfill; complete 执行;落实;实现

30. take on/teikɔn/to begin to have a quality or appearance 呈现;具有(⋯⋯特征)

31. interact with/ˌintər'ækt wið/react together and affect each other's development or nature 相互作用;相互影响

32. be concerned about/biːkən'səːnd ə'baut/be worried about 担心 give attention to something 考虑;关注

33. in terms of/in təːmz əv/considering 在⋯⋯方面 with a certain mode of expression 用⋯⋯的话

Notes

1. This text is selected and adapted from *International Business* written by Ricky W. Griffin and Michael W. Pustay.

2. international business ① (国际商务):A term used to collectively describe topics relating to the operations of companies with interests in several countries. Such companies are sometimes called multinational corporations(跨国公司). Points of discussion with this topic may include cultural considerations, which itself may include differences in law and legal systems, language barriers, living standards, climate and more. These have to be overcomed for a multinational corporation to be successful in an overseas venture. ② (国际性企业)A business that is primarily based in a single country but acquires some meaningful share of its resources or revenues (or both) from other countries.

3. joint venture(合资企业):A special type of strategic alliance when the partners share in the ownership of an operation on an equity basis.

4. isolationism（孤立主义）: A diplomatic policy whereby a nation seeks to avoid alliances with other nations. Most nations are not in a political position to maintain strict isolationist policies for extended periods of time, even though most nations have historical periods where isolationism was popular.

5. currency（货币）: A currency is a unit of exchange, facilitating the transfer of goods and services. It is a form of money, where money is defined as a medium of exchange.

6. Saudi Arabia（沙特阿拉伯）: The full name for it is the Kingdom of Saudi Arabia, the largest country on the Arabian Peninsula（阿拉伯半岛）, with its capital named as Riyadh（利雅德）. It is called "the land of the two holy mosques", a reference to Mecca（麦加）and Medina（麦地那）, Islam's two holiest places.

7. target audience（目标受众）: A specified audience or a group of people for which an advertising message is designed.

8. Successful participation in international business, however, holds the promise of improved quality of life and a better society, even leading, some believe, to a more peaceful world. 这句中的 even leading to a more peaceful world 为主语 successful participation in international business 的补语,说明主语的行为。some believe 为插入语,它将 even leading to a more peaceful world 分隔开来,形成了分隔现象。

Word Study

1. finance

v. to provide money for 为……提供资金

The concert is financed by a big company.

音乐会是由一家大公司资助的。

Sam financed his study at a vocational school by working all summer.

山姆一个夏天都在打工以补贴职业学校学习的费用。

n. ①（the science of）the control of money 财政;金融

public finance 公共财政;财政学; business（company, private）finance 商业（公司,私人）财务

②［复数］the amount of money owned especially by an organization 资金;财务状况

Are the company's finances sound?

公司的财务状况良好吗?

The company's finances are very limited.

公司的资金很有限。

2. adjust *v.*

① to make small changes to something to make it more effective 调整;调节

I must adjust my watch, it's slow.

我的表慢了,要调一下了。

to adjust the price to... 将价格调整到······

② to gradually get used to a new situation by making small changes 使适合;适应

He adjusted himself very quickly to the heat of the African country.

他很快适应了这个非洲国家的炎热气候。

3. promote *v.*

① to advance someone in position or rank 提升;提职

Helen was promoted to general manager.

海伦被提拔为总经理。

You will get promoted in this company if you work hard.

如果工作努力,你在这个公司会升职。

② to help something to develop and be successful 促进;增进

The meeting is to promote trade between China and Australia.

会议是为了促进中国与澳大利亚之间的贸易。

③ to bring goods to public notice in order to increase sales 促销;推销

The company are promoting their new sort of medicine on television.

公司通过电视促销新药。

How can we promote the sales of this product?

我们如何才能促进该产品的销售呢?

④ to be responsible for arranging a large public event 主办;筹办

Who is promoting the football match between the two colleges?

谁主办了这两所大学之间的足球赛?

4. lack *v.*

① to be without; not have 缺乏

We lacked food.

我们缺乏食物。

Tom's real problem is that he lacks confidence.

汤姆的真正问题是缺乏自信。

② lack for nothing—to have everything that a person needs 应有尽有

Smith's parents made sure that he lacked for nothing.

史密斯的父母让他什么都不缺。

n. ① the state of not having something or not having enough of it 缺乏

Lack of vitamin C can cause diseases.

缺乏维生素 C 会生病。

a lack of care, money, water, etc.

② a complete lack of 完全缺乏

Rosie was showing a complete lack of interest in her school work.

罗西对学习一点也不感兴趣。

③ for/through lack of—because there is a lack of 由于缺乏

The worker felt very tired for/through lack of sleep.

由于缺少睡眠,这位工人感到很困。

5. interact *vi.*

① to have an effect on each other 相互作用;相互影响

Social and economic factors interacting with each other produce certain results.

社会和经济因素的相互作用会产生一定的结果。

The two ideas interacted, which changed our point of view.

这两种观念相互影响,改变了我们的观点。

② to talk to each other and understand each other 相互交流,相处

The student from England interacts well with his classmates.

来自英国的这个学生和他的同学们相处得很好。

Post-reading Activities

Ⅰ. **Comprehension Questions.**

1. What is the definition to international business according to the passage?

2. Could you give some examples of international transactions?

3. How many reasons are mentioned in the passage that international business is different from domestic business? What are they?

4. What should a company do if it wants to expand itself and grow larger?

5. How international business people should be to be successful?

Ⅱ. **Fill in the blanks with the words or phrases given in the box. Change the forms if necessary.**

participation	expansion	competition	domestic
potential	be related	a variety of	lead to
as a result	in most cases		

1. The company's _____ into Asia was a failure because of careless planning.
2. The increasing global _____ is one of the reasons that many companies seek international business.
3. China is moving from planned economy to market economy. _____, China will see great changes in its economy.
4. He is not a good salesman. _____, he did not know how to decide a reasonable price for his products.
5. There is a _____ market for our new product in France as its design is so popular among young French people.
6. Today's companies offer consumers _____ wider _____ product choices and places to buy.
7. The workers wanted more direct _____ in the management of the business and its profit.
8. The sense of success _____ closely _____ to material achievement.
9. International business has increased rapidly in recent years, _____ the fast growth of China's economy.
10. We did badly in the European market so at last we decided to concentrate on the large _____ market.

Ⅲ. **Fill in the blanks with suitable words to complete the summary of the text.**

The author first tells us _____ is international business. International business is _____ that involve two or more countries. These transactions take on various _____. The author also points out the _____ and necessity of international business. Then the author lists four _____ to tell the _____ between international business and _____ business. The author next explains the reasons that _____ engage in international business. At the _____ of the text the author tells us how to be _____ international businesspeople.

Ⅳ. **Translate the following sentences into English.**

1. 国际间的交易是通过银行体系(banking system)来实现的。(carry out)
2. 英语使得来自不同国家的人们能够交往。(interact with)
3. 居民们希望得到更多更低价的商品(goods)和服务。(a variety of)
4. 我们应该调整价格以满足普通消费者(consumer)的需要。(adjust...to...)

5. 国际法和国内法由于以下原因是很不相同的。(differ from, to a great extent)

Text B

Why Study International Business?

There are many different reasons why students today choose to study international business. First, almost any large organization people work for will have international operations or be affected by the global economy. People need to understand this increasingly important area in order to better assess career opportunities and to interact effectively with other managers. For example, as part of your first job task, you could be part of a project team that includes members from different countries. A basic grasp of international business would help you to understand more fully why this team was formed, what the company expects it to achieve, and how you might most effectively interact with your colleagues.

Small businesses are also becoming more involved in international business. If after graduation you plan to start your own business, you may find yourself using foreign-made materials or equipment, competing with foreign firms, and perhaps even selling in foreign markets. For example, a small U. S. firm may buy raw materials from a German company, communications equipment from a Canadian company, office equipment from a Japanese company, manufacturing equipment from a Korean company.

You also need to study international business because you may finally work for a firm that is owned by a corporation headquartered in another country. A total of 4. 9 million U. S. citizens work for U. S. branch company of foreign-owned corporations.

Still another reason for you to study international business is to keep pace with your future competitors. Business students in Europe have traditionally learned multiple languages, traveled widely, and had job experiences in different countries. And more European universities are launching business programs, many of which require students to spend one or more semesters in different countries. Japanese students, too, are actively working to learn more about foreign markets and cultures, especially those of the North American and European countries. These students will soon be in direct competition with you. You need to ensure that your global skills and knowledge will aid your career.

You also need to study international business in order to stay abreast of the latest business techniques and tools, many of which are developed outside your own country.

For example, Japanese firms have been the first to use inventory management techniques such as just-in-time systems under which suppliers are expected to deliver necessary inputs just as they are needed.

Finally, you need to study international business to know different cultures. As global cultures and political systems become even more joined together, understanding and appreciating the similarities and differences of the world's peoples will become increasingly important. You will more often encounter colleagues, customers, suppliers, and competitors from different countries and cultural backgrounds. Knowing something about how and where their countries and companies fit into the global economy can help you earn their respect and confidence as well as give you a competitive advantage in dealing with them. If you know little or nothing about the rest of the world, you may be considered as provincial, arrogant, or simply absurd. And this holds true regardless of whether you are a manager, a consumer, or just an observer of world events.

Words & Expressions

1. affect/əˈfekt/*v.* to cause some result or change in; influence 影响
2. assess/əˈses/*v.* to judge the quality or worth of 评估;评价
3. colleague/ˈkɔliːg/*n.* a fellow worker 同行;同事
4. equipment/iˈkwipmənt/*n.* things needed for a purpose 设备;设施
5. raw material/rɔːməˈtiəriəl/*n.* the natural substance from which an article is made [常用复数] 原材料
6. manufacture/ˌmænjuˈfæktʃə/*v.* to make or produce by machinery in large quantities 制造
7. Korean/kəˈriən/*a.* 韩国的;韩国语的;韩国人的
8. corporation/ˌkɔːpəˈreiʃən/*n.* company 公司
9. headquarters/ˈhedˈkwɔːtəz/*n.* head office; the chief or central office of a business organization [常用复数]总部;总公司
10. multiple/ˈmʌltipl/*adj.* including many different parts, types, etc. 多种的;多样的
11. semester/siˈmestə/*n.* a term; either of the two periods of a school year 学期
12. ensure/inˈʃuə/*v.* to make something certain to happen 保证
13. global/ˈgləubl/*adj.* concerning or including the whole world 全球的 globe *n.*

14. technique/tek'ni:k/*n.* a method, manner or skill in doing something 技巧；工艺

15. inventory/'invəntri/*n.* a detailed list of things 存货；库存

16. deliver/di'livə/*v.* to send something to the intended place 交付；送（货）

17. appreciate/ə'pri:ʃieit/*v.* to understand fully 理解

18. similarity/ˌsimi'læriti/*n.* the quality of being alike 相似性

19. provincial/prə'vinʃəl/*adj.* old-fashioned；narrow-minded ［贬］土气的；偏狭的

20. arrogant/'ærəgənt/*adj.* too proud and self-important ［贬］傲慢的

21. keep pace with/ki:p peis wið/to go forward at the same rate as 与……齐步；跟上

22. stay abreast of/stei ə'brest əv/to know all the time the most recent facts about something 了解（最新的情况）；跟上 keep/be abreast of

23. regardless of/ri'gɑ:dlis əv/careless of；without worrying about 不顾；不管

Notes

1. This text is also selected and adapted from *International Business* by Ricky W. Griffin and Michael W. Pustay.

2. inventory management（库存管理）：A term used to refer to the direction and control of activities with the purpose of getting the right inventory in the right place at the right time in the right quantity in the right form at the right cost.

3. just-in-time systems（及时盘存控制存货的生产制度）：Or JIT, a management philosophy aimed at eliminating manufacturing wastes by producing only the right amount and combination of parts at the right place at the right time. JIT finds its origin in Japan, where it has been in practice since the early 1970's. It was developed and perfected by Taiichi Ohno of Toyota, who is now referred to as the father of JIT.

Word Study

1. affect *vt.*

① to do something that produces and effects or changes in somebody or something 影响

The quality of the products would not be much affected if the process of production is under careful control.

如果生产过程得到严格控制，那么产品的质量就不会受到影响。

How will the tax affect people on low incomes?

税收对低收入者有什么影响?

② (usually passive)to make someone feel strong emotions 感染;使……感动

The audience was deeply affected by the president's speech.

听众被主席的讲话所深深打动。

Pictures displayed with music affect people very strongly.

配有音乐的画面能深深打动人们。

③ to pretend to have a particular feeling, way of speaking, etc. 假装

He affected ignorance of the law.

他假装不懂法律。

His secretary affected not to hear him.

他的秘书装着没听见他。

2. assess *vt.*

① to make a judgment about a person or situation after thinking carefully about it 评价;评定

It's very difficult to assess the present state of the economy.

很难对当前的经济形势做出评价。

We've tried to assess what went wrong.

我们尽力找出错误。

② to calculate the value or cost of something 估价;估计

assess something at

They assessed the value of the house at over $ 50,000.

他们估计此房值五万多美元。

The damage was assessed at about $ 2,500.

估计损失为2,500美元。

3. ensure *vt.* to make it certain that something will happen 保证;确保

to ensure something/that-clause

All the necessary steps had been taken to ensure their safety.

采取了所有的措施,以确保他们的安全。

His wife ensured that he took all his pills every day.

他妻子确保他每天都服药。

The seller cannot ensure that the shipment will be completed in time.

卖方不能保证及时装运。

to ensure delivery 保证交货

4. launch *v.*

① to cause (an activity, plan, way of life, etc.)to begin 发动；发起

The soldiers launched a fierce attack upon the enemy.

士兵们对敌人发起了猛烈的进攻。

The government launched a mass movement against stealing.

政府开展了反盗窃的群众运动。

to launch an enterprise/a new business 开办企业/新商行

② to make a new product,book, etc. available for sale for the first time 推出；发行

The party was held to launch her new novel.

举办此晚会是为了推出她的新小说。

The company is spending thousands of dollars launching a new brand of soap.

公司花了数千元来推出一款肥皂。

③ to launch a boat to set a boat into water 使船下水

n. 推出；发行；(产品)首次投放市场

the launch of a new car 新车面市

The launch of the new model has been put back three months.

新款的面市推迟了三个月。

5. appreciate *vt.*

① to understand how good or useful someone or something is 欣赏；赏识

Her abilities are not fully appreciated by her employer.

她的才能没有完全受到老板的赏识。

A sensitive mouth is necessary to appreciate good wine.

鉴赏好酒需要敏感的味觉。

② to be thankful or grateful for 感激

I would appreciate it if you would turn the music down.

如果你把音乐放小点声,我将深表感激。

I appreciate your help.

感谢你的帮助。

③ to understand fully 充分理解；明白

I don't think you appreciate the dangers of this job.

我认为你不了解此工作的危险性。

I don't think you appreciate the difficulties his absence will cause.

我认为你不明白他的缺席会带来的困难。

④ to increase in value 增值

Most investments are expected to appreciate at a steady rate.

Vocabulary Building

multinational business/enterprise/corporation 跨国企业

global business 全球企业

wholly foreign venture 外国独资经营企业

mixed venture 政府参与投资的合资企业

parent company/firm 母公司；总公司

subsidiary/affiliate firm 子公司；分公司

business behavior 企业(营业)行为

business risk 企业(经营)风险　　business rivalry 商业竞争

market economy 市场经济　　　　market share 市场份额

market potential 市场潜力　　　　market price 市场价格

market research 市场调查　　　　money market 货币市场

futures market 期货市场　　　　　securities market 证券市场

stock market 股票市场　　　　　　economic community 经济共同体

Word Formation：Negative Prefixes and Reversative Prefixes(否定和逆转前缀)

Negative Prefixes	Meaning	Added to	Examples	Illustrative Sentences
un-	the opposite of, not	adjectives, participles, adverbs, nouns, verbs	unconscious, unfair, unrest, unmanageable, unfruitful, unlikely, unexpected, unlisted,	The city's traffic problems will soon become unmanageable.
non-	not	adjectives, nouns	non-existent, nonproductive, non-smoker, nonstop	We must reduce our nonproductive spending.
in-, il-, im-, ir-	the opposite of, not	adjectives	indirect, illogical, illegal, impossible, irresponsible, irregular	The procedure is highly irregular.

（续表）

Negative Prefixes	Meaning	Added to	Examples	Illustrative Sentences
dis-	the opposite of, not	adjectives, verbs, nouns	dishonest, disobedient, disagree, disobey, displeasure, disorder, disadvantage	The price has declined, putting us at a disadvantage.
a-	lacking in, lack of	adjectives, nouns	apolitical, atypical, asexual, amoral, apathy	Don't discuss politics with him. He is apolitical.

Reversative Prefixes	Meaning	Added to	Examples	Illustrative Sentences
un-	to reverse the action, to deprive of, to release from	verbs, nouns	untie, unpack, undo, undress, unhorse, unman	We unpacked the goods at once and examined them carefully.
de-	to reverse the action, to get rid of	verbs, nouns	defrost, decode, demonopolize, denationalize, decentralize, decentralization	The government has denationalized the steel industry.
dis-	to reverse the action, to deprive of, to release from	verbs, participles, nouns	disconnect, discontinue, disown, discolored, disheartening, discontent, disbenefit	Your failure to open L/C in time will be of disbenefit to our future business.

Post-reading Activities

I. True or false questions.

1. Six reasons for students' learning international business are discussed in the text.

2. If you work in a small company you need not study international business for your company has no opportunity to get involved in international business.

3. According to the passage a total of 4.9 million U. S. citizens work in foreign

countries for foreign-owned companies.

4. International business helps you to compete with your future competitors and to be in an advantageous position.

5. International business also helps you to get familiar with the latest business techniques and tools.

6. According to the passage culture is of great importance in international business.

II. **Fill in the blanks with the words or phrases given in the box. Change the forms if necessary.**

| affect | keep pace with | launch | regardless of |
| a total of | a grasp of | involve | in order to |

1. Visible trade(有形贸易) _____ the import and export of goods while invisible trade(无形贸易) includes the exchange of services.

2. Any country which fails to _____ these developments will soon be in trouble.

3. The company _____ a new product three days ago and it sold well.

4. The Chinese manager communicated well with the English businessman for he had _____ good _____ English.

5. _____ US $ 2,000 was paid for the computer imported from Japan.

6. _____ win the election again the president made some changes in his economic policy.

7. The advance of technology continues _____ international business.

8. The general manager bought his wife a new car _____ the expenses.

III. **Dictation.**

Exercises

I. **Structures：Subject-predicate Concord**

一致关系是指句子成分之间在人称、数、性等方面保持一致。英语中最主要的一致关系是主语和谓语动词之间的一致,即主谓一致。主谓一致一般遵循如下原则:语法一致原则、意义一致原则和就近原则。

The subject of a sentence should agree with its predicate in number. This rule is called the principle of subject-predicate concord. Subject-predicate concord should follow the three principles：grammatical concord，notional concord(意义一致)，and concord of proximity(就近原则).

Generally speaking, grammatical concord is that the verb matches its subject in number. The most important type of concord in English is concord of the 3rd person number between subject and predicate. Usually, a singular subject requires a singular verb, while a plural subject requires a plural verb. For example: My son has no intention of spending a vacation with me. Two letters have been sent to every applicant. Difficulties over concord may arise through occasional conflict between the principle of grammatical concord and the principles of notional concord and of proximity.

Notional concord is agreement of verb with subject according to the notion of number rather than the actual presence of the grammatical marker for that notion. For example, collective nouns such as "government" in British English are often treated as notionally plural: The government have broken all their promises.

The principle of proximity, also termed "attraction", denotes agreement of the verb with a closely preceding noun phrase in preference to agreement with the head of the noun phrase that functions as subject. For example: A year and a half has passed since we last met. Not only the students but also the teacher is enjoying the movie.

Study the following examples and do the exercises afterwards.

Examples:

1. A number of students are majoring in business English.

2. The number of failures in the examination is surprisingly large.

3. General Motors, a huge automobile company, makes thousands of cars each month.

4. Using familiar words means using the language that most of us use in everyday conversation.

Exercises:

1. Ten thousand dollars _____ (be) a large sum of money.

2. Each president and chairman _____ (invite) to the meeting yesterday.

3. Much of Africa's economy _____ (depend) on its natural resources.

4. Chinese and Japanese silk _____ (be) of good quality.

5. The factory, with all its equipment, _____ (burn) in the fire the day before yesterday.

6. Gold, as well as silver, _____ recently _____ (rise) in price.

7. The United Nations _____ (form) in 1945.

8. To become an actress _____ (be) her dream.

9. Every male and female employee in the same position _____ (pay) the same

in the corporation.

10. Not only the students but also the teacher _____ (know) something about business principles.

II. Vocabulary

appreciate	ensure		technique	stay abreast of	interact
carry out	be concerned about	take on	quantity		promote

1. When the word appears in this context, it _____ a different meaning.

2. He is a basketball player with good _____.

3. Political and social factors often _____ with each other.

4. The government could do more _____ the economic growth.

5. It's a lot cheaper if you buy the pens in _____.

6. I will try _____ that your stay here is pleasant.

7. A good manager has _____ the latest developments in his industry.

8. We would much _____ the help from a professor.

9. You will succeed if you _____ the plan you've made for your study.

10. The letter says that your mother _____ very _____ your health.

III. Word Formation

Fill in the blanks with the proper forms of the words given in the parentheses.

1. If you work in our company, you will have more chances of _____ (promote).

2. Everyone seeks success in their career, but it is difficult to _____ (combination) family life with career.

3. The information industry is an _____ (expansion) industry that is increasing in size and output.

4. The _____ (analyze) of the food showed the presence of poison(毒物).

5. Dozens of _____ (competition) are applying for the position of sales manager.

6. There is much _____ (similar) between men and women. For example, they both want to do a good job, a creative job.

7. Today's marketplace is becoming more and more _____ (globe) because of information technology.

8. Tomorrow's market leaders will be companies who can effectively deal with the _____ (complex) of the changing business situations.

9. The _____ (participate) in international business allows corporations to

achieve more successes that cannot be achieved in domestic markets.

10. There were _____ (variety) questions he wanted to ask when he met a foreign teacher for the first time.

IV. Translation

1. 她很快适应了北方的寒冬。(adjust. . . to. . .)
2. 很多中国人今天在学英语,原因各异。(reasons why)
3. 在电视上推销某一产品是最好的方法之一。(promote).
4. 大多数情况下他的想法和我的是相似的。(in most cases,similar)
5. 就速度而言飞机比火车快得多。(in terms of)
6. 如果你参与了这项犯罪你就会受到惩罚。(be involved in)
7. 这家公司花了两年时间推出了一款新车。(launch)
8. 很多人都想成为电影明星、歌手、作家诸如此类的名人。(such as)
9. 如果你们停止制造噪音,我将不胜感激。(appreciate)
10. 熟练的掌握英语能让你有更多成功的机会。(a grasp of)

V. Cloze

Calvin Klein is the president of the firm, Nature of Business, which helps individuals and companies use the __1__ of nature to __2__ success. He thinks __3__ happens when we live according to those principles and laws.

Today's business world is mostly market-driven. Companies look outward to see where the opportunities are and then make the necessary changes to __4__ after those opportunities. "That's not what happens __5__ nature," Klein points __6__. "Don't look outward to find what you can get. Look __7__ to discover what you have to give."

Apple Computers is one of many examples. Apple has always been about great design and putting that design to __8__ in education. A while ago, Apple's leaders decided they wanted to build big computers and servers and compete __9__ companies like IBM. That decision almost __10__ their complete failure. They finally decided to go back to __11__ they really were, and they became successful again.

Our true natures show up in two ways: in our passions and in our natural abilities, that is, talents. If you have a natural talent __12__ something, you can do it happily, successfully, and return to it over and over again __13__ getting sick of it. You tend to lose your __14__ of time when you do it.

Everyone has a natural talent. It's a natural law. If they think they don't have one, they just haven't __15__ it yet.

1. A. principles   B. theories   C. ideas   D. discoveries

2. A. finish   B. achieve   C. create   D. discover

3. A. failure   B. defeat   C. success   D. achievements

4. A. look   B. obtain   C. get   D. go

5. A. on   B. in   C. inside   D. into

6. A. forward   B. to   C. out   D. at

7. A. inward   B. outward   C. inside   D. into

8. A. useful   B. used   C. use   D. useless

9. A. to   B. in   C. over   D. with

10. A. led   B. resulted   C. wasted   D. caused

11. A. what   B. why   C. how   D. which

12. A. of   B. for   C. on   D. with

13. A. with   B. but   C. without   D. except

14. A. sense   B. content   C. feeling   D. consideration

15. A. invented   B. discovered   C. recovered   D. required

VI. Reading Comprehension

The buying and selling of goods and services across national borders is known as international trade. International trade is the <u>backbone</u> of our modern, commercial world, as producers in various nations try to profit from an expanded market. Many factors lead to international trade, including lower production costs, specialized industries, different natural resources and consumer tastes.

One of the factors that promote international trade today is the lower production costs of "developing" nations. There is currently a great deal of concern over jobs being taken away from the United States, member countries of the European Union and other "developed" nations as countries, such as China, Korea, India and others, produce goods and services at much lower costs.

Even though many consumers prefer to buy less expensive goods, some international trade develops because of a specialized industry that has developed due to national talent and/or tradition. <u>Swiss watches, for example, will never be price-competitive with mass produced watches from Asia.</u> Scottish wool, fine French silks and other such products always find their way onto the international trade scene.

One of the biggest parts of international trade is oil. Total net oil imports in 2005 are over 26 million barrels per day. The natural resources of those nations, mostly the nations of OPEC, the Organization of Petroleum Exporting Countries, are swept onto the international trade scene, and consumer nations continue to absorb this flow. Diamonds from Africa, wheat and other agricultural products from the United States and Australia, coal and steel from Canada and Russia, all flow across borders from these nations to the nations that lack these natural resources.

1. The underlined word "backbone" in the first paragraph means " _____ ".
   A. chief support   B. strength
   C. firmness   D. main bone

2. _____ is not one of the goods which are produced by specialized industries according to the passage.
   A. Swiss watch   B. Scottish wool
   C. Canadian coal   D. French silk

3. According to the passage the lower production costs of "developing" nations may cause _____ .
   A. more and more unemployment in the developing countries
   B. more and more factories and plants built up in the developed countries
   C. more and more unemployment in the developed countries
   D. more and more workers of developing countries to work in the developed countries

4. The sentence in the third paragraph "Swiss watches, for example, will never be price-competitive with mass produced watches from Asia" means that " _____ ".
   A. the mass produced watches from Asia are very popular in the developed countries
   B. the mass produced watches from Asia cannot be compared with Swiss watches
   C. Swiss watches are made with more expensive materials
   D. Swiss watches are much more expensive than those produced from Asia

5. The passage seems to tell us _____ .
   A. how international trade develops
   B. what contributes to the development of international trade
   C. why international trade is different from domestic trade
   D. that we cannot live without international trade

VII. Writing

(I) Writing Basics: Types of Sentences According to Structures

A sentence is a complete, independent unit of thought made up of a group of words. Sentences can be classified from different angles, for example, from the angles of grammar/structure, function, or rhetoric.

Grammatically, sentences are classified into four categories on the basis of the clauses they contain. They are simple, compound, complex and compound-complex sentences.

A simple sentence is one that consists of a single independent clause. For example: The storm is over.

A compound sentence consists of two or more independent clauses with no dependent clauses. For example: The storm is over, but the ground is still wet.

A complex sentence consists of one independent clause and one or more dependent clauses. For example: Although the storm is over, the ground is still wet.

A compound-complex sentence is both compound and complex; it consists of two or more independent clauses. For example: Although the storm is over, the ground is still wet; we can not go for a walk.

Each kind of sentence has its own advantages. Generally speaking, a simple sentence gives prominence to the idea expressed; a compound sentence conveys the equal importance of the ideas stated in the independent clauses that compose it; a complex sentence reveals various relationships between the ideas expressed by the clauses; and the compound-complex sentence reflects the complexity of the matter.

Now, rewrite the following by combining the short sentences into compound or complex sentences by using conjunctions or punctuation.

1. Most of his movies are liked by the audience. Most of his movies are ignored by critics.

2. Mr. Howe owned a plant. He came to ask me to help him with his work.

3. I was watching TV. Someone knocked at my door violently.

4. I was waiting for my train. I read a magazine. I borrowed it from a library.

5. He went abroad. He graduated from university. He looked forward to having a new life.

6. What surprised me? It is this. They gave me a toy as my birthday present. The toy was bigger than I.

(Ⅱ) **Writing Assignment**

You are supposed to write a composition on the topic How to Learn Business English Well. Write about 100 to 120 words and base your composition on the following outline.

1. English is called the "language of communication", and we can learn Business English well if we communicate in English with people.

2. Business English is English especially related to international trade, so we

should have a grasp of the knowledge and techniques of international trade.

3. Language learning, including Business English learning, requires persistence.

Ⅷ. Presentation(Speaking)

Work in pairs and talk about your job. You and your partner are supposed to be a marketing manager and human resources manager. Go to the library or visit the Internet to find out your duties by referring to some materials or books. Write down your duties and give a presentation next time. You may refer to the following expressions: I'm responsible for employing most of the people in the company. My job involves giving financial advice. I deal with questions people have for their jobs. As part of my job I have to produce financial report.

Enjoy Your Time

A Second Language

A mother mouse was out for a stroll with her babies when she spotted a cat crouched behind a bush. She watched the cat, and the cat watched the mice.

Mother mouse barked fiercely, "Woof, woof, woof!" The cat was so terrified that it ran for its life.

Mother mouse turned to her babies and said, "Now, do you understand the value of a second language?"

Unit 2

Jobs and Occupations

Learning Objectives

In this unit you will ◆ know something about current urgently needed jobs;

◆ know something about the busy life of a CEO;

◆ and review the grammar item: subjunctive mood (虚拟语气).

Pre-reading Activities

New Words: flextime   designated   supervisor   alternative   dynamic   participant

I. **Listen to the following short passage twice and fill in the blanks with the words you've heard.**

"Flextime" means a work arrangement that includes designated hours during which an employee may, with the ___1___ of the supervisor and under work unit plans approved by the department head, ___2___ an alternative time of ___3___ and leave from work. It may also include ___4___ days or hours during which an employee must be ___5___ for work. Working hours must be balanced to meet the ___6___ needs of the department and, if possible, an employee's own personal choices as to work hours.

The process for planning and developing a flextime arrangement is a dynamic process that ___7___ employees as well as supervisors. Without the ___8___ of all staff members, including those who choose not to join in, flextime will be ___9___.

Each participant should organize his/her work arrangement to make that the operating requirements for the department are ___10___.

Ⅱ. **What kind of job are you expecting to take up after graduation? When you are making your choice, which one do you think is the most important, the salary, the working environment or the potential for further promotion? Discuss with your partner, and list your reasons.**

Text A

5 Careers: Big Demand, Big Pay

Recent surveys show that a lot of people are eager to find new jobs and human resource managers are expecting a lot of movement. There also have been predictions that the labor market may start to be in favor of job seekers due to a shortage of skilled workers. Let's look at what these careers are.

In the accounting area, those who have a few years of auditing experience working for a large public accounting firm can negotiate a satisfactory salary for themselves when they change jobs. That applies whether they're leaving the accounting firm to go work for a corporation or if they're seeking to return to the public accounting firm from an auditing job at an individual company.

College graduates with an accounting degree but not yet a CPA might make between \$35,000 and \$45,000 a year, or up to \$50,000 in large cities like New York. After a couple of years they can get a substantial pay hike if they move again.

The healthcare and biomedical fields also offer some earnings opportunities for those on the business side. Business development directors, product managers and associate product managers working for medical device makers, for instance, can do quite well for themselves if they develop a successful track record before jumping ship.

Typically, they have an MBA in marketing plus at least two to three years' experience on the junior end to between five and eight years' experience at the more senior levels. That experience ideally will be in the industry where they're seeking work.

An associate product manager might make a base salary of \$55,000 to \$75,000. A product manager can make a base of \$75,000 to \$95,000, while a business development director may make \$120,000 to \$160,000. Those salaries don't include bonuses.

In the legal sector, intellectual property lawyers specializing in patent law and the legal secretaries who have experience helping to prepare patent applications are highly desirable these days.

The most in demand are those lawyers who also have an advanced degree in electrical and mechanical engineering, chemical engineering, etc.

Patent lawyers working for a law firm might make $ 125,000 to $ 135,000 to start or about $ 90,000 if they work for a corporation that's trying to get a patent or to protect one they already have. With a couple of years' experience, they can expect a 10 percent jump or better when they get another job.

Two tech jobs in high demand these days are developers and quality assurance analysts.

Developers who are expert users of Microsoft's software programming language can make between $ 75,000 and $ 85,000 a year in major cities. If they pursue a job at a company that seeks someone with a background in a given field, they might achieve a salary hike of 15 percent or more when they switch jobs.

Those who work in software quality management, meanwhile, might make $ 65,000 to $ 75,000 a year and be able to negotiate a 10 percent to 15 percent jump in pay if they switch jobs.

Despite the above areas, though job cuts in the automotive industry, quality and process engineers, as well as plant managers certified in what's known as "Lean Manufacturing" techniques, are hot commodities. The same applies to professionals in similar positions at other types of manufacturers.

One Lean Manufacturing technique is to use cameras to rake down the manufacturing process. A quality engineer will analyze the tapes to identify areas in the process that create inefficiencies or overmuch waste, both in terms of materials and workers' time.

Process and manufacturing engineers might make between $ 65,000 and $ 75,000 a year. With a certification in Lean Manufacturing and a few years' experience, they can get pay hikes of between 15 percent and 20 percent if they choose to switch jobs.

A plant manager making between $ 90,000 and $ 120,000 may expect to get a 10 percent raise or more.

Words & Expressions

1. survey/sə'vei/n. a set of questions that you ask a large number of people in

order to find out about their opinions or behaviors 调查

2. prediction/priˈdikʃən/*n.* something that you say is going to happen, or the act of saying what you think is going to happen 预言的事物,预言,预告

3. job seeker   a person who is looking for a job 求职者

4. audit/ˈɔːdit/*v.* to officially examine a company's financial records in order to check that they are correct 查……的账,审计,稽查

5. negotiate/niˈgəuʃieit/*v.* to discuss something in order to reach an agreement, especially in business or politics 谈判,协商,商定（+with）

6. corporation/ˌkɔːpəˈreiʃən/*n.* a big company, or a group of companies acting together as a single organization 法人,社团;公司

7. individual/ˌindiˈvidʒuəl/*n.* one person, considered separately from the rest of the group or society that they live in 个人,个体

8. CPA（Certified Public Accountant）*n.* 注册会计师;（经考试获得证书的）职业会计师

9. substantial/səbˈstænʃəl/*adj.* large enough to be satisfactory 多的,可观的

10. hike/haik/*n.* [especially AmE informal] a large increase in prices, wages, taxes, etc. 【尤美,非正式】（价格、工资、税率等的）大幅度上升

11. healthcare /ˈhelθkɛə/*n.* the service of looking after the health of all the people in a country or an area 医疗保健（服务）

12. biomedical/ˌbaiəuˈmedikəl/*adj.* the scientific study of the medicine 生物医学的

13. opportunity/ˌɔpəˈtjuːnəti/*n.* a chance to do something or an occasion when it is easy for you to do something 机会,时机

14. device/diˈvais/*n.* a piece of equipment intended for a particular purpose, for example for recording or measuring something【用于专门用途的】装置,设备

15. ideally/aiˈdiəli/*adv.* used to describe the way you would like things to be, even though this may not be possible 理想地

16. associate/əˈsəuʃiit/*adj.* having a lower level of rights or responsibilities than somebody else 副的;准的

17. legal/ˈliːgəl/*adj.* [only before noun] concerned with or connected with the law（有关）法律的

18. intellectual property/ˌintiˈlektʃuəl ˈprɔpəti/*n.* [law] something which someone has invented or has the right to make or sell, especially something protected by a patent, trademark, or copyright【法律】知识产权

19. specialize/ˈspeʃəlaiz/*v.* to limit all or most of your study, business, etc. to a

particular subject or activity 专门研究,专门从事,专攻

20. patent/'peitənt/*n.* a special document that says that you have the right to make or sell a new invention or product and that no one else is allowed to do so 专利证书,专利

21. advanced/əd'vɑːnst/*adj.* using the most modern ideas, equipment, and methods 高级的,先进的

22. electrical and mechanical engineering *n.* 电子和机械工程

23. in high demand   be wanted by a lot of people 广受欢迎

24. pursue/pə'sjuː/*v.* to continue doing an activity or trying to achieve something over a long period of time 追求,继续进行

25. switch job   change job 跳槽,换工作

26. certified/'səːtifaid/*adj.* formally declared, esp. in writing or on a printed document 证明的

27. apply to   to use something such as a method, idea, or law in a particular situation, activity or process 使用,应用,运用

28. professional/prə'feʃənl/*n.* someone who works in a job that requires special education and training 专业人士,专家

29. identify/ai'dentə,fai/*v.* to recognize something or discover exactly what it is, what its nature or origin is, etc. 确定,发现

30. inefficiency/,ini'fiʃənsi/*n.* something that does not work well, or waste time, money or energy 效率低,不称职

Notes

1. This text is selected and adapted from CNNMoney. com by Jeanne Sahadi, a senior writer.
2. MBA = Master of Business Administration 工商管理学硕士

Word Study

1. audit/'ɔːdit/*v.*

① to officially examine a company's financial records in order to check that they are correct 查……的账,审计,稽查

the annual audit 年度审计 audit on banking business 银行业务检查; purchase audit 进货审计; quality audit 品质监察[稽核]

②（AmE）to attend a university course without having to take any examinations【美】旁听(大学课程)

auditor/ˈɔːditə/n. 稽核员,查账员,审计员

2. negotiate/niˈgəuʃieit/v.

① to discuss something in order to reach an agreement, especially in business or politics 谈判,协商,商定(+ with)

The government refused to negotiate with foreign traders. 政府拒绝与外商谈判。

② arrange or settle something in this way 商订,洽谈

Union leaders have negotiated an agreement for a shorter working week.

工会领袖已经商定了一份缩短每周工作时间的协议。

come to the negotiating table 开始正式谈判

negotiator n. 商议者;谈判者

negotiation n.【尤指商业或者政治上的】谈判,协商

be open to negotiation 可以协商谈判

enter into negotiation 开始【进入】

3. specialize /ˈspeʃəlaiz/v. to limit all or most of your study, business, etc. to a particular subject or activity 专门研究,专门从事,专攻

specialize in agriculture 专攻农业

This travel firm specializes in charter flights. 这家旅游公司专营包机业务。

＊antonym：generalize v.

① 使一般[普通,统一]化

② 概括,综合;归纳,做出结论

③ 泛泛论述,概括地说

④ 推广,普及

generalize a conclusion from the facts 从这些事实中归纳出结论

generalize the use of a new invention 普及一项新发明

4. pursue/pəˈsjuː/v. to continue doing an activity or trying to achieve something over a long period of time 追求,继续进行

pursue the matter/argument/question 追究某件事/继续争论/追查某问题

pursue a discussion 继续讨论

pursue one's studies 从事研究

She pursued the study of English for five years. 她持续不断地学了五年英语。

Post-reading Activities

I. Comprehension Questions.

1. According to the passage, what are the five areas that are in need of workers?

2. For the accounting area, what do you need if you want to be able to discuss your salary with your boss?

3. What kind of persons is in high demand in the legal field?

4. What are the two technology jobs that are in need of workers?

5. List one example to show the meaning of "Lean Manufacturing techniques".

II. Fill in the blanks with the words or phrases given in the box. Change the forms if necessary.

```
pursue  apply  individual  hike  in high demand
specialize in  negotiate  in terms of  manufacture  survey
```

1. We have always _____ a friendly policy towards the people all over the world.

2. We must _____ our energies to finding a solution.

3. _____ customer satisfaction, the policy cannot be criticized.

4. According to a recent _____ , in Shanghai alone there are more than 2.5 million migrant workers.

5. Teachers are _____ in this area.

6. But to develop _____ to the utmost, China must have new markets for her products.

7. We've decided to _____ with employers about the working hours.

8. The rights of the _____ are considered to be the most important in a free society.

9. That doctor _____ children's illnesses.

10. There's a _____ in living expenses because of the high unemployment.

III. Fill in the blanks with suitable words to complete the summary of the text.

Recent __1__ show that a lot of people are eager to find new jobs and human resource managers in each company are __2__ a lot of people to change their jobs. Because of a __3__ of skilled workers, there are also signs that the situations are more __4__ for the job seekers.

If you have a few years of __5__ experience working for a large public accounting company, you can get a ___6___ salary when you change jobs.

If you have an ___7___ in marketing and at least two to three years' experience, you can easily find a job in the ___8___ and ___9___ field. Your annual salary can reach $ 160,000 at the most excluding ___10___.

Ⅳ. Translate the following sentences into English.

1. 他从银行获得了大笔贷款。(substantial)
2. 这项研究成果可以应用于新产品的开发。(apply to)
3. 他能胜任他的工作。(efficient)
4. 国家应该立法保护知识产权。(intellectual property)
5. 他预料(prediction)经济会受影响,你认为这话靠得住吗?(take sth seriously)

Text B

How I Work

I go from Paris to Tokyo every month and spend between one and two weeks there. The week when I am in Tokyo is the week when I have the Nissan executive committee meeting, the design meeting, the product decision meeting, the investment meeting, the board meeting—all the important meetings are taking place during this week. I do the same thing at Renault. To put decisions into action, I hand them to the executive committee.

Every month is different. In March, I will be one week in the US (I'm also head of Nissan's North American operations), one week in Japan, two weeks in France. But everybody knows that the first week of the month I am in Paris and the third week of the month I'm in Japan.

I have an assistant in France, one in Japan, and one in the US. They are all bi-lingual: Japanese and English, French and English. My assistants screen all the mails and documents. I'm very selective. They know exactly the topics I am interested in and what should be given to other members of the executive committee. For meetings on a single topic that aren't regular operational meetings, I'm very strict. The maximum is one hour and 30 minutes. Fifty percent of the time is for the presentation, 50% is for discussion.

I do my best thinking early in the morning. I always ask that my first meeting not happen before eight. When I need more time to think, I wake up earlier. If I don't do six hours of sleep I'm in bad shape, but I'm usually up by six.

The risk in holding two jobs is that you are going to lose some details. We have organized ourselves in a way where I still see many, many people in both companies, so I consider myself in really good contact with reality. Some things I have to sacrifice. When I was in Japan running Nissan, I used to visit one dealer a month and one plant every two or three months. Now dealer visits are once every six months, and plants are once every year.

It is also important to take a distance from the problem. I do not bring my work home. I play with my four children and spend time with my family on weekends. When I go to work on Monday, I can look at the problem with more distance. I come up with good ideas as a result of becoming stronger after being recharged.

Stress builds up when you know that there is a problem but you do not clearly see it, and you do not have a solution. We're all human. I want to assure you I feel the same pain and the same stress and the same jet lag as anybody else. You have nights when you cannot sleep, and the stress is unbearable. It happens to every single person in a job like this.

Words & Expressions

1. board/bɔːd/*n.* a group of people in an organization who make the rules and important decisions 理事会,委员会,董事会;(官方的)局,部
2. put...into action to begin to use a plan or idea that you have and to make it work 使……投入运作,启动
3. the executive committee 执行委员会
4. operation/ˌɔpəˈreiʃən/ *n.* the work or activities done by a business, organization, etc. 经营,业务
5. bilingual/baiˈliŋgwəl/*adj.* written or spoken in two languages 双语的,包含两种语言的
6. screen/skriːn/*v.* examine or test somebody/something to find out if there is any disease, defect, etc. 检查或测验某人/某事物(有无疾病,缺陷等)
7. selective/siˈlektiv/*adj.* careful about what you choose to do, buy, allow, etc. (做事、购物等)认真选择(挑拣)的
8. maximum/ˈmæksiməm/*n.* (plural maxima, or maximums) the largest number or amount that is possible or is allowed (可能的或可允许的)最大量,最大值
9. presentation/ˌprizenˈteiʃən/*n.* an event at which a new product or idea is described and explained 报告,(新产品的)介绍,(观点的)陈述,说明

10. in bad shape in a bad condition 情况不好

11. sacrifice/'sækrifais/ v. to willingly stop having something you want or doing something you like to get something more important 牺牲,献出

12. plant/plɑːnt/ n. a factory or building where an industrial process happens 工厂,车间

13. come up with to think of an idea, plan, reply, etc. 想出,提出(主意、计划、回答等)

14. recharge/ri'tʃɑːdʒ/ v. get back your strength and energy again 使自己恢复精力

15. assure/ə'ʃuə/ v. to tell someone that something will definitely happen or is definitely true so that they are less worried 向……保证,使确信,让……放心

16. jet lag the tired and confused feeling that you can get after flying a very long distance 飞行时差反应

17. unbearable/ʌn'bɛərəbl/ adj. too unpleasant, painful, or annoying to bear 忍受不了的,承受不了的,无法容忍的

Notes

1. This text is selected and adapted from *Fortune* by Alex Taylor Ⅱ, etc.

2. The narrator here is Carlos Ghosn. He's CEO of Renault (France) and Nissan (Japan). Renault and Nissan are both listed among Global 500 companies.

3. Nissan: A famous Japanese automobile manufacturer.

Word Study

1. sacrifice

v. to willingly stop having something you want or doing something you like to get something more important 牺牲,献出

sacrifice sth for...

It's not worth sacrificing your health for your career. 你为事业而牺牲健康是不值得的。

sacrifice sth to do sth

n. something valuable that you decide not to have, in order to get something that is more important 牺牲

make sacrifices 做出牺牲

sell sth at a sacrifice 亏本出售某物

the need for economic sacrifice 在经济上作出牺牲的必要性

2. assure *v.* to tell someone that something will definitely happen or is definitely true so that they are less worried 向……保证,使确信,让……放心

assure sb of sth

I can assure you of the reliability of the news. 我可以向你保证这消息是可靠的。

assure sb that...

He assured me that he had finished. 他向我保证他已经完成了。

assure sth

Nothing can assure permanent happiness. 没有什么东西能确保永久的幸福。

be assured of 对……确信,有把握

3. come up with   to think of an idea, plan, reply, etc. 想出,提出(主意、计划、回答等)

He couldn't come up with an answer. 他答不上来。

He couldn't come up with an appropriate answer just at the time.

那时他想不出一个合适的答案。

与 come 相关的其他短语:

come about

to take place; happen 发生

Can you tell me how the accident came about?

你能告诉我事故是怎样发生的吗?

come across

to meet or find by chance 偶然遇见或发现

I came across my old college roommate in town today.

今天在城里我遇到了我以前的大学室友。

come along

① to make advances to a goal; progress 进展

Things are coming along fine. 事情进展顺利。

② to show up; appear 出现

Don't take the first offer that comes along. 不要接受出现的第一个建议。

come round

① to recover, revive 恢复

He fainted but soon came around. 他昏倒了,但很快苏醒了。

② to change one's opinion or position 改变某人的看法或立场

You'll come around after you hear the whole story.

你听完整个故事将会改变看法。

come at

① to obtain; get 获得

You'll come at an education through study. 通过学习你将获得教育。

② to rush at; attack 攻击

She came at me with a stick. 她用棒子向我打来。

come back

① to retort; reply 回嘴式答复

She came back at the speaker with some sharp questions.

她用一些尖锐的问题反驳演讲者。

② to recur to the memory 回想起

When I saw the picture, happy memories came back.

当我看见照片,回想起美好的过去浮现在眼前。

come by

to gain possession of; acquire 得到某物(通常依靠努力)

Jobs are hard to come by these days. 近来很难找到工作。

come down

① to lose wealth or position 失去财富或地位

He has really come down in the world. 他真的潦倒了。

② to pass or be handed down by tradition (根据习俗)传递

customs coming down from colonial times 殖民时代传下的习俗

③ (of prizes, temperature, etc) become lower; fall 下降

The prizes of petrol is coming down. 汽油价格在下跌。

Vocabulary Building

talent capital 人才资本	eight-hour working system 八小时工作制
pioneering talent 开拓型人才	incorporeal capital 无形资本
business manager 业务经理	production manager 生产经理
regional manager 地区经理	white-collar 白领
labor contract system 劳动合同制	ideas about job-seeking 择业观念

Word Formation：Pejorative Prefixes（贬义前缀）and Prefixes of Degree or Size

Pejorative Prefixes	Meaning	Added to	Examples	Illustrative Sentences
mis-	wrongly, astray	verbs, participles, abstract nouns	misbehave, misbehavior, mishear, miscalculate, miscalculation, misconduct, misfire, misfortune, mishap, misinformation, misinform, mislead, misleading, mistreat, misunderstanding	The misconduct of the business resulted in a loss of one million dollars. Misleading advertisements are prohibited by law.
mal-	badly, bad	verbs, participles, adjectives, abstract nouns	malformation, malformed, malfunction, malnutrition, malpractice, maltreat	The data was incorrectly processed because the computer was misfunctioning yesterday.
pseudo-	false, imitation	nouns, adjectives	pseudo-guarantee pseudo-Christianity pseudo-classicism pseudo-intellectual pseudo-scientific	A pseudo-scientific definition to a term sounds scientific but does harm to people who want to understand science.

Prefixes of Degree or Size	Meaning	Added to	Examples	Illustrative Sentences
arch-	supreme, most	nouns	archbishop, arch-criminal, arch-enemy, arch-fascist, arch-hypocrite	The man was no common muderer, for he was the creator of the crime. He was the arch-criminal.
super-	more than, very special, on top	nouns, adjectives, verbs	supercomputer, superman, superpower, supermarket, superprofit, supernatural, supersensitive, supersonic, superimpose	Global capitalists allow workers in their home countries to share in their superprofits.
out-	doing better, surpassing	nouns, intransitive verbs	outclass, outdistance, outgrow, outlive, outnumber, outrun, outweigh	We outnumbered them by four to one.

（续表）

Prefixes of Degree or Size	Meaning	Added to	Examples	Illustrative Sentences
sur-	over and above	nouns	surcharge, surname, surtax	The express company made a surcharge for delivering the parcel outside of the province limits.
sub-	below	adjectives	subatomic, subconscious, subnormal	The temperature this winter is subnormal.
over-	excessive, too much	verbs, adjectives	overconfident, overspend, overdressed, overdue, overeat, overreact, overestimate, overflow, overplay, oversimplify, overdo, overwork	They are encouraged to overspend and borrow money.
under-	too little	verbs, participles	undercharge, undercook, underestimate, underfeed, underspend, underprivileged, understatement	He has underspent his budget. The company support the children from underpriviledged homes.
hyper-	extreme	nouns, adjectives	hypermarket, hyperactive, hypercritical, hypersensitive	This hypermarket sells many kinds of commodities.
ultra-	extreme, beyond	adjectives, nouns	ultra-conservative, ultra-high, ultralight, ultra-modern, ultrasonic, ultrasound, ultraviolet	An ultrahigh skyscraper of 120 stories will be built in Shanghai.
mini-	little	nouns	minibus, mini-cab, mini-market, mini-computer, mini-mall, mini-skirt	Mini-computers are on sale and I have bought one.
co-	jointly, on equal basis	nouns, verbs	co-education, coexist, cohabit, cooperate, coordinate	The government is cooperating with businesses in the fight against piracy.

Post-reading Activities

I. True or False Questions.

1. The author spends his time dealing with the business in Japan and France.

2. The author has three assistants in all, who are bilingual.

3. The author thinks best early in the morning.

4. The author is always in good shape even if he sleeps less than six hours.

5. The author finds that holding two jobs makes him very busy. He has to spend less time on the detailed information.

6. The author sometimes takes work home, and he thinks that it is a good way.

II. Fill in the blanks with the words or phrases given in the box. Change the forms if necessary.

sacrifice assure screen maximum come up with presentation plant

1. There are more and more power _____ in China to provide energy for the society.

2. The applications were carefully _____ in case any of them contained false information.

3. Someone had better _____ a solution fast.

4. His parents made _____ to pay for his education.

5. I've been asked to give a short _____ on the aims of the project.

6. The _____ score on this test is 100.

7. The dealer had _____ me of its quality.

III. Dictation

I spend my time in the US, Japan and France separately every month. I have __1__ assistants, one is in France, one in Japan, and one in the US. They are all __2__. They deal with all the mails and __3__ for me.

I have to lose some __4__ after I have held two jobs. When I was in Japan running Nissan, I used to visit one __5__ a month. Now dealer visits are once every six months.

I think __6__ early in the morning. If I don't sleep well enough, I will be in __7__ shape next day. It is also important to take a __8__ from the problem. I do not __9__ my work home. Instead, I spend the time with my family. I usually have __10__ ideas after I come back from home.

Exercises

Ⅰ. Subjunctive Mood（虚拟语气）

虚拟语气是动词的一种特殊形式，用来表达说话者的愿望、请求、意图、建议、惊奇、假设、怀疑等未能或不可能成为事实的情况。虚拟语气的三种主要用法如下：

1. In Conditional Sentences（用于条件句中）

虚拟语气用于非真实条件句时谓语动词的主要形式见下表：

情况	非真实条件句	主句
与现在事实相反	过去时（be 用 were）	would + 动词原形
与过去事实相反	过去完成时	would have + 过去分词
与将来事实相反或推测	A. 过去时（be 用 were） B. were to + 动词原形 C. should + 动词原形	would + 动词原形

If I knew French, I would read the book in the original.

If I were/Were I in your position I would tell her the truth.

If you had/Had you come a few minutes earlier, you would have caught the train.

If he came tomorrow, I might have time to see him.

If we should/Should we fail again, we wouldn't lose courage.

以上结构中，主句谓语动词除了用 would 外，有时还可用 might 或 could，第一人称还可用 should，但美国英语都用 would。

如果条件句的谓语中含有 were, had 或 should 时，有时可省略 if 而用把 were, had 或 should 放到主语之前使用倒装句。

2. In the That-Clauses（用于 that 从句中）

I wish that you didn't smoke too much.

I wish that I had paid more attention to my spelling.

He wishes that we would help him in the work.

He suggested that the meeting (should) be held at once.

It is desired that Tom (should) get everything ready by ten o'clock.

Our decision is that the school (should) remain closed.

It's a pity that he (should) call Black White.

He made a request that the new electronic instrument (should) be tested at once.

It is necessary that the problem (should) be solved at once.

3. **In the Clauses and Constructions**（用于从句和结构中）

He treated me as if I were a child.

He acted as if nothing had happened.

It's（high）time you went to bed.

I would rather（sooner）that you started the work at once.

4. 用在含有 **without, but for, in the absence of** 等介词或介词短语的句中，表示"要不是"，句子谓语形式和 **wish** 后的从句相同。

Without/But for/In the absence of the rain, we should have had a pleasant journey.

5. **Multiple choices**

1. If you hadn't gone with Tom to the party last night, _____.

    A. you would meet John already   B. you won't have missed John

    C. you will have met John   D. you would have met John

2. The teacher suggested that each student _____ a plan for the vacation.

    A. made   B. make   C. makes   D. will make

3. "If I hadn't practised when I was younger," the musician says, " I _____ able to play so well now."

    A. wouldn't be   B. won't be

    C. wouldn't have been   D. couldn't have been

4. I wish our teacher _____ to give another test. I haven't got prepared yet.

    A. isn't going   B. weren't going

    C. will not going   D. could have gone

5. It is required that the machine _____ as frequently as necessary.

    A. be oiled   B. must be oiled

    C. is oiled   D. will oil

6. The doctor's advice is that the patient _____ about his real physical condition.

    A. be not told   B. not be told

    C. will not be told   D. must not be told

7. _____, we could not have finished the work on time.

    A. If they do not help us   B. Was it not for their help

    C. Should they offer to help us   D. But for their help

8. If we had been more careful, we _____ much better results now.

    A. got   B. had got

    C. would be getting   D. would have got

9. There is a general understanding among the members of the Board of Directors that chief attention _____ to the undertaking that is expected to bring in highest profit.

    A. is given   B. gives

    C. should be given   D. must be given

10. He told me how he had given me shelter and protection without which I _____ of hunger and cold.

    A. would be died   B. would have died

    C. would die   D. will have died

Ⅱ. Vocabulary

out of action	bilingual	audit	ideal	presentation
advance	sacrifice	come up with	assure	selective

1. A person who can speak two languages, is called a _____ and is preferred in our company.

2. Sometimes you will meet some very _____ customers who want to find faults with the products, at this time, you should be patient.

3. Will you please write a company _____ so that the customers can know more about our company history and our products?

4. If you want to be very successful, you will have to _____ a lot of free time and devote it to your job.

5. I've been _____ for several weeks with a broken leg.

6. They were _____ that everything possible was being done.

7. During Newton's time, some of his _____ theories couldn't be accepted.

8. Today is sunny. It is an _____ day for outgoing.

9. The accounts in this company are being _____ twice a year to make sure there're no mistakes.

10. She _____ a new idea for increasing sales.

Ⅲ. Translation

1. 这个大厅最多能够容纳100人。(maximum)

2. 只有少吃多锻炼才能健康。(in good shape)

3. 求职者只要有能力总能找到合适的工作。(job seeker)

4. 在美国人们频繁地换工作。(switch jobs)

5. 每年有很多从事会计职业的人报考注册会计师。(CPA)

6. 人们更希望在大公司工作,因为那里给他们提供了更多的机会。

（corporation）

7. 董事会每两周召开一次会议。（the board of directors）

8. 弹性工作制还没有被广泛采纳。（flextime）

9. 公司雇员年终时根据表现得到不同数额的奖金。（bonus）

10. 另一种办法就是提高生产率。（alternative，productivity）

Ⅳ. Cloze

While every business faces obvious competition in the marketplace, the most ___1___ competition comes from the war for excellent ___2___. Usually lacking the strong economic resources enjoyed by the Fortune 500 companies, the success and indeed the ___3___ of the emerging business is ___4___ dependent upon excellent people. Common people may be buried within a large organization, but mediocrity（庸才）cannot be ___5___ in the emerging business. Each person must carry his or her ___6___.

In Year 2000, men as well as women are willing to ___7___ their job responsibilities and family duties. The most ___8___ people are not hesitant to give up employment chances that make it uncomfortable for them to meet many situations ___9___ when playing with younger children, or caring for elderly parents. As women and men are ___10___ great family duties, their employer is no longer their only workday commitment. The ___11___ rules of yesterday are being bent; in many instances, they are ___12___ and no longer ___13___. This difficulty often ___14___ upon what is termed face time—the periods when an employee is required to be ___15___ and seen in the workplace.

1. A. healthy　　B. small　　　C. serious　　　D. unhealthy

2. A. employers　B. employees　C. workers　　　D. teachers

3. A. development　　　　　　B. survival
   C. difficulty　　　　　　　D. failure

4. A. lightly　　B. seldom　　　C. never　　　　D. heavily

5. A. produced　B. found　　　C. borne　　　　D. happened

6. A. load　　　B. life　　　　C. rights　　　　D. responsibility

7. A. balance　　B. share　　　C. define　　　　D. combine

8. A. hardworking　　　　　　B. persistent
   C. competent　　　　　　　D. selective

9. A. raising　　B. coming　　　C. arising　　　D. happening

10. A. holding　　B. taking　　　C. carrying　　　D. bearing

11. A. loose　　　B. humane　　　C. strict　　　　D. impossible

12. A. up-to-date　　　　　　　B. out-of-date
    C. in fashion　　　　　　　D. silly

13. A. emphasized   B. existed
     C. needed   D. found

14. A. connects   B. comes   C. centers   D. falls

15. A. absent   B. working   C. talking   D. present

V. Reading Comprehension

For many of you it will be your last year at school and now is the time for you to begin thinking seriously about future careers. In order to give you as much help as possible, I have drawn up a list of questions that you ought to ask yourself.

"Have I given thought to what I would like to do 15 or 20 years from now?" Bear in mind that the career you choose will affect the future course of your life. It will partly determine your range of friends and other important aspects of your life.

"Have a clear knowledge of my abilities, as well as my interests and aims?" Be honest about your weak points as well as your strong ones. Think about what kind of person you are, and what kind of person you want to be.

"Have I weighed carefully the immediate advantages against the long term prospects offered by the jobs I am considering?" Will the occupation you select give you satisfaction, not just when you start, but in the years to come?

How do I regard my job? Is it just a means of getting money to do the things that I want to do? Is the work important to me and my future happiness? Is it a combination of both these things? The above questions and their answers should give you some better ideas about how you should start planning your career. It must be considered carefully, examined from every angle, talked over with those who know you and those who can help you in any way.

1. Who is supposed to be the audience of this talk?

    A. Businessmen.   B. Teachers.

    C. Parents.   D. Students who are to graduate.

2. What do the underlined words in Paragraph 1 mean?

    A. 总结   B. 草拟   C. 指出   D. 提问

3. Paragraph 2 tells us that when you choose a career, you'd better _____.

    A. think about what kind of person you want to be

    B. try to foresee how your future life will be affected by your career

    C. just consider the short-term benefits

    D. make up your mind quickly and change it after some time

4. To have a clear knowledge of yourself you must _____.

    A. decide what you want to be in the future

    B. be honest

    C. be aware of your advantages and disadvantages

    D. examine yourself

5. What does the underlined word in Paragraph 4 mean?

    A. 权衡   B. 称重   C. 参考   D. 了解

6. Which one is false according to the above text?

    A. It takes a long time to choose a job.

    B. Luck is important to find a good job.

    C. The job-seeker must ask himself a lot of questions to be well prepared.

    D. You must examine every possibility before you make decisions.

Ⅵ. Word Formation: The Prefix in-, im-, un-

In our text, we have learned the following words: efficiency – inefficiency, bearable – unbearable.

We also have learned in our middle school: able – unable, possible – impossible complete – incomplete, etc. (Can you show more examples?)

So, "in-, un-, im-" are prefixes which are often used before the adjectives, verbs, or nouns to show opposite meaning, which means: "not", "no", etc.

Fill in the blanks below, using the correct forms of the given words.

1. He is _____ for the job. He never has related experience. (fit)

2. The manager thinks he is _____ though he graduated from a famous university. (competent)

3. The answer is _____. Please think it over. (correct)

4. He is very strict with his employees, so they all think that he is _____. (personal)

5. The Japanese think it _____ if you ask some personal questions at the first time. (polite)

6. It is _____ (adequate) if you only have some book knowledge. You should make yourself suit to the changes of the times.

7. When the customer asked for the third time about the effects of the machine, the salesman became _____. (patient)

8. Had the accountant not found the mistake, the loss would be _____ (measurable).

9. Though has been told how to do the job, she is still _____ (certain).

10. After a day's hard work, he _____ (dress) and went to bed.

Ⅶ. Writing

1. Writing Basics

Sentence Building: Coordination

Coordination is a technique of writing to show that in a sentence two or more ideas are of the same importance. You can coordinate single words or phrases, and you can coordinate clauses. Here, we show four ways to link two or more main clauses together in a single sentence.

(1) **Using Coordinating Conjunctions**

There are seven coordinating conjunctions: **and, but, yet, or, nor, so, and for.**

Eg: Sentences: We did not feel comfortable sitting in the empty restaurant.

We could not decide what to order.

Combined: We did not feel comfortable sitting in the empty restaurant, nor could we decide what to order.

(2) **Using Correlative Conjunctions**

The correlative conjunctions—**either... or...** , **neither... nor...** , **both... and...** , and **not only... but also...** —can be used to join sentences of equal importance.

Eg: Sentences: You will have to turn up the heat in the building.

I will be forced to complain.

Combined: Either you will have to turn up the heat in the building, or I will be forced to complain.

(3) **Using Conjunctive Adverbs**

Conjunctive adverbs are adverbs or short phrases that also show equal relationship between the joined clauses, as coordinating conjunctions do, but they are more emphatic and formal than the latter.

The following are some most frequently used conjunctive adverbs:

Indicating contrast—**however, instead, on the other hand, nevertheless, otherwise, in contrast**

Indicating cause and effect—**therefore, thus, hence, consequently, as a result, for this reason**

Indicating a similar idea follows—**besides, moreover, furthermore, in addition, similarly**

Indicating emphasis and illustration—**indeed, in fact, in particular, for example, for instance**

Indicating time—**then, meanwhile, at the same time, afterward, later**

Eg:Sentences: Six inches of snow fell last night.

Chris and I will have to clear the walkway this morning.

Combined: Six inches of snow fell last night; consequently, Chris and I will have to clear the walkway this morning.

(4) **Using the Semicolon**

The use of semicolon often gives emphasis to 1) two similar ideas; 2) two opposite ideas, or 3) strong cause-effect relationship.

Eg:Sentences:John is a beggar.

His father was a millionaire.

Combined: John is a beggar; his father was a millionaire. (two opposite ideas)

Exercise: Combine the following sentences according to the instructions given.

1. The workers accepted the contract.

   It was in their best interests. (use proper coordinating conjunctions)

2. Ancient Greece gave the world the great culture.

   It gave the world an incomparable architecture(建筑).

   It gave the world great works of music we study today. (use proper coordinating conjunctions)

3. New sources of income will have to be found.

   Local government will have to increase taxes. (use correlative conjunctions)

4. This building is too old.

   People have decided to pull it down. (use a conjunctive adverb)

5. I need a ride home after school.

   My sister can't pick me up. (use a semicolon)

2. **Writing Assignment**

You are supposed to write a composition on the topic **Flextime Is _____ (Bad/ Good/Suitable, etc.) for Today's Business.** Choose one adjective to complete the title and then write about 100 to 120 words. You can base your composition on the information that has been given in this lesson, or you can just express your own opinions, but try to use some examples or reasons to make your composition convincing.

VIII. Presentation(Speaking)

Work in groups and try to find information for three of the following companies:

First Direct   IKEA Business   Reuters   BMW   Marks & Spencer

Write a simple company history for two of them. When writing, try to include:

1. The founder's name.
2. The date of foundation.
3. Important incidents in the company's history.
4. The company's business scope(eg. what goods or services does it provide?).
5. The company's present position in the market.

Enjoy Your Time

Sailing

I am sailing, I am sailing
home again cross the sea.
I am sailing stormy waters,
to be near you, to be free.

I am flying, I am flying
like a bird cross the sky.
I am flying passing high clouds,
to be near you, to be free.

Unit 3

Company History and Activities

Learning Objectives

In this unit, you will ◆ learn the history of a company growing into a giant;

◆ review the grammar item: subjunctive mood;

◆ grasp one of the basic writing skills: subordination.

Pre-reading Activities

Ⅰ. **Listen to the following passage and fill in the blank with the words you hear from the tape.**

New Words: development experience founders reputation key turn prove

Any company with a certain kind of ___1___ prefers to list his history in the company literature. A long history, in most cases, is accepted to ___2___ that this company or corporation is established and has special ___3___. Therefore, compared with a young company, people always ___4___ to those with a longer history and more experience.

In the showroom of a company, people will probably present the ___5___ dates and the key events during his ___6___. The information about the ___7___ and the backers is also necessary sometimes.

Ⅱ. **Discussion: Think about the following questions and try to exchange ideas with your partner.**

1. Why do you think people pay so much attention to the history of a company?

2. Can you think of any examples of promotion by representing a company's history?

Walt Disney

You may know those non-human superstars in movies, like Mickey Mouse, Pooh, and Nemo. These are all produced by a famous cartoon producer—Disney Company. Named after his founder, the company has just celebrated his 80th birthday. How did this giant come into being? The following is the history of Disney Company.

Walt Disney arrived in California in the summer of 1923 with a lot of hopes but little else. He had made a cartoon in Kansas City about a little girl in a cartoon world, called Alice's Wonderland, and he decided that he could use it as his pilot film to sell a series of these Alice Comedies to a distributor. Soon after arriving in California, he was successful. A distributor in New York contracted to publish the Alice Comedies on October 16, 1923, and this date became the start of the Disney Company. Originally known as the Disney Brothers Cartoon Studio, with Walt Disney and his brother, Roy, as equal partners, the company soon changed its name, at Roy's suggestion, to the Walt Disney Studio.

Walt Disney made his Alice Comedies for four years, but in 1927, he decided to move instead to an all-cartoon series. To start in this new series, he created a character named Oswald the Lucky Rabbit. Within a year, Walt made 26 of these Oswald cartoons, but when he tried to make more money from his distributor for a second year of the cartoons, he found out that the distributor had broken the contract and signed up almost all of his animators, hoping to make the Oswald cartoons in his own studio for less money without Walt Disney. On studying his contract, Walt realized that he did not own the rights to Oswald, while the distributor did. It was a painful lesson for the young cartoon maker to learn. From then on, he saw to it that he owned everything that he made.

It was at the Hyperion Studio, after the loss of Oswald, that Walt had to come up with a new character, and that character was Mickey Mouse. With his chief animator, Ub Iwerks, Walt designed the famous mouse and gave him a kind personality. Ub made two Mickey Mouse cartoons, but Walt was unable to sell them because they were silent films, and sound was revolutionizing the movie industry. So, they made a third Mickey Mouse cartoon with the name of Steamboat Willie, this time with fully synchronized sound in New York November 18, 1928. The new character was immediately popular, and a lengthy series of Mickey Mouse cartoons followed. A cartoon star, Mickey Mouse, was born.

Walt Disney did not stop. He soon produced another series—the Silly Symphonies—to go with the Mickey series. It featured different characters in each film and enabled the animators to experiment with stories that relied less on the humor of the Mickey cartoons and more on mood, emotion, and musical themes. Eventually the Silly Symphonies turned into the training ground for all Disney artists as they prepared for the advent of animated feature films. Flowers and Trees, the first full-color cartoon, and the Silly Symphony, won the Academy Award for Best Cartoon for 1932, the first year that the Academy offered such a category. For the rest of that decade, a Disney cartoon won the Oscar every year.

Walter Disney was not satisfied with this. He thought that there should be a place for children and the whole family where they could share the world of cartoons and comics. His idea soon came into reality—in 1955, the first Disneyland was built in Los Angeles. Children can see Snow White, Mickey Mouse and other cartoon stars they could see only on TV or in cinema. This attracted millions of people every day. Until now, Walter Disney and his inheritors have already opened 5 Disneylands all over the world. In 2005, when Disneyland celebrated her 50th birthday, the 5th Disneyland was built in Hong Kong, China.

There is no doubt that Disney Company is playing and will play a leading role in the cartoon movie producing industry, for they have created such a brilliant history. Children, as well as their family, all over the world can wait and see Mickey and Donald, or whoever in the future.

Words & Expressions

1. giant/'dʒaiənt/n. somebody or something that is of extraordinary power, significance, or importance 巨人,巨大的物
2. producer/prə'djuːsə/n. one that produces 生产者,制造者
3. pilot/'pailət/adj. serving as a tentative model for future experiment or development 试验性的
4. series/'siəriːz/n. a number of objects or events arranged or coming one after the other in succession 一系列
5. comedy/'kɔmidi/n. a dramatic work that is light and often humorous or

satirical in tone 喜剧

6. distributor/dis'tribjutə/*n.* one that markets or sells merchandise, especially a wholesaler 贩卖或出售商品的人,尤指批发商

7. contract/kən'trækt/*v.* establish or settle by formal agreement 定约,订合同 /'kɔntrækt/*n.* 合同,契约

8. originally/ə'ridʒənəli/*adv.* at first 最初;开始

9. character/'kærəktə/*n.* a person portrayed in an artistic piece, such as a drama or novel 人物,角色

10. animator/'ænimeitə/*n.* one, such as an artist or a technician, who designs, develops, or produces an animated cartoon 动画片绘制者

11. see to to attend to; to take care of 负责,注意

12. personality/ˌpəːsə'næləti/*n.* the pattern of collective character, behavioral, temperamental, emotional, and mental traits of a person 个性

13. revolutionize/ˌrevə'l(j)uːʃənaiz/*v.* to bring about a radical change in 在……中引起根本改变;革命

14. synchronize/'siŋkrənaiz/*v.* to cause to occur or operate with exact coincidence in time or rate 使同步

15. lengthy/'leŋθi/*adj.* of considerable length, especially in time; extended 拥有相当长度的(尤指在时间上);延长的

16. feature/'fiːtʃə/*v.* to have or include as a prominent part or characteristic 包含……作为主要部分或特点

17. enable/i'neibl/*v.* to supply with the means, knowledge, or opportunity; make able 使能够

18. experiment/iks'perimənt/*v.* to try something new, especially in order to gain experience 尝试;试用新事物(尤指获得经验)

19. rely/ri'lai/*v.* to be dependent for support, help, or supply 依靠

20. mood/muːd/*n.* a state of mind or emotion 心情,心境,情绪

21. emotion/i'məuʃən/*n.* the part of the consciousness that involves feeling; sensibility 情绪;感情

22. advent/'ædvənt/*n.* the coming or arrival, especially of something extremely important 出现,来临

23. category/'kætəgəri/*n.* a specifically defined division in a system of classification; a class 种类

24. comic/'kɔmik/*n.* comics, comic strips 连环画杂志;连环漫画 *adj.* of or relating to comic strips 连环画的,漫画的

25. inheritor/in'heritə/n. one who receive property（a title, etc.）left by someone who has died 继承人，后继者

Notes

1. Walt Disney（沃特·迪斯尼）：Walt Disney（1901 – 1966），born in Chicago, the great film-maker, the founder of Disney Company. He created many world famous cartoon stars, among which Mickey Mouse and his friends are the most famous ones. The company named after him is now playing as the leader in this sector.

2. pilot：Companies prefer to making an advertisement or a market research questionnaire or something else, before a product is really launched. This product is called pilot product. And "pilot" can be used as a verb as well.

3. Mickey Mouse, Pooh, and Nemo：Here they refer to some famous stars in movies. In Chinese, they are called "米老鼠、维尼熊、小丑鱼尼莫".

4. Academy Award（美国电影艺术与科学学院奖暨奥斯卡奖）：（also known as Oscar Award）Awarded by Academy of Motion Picture Arts and Sciences（美国电影艺术与科学学院）since 1928.

5. contract（合同）：Any legal binding agreement between two or more parties. To be effective according to law, it is essential that the parties to a contract have legal capacity（powers）and freedom of contract; they must intend it to be binding; they must be agreed on the purpose of the contract and the purpose must not be illegal; there must be valuable consideration, i. e. some payment or service or sacrifice must be promised by each party; and the meaning of the agreement must be clear enough to be understood. It needs not necessarily be in writing unless it is required by law or under seal.

6. distributor（分销商）：A retailer who has arranged with one or more suppliers to sell a product or range of products. Where he is the only seller in a particular place or area, he is known as the sole distributor. He is often said to have a sole agency or exclusive agency, but he is strictly not an agent because he buys and sells for himself and not as the respective of another party.

7. Hyperion（希腊神话中的亥伯龙神）：According to ancient Greek stories, Hyperion is the Titan of light, an early sun god. He is the son of Gaea(大地之母盖娅)and Uranus(天神乌拉诺斯). Walt Disney named his studio with the name of him.

8. Alice's Wonderland, Oswald the Lucky Rabbit, Steamboat Willie, the Silly

Symphony, Flowers and Trees: Some cartoons made by Disney and his friends. They are "爱丽丝在卡通国", "幸运兔子奥斯华", "威利汽船", "糊涂交响曲", "花与树".

9. Ub Iwerks（乌布·伊沃克斯）: One of Disney's early partners and good friends. He was also famous for his talent in movie directing.

Word Study

1. pilot *n.* one who operates or is licensed to operate an aircraft in flight 飞行员

   The airline is planning to dismiss some pilots to lower the cost.

   航空公司准备解雇一些飞行员来降低成本。

   v. ① to serve as the pilot of 当引航员

   The government piloted many small companies in the depression.

   在经济衰退期,政府曾引导许多小企业经营。

   ② to steer or control 导引或控制(进程)

   The servant piloted the old man to his seat before the meeting started.

   会议开始前,服务生把老人带到他的位置上。

   adj. serving as a tentative model for future experiment or development 试验性的

   That's nothing but a pilot product—we welcome any complaint and suggestion.

   那只是个实验产品——我们欢迎任何的投诉和建议。

2. contract *n.* an agreement between two or more parties, especially one that is written and enforceable by law 合同,契约

   The contract they signed 10 years ago still holds.

   他们十年前签的和同,现在仍然有效。

   v. ① to enter into by contract; establish or settle by formal agreement 定约

   The residents contracted for garbage collection with the public service company.

   居民们与公共服务公司签订了收集垃圾的合同。

   ② to reduce in size by drawing together; shrink 通过收紧使……尺寸缩小;收缩

   Metal contracts as it cools.

   金属在遇冷时体积会收缩。

3. feature *n.* a prominent or distinctive aspect, quality, or characteristic 特征;显著的或有特色的方面、品质或特点

   Her features in her personality made her not able to win trust among the staff.

她性格上的特点使得她在员工中得不到信任。

v. to have or include as a prominent part or characteristic 包含……作为主要部分或特点的

Excited buying industrials features largely in the stock market this afternoon.

大量购买工业股票成为今天下午股市的主要特点。

4. experiment *n.* a trial made in order to learn something or prove the truth of an idea 试验,实验

After many times of experiments, they finally pointed out the fault of design.

经过多次试验后,他们终于找到了产品设计上的缺陷。

v. ① to conduct an experiment 进行试验

They were experimenting on the assembly line.

他们正在对装配线进行试验。

② to try something new, especially in order to gain experience 尝试;试用新事物,尤指获得经验

The company is experimenting a new way of administrating its staff members.

公司正在尝试一个新的员工管理模式。

Post-reading Activities

Ⅰ. **Read the passage quickly and try to find the correct answers.**

1. When was Disney Company set up?

2. What was the original name of Disney Company? Why was it named like that?

3. Did Disney earn a lot by creating his first cartoon character? Why or why not?

4. Was Disney an experienced businessman when he was producing Oswald? How do you know?

5. Were the first Mickey Mouse films successful? Why or why not?

6. When did Disney firstly win Oscar Award? Who was the hero of that film?

7. When and where was the first Disneyland built?

8. Was the Disneyland well accepted by the public?

Ⅱ. **Fill in the blanks with the words or phrases given in the box. Change the forms if necessary.**

series	feature	contract	pilot	category	distributor
sign up	experiment with		contract to	see to it	

1. They _____ the new way of storage, and this was proved to be very

successful.

2. A _____ of new regulations have been published after the incorporation.

3. According to the _____, nobody but our company has the right to sell this brand in China.

4. Before turn on the machine, _____ that the power line is properly connected.

5. It's just a _____ product—it needs to be developed.

6. Exporting _____ in the business of that joint venture.

7. Drinks generally fall into two _____, namely soft drink and hard drink.

8. We have noticed the _____ to delay the delivery (交货) of our order.

9. China and EU had _____ agreement on commercial cooperation.

10. They have _____ build a railway across Africa.

Ⅲ. Fill in the blanks with suitable words to complete the summary of the text.

Disney Company, __1__ named as Disney Brothers Cartoon Studio, is now playing the leading role in cartoon making and publication. When Walt Disney, the founder of this giant, firstly stepped into the world of cartoon, he proved himself to be a successful __2__. He created a __3__ of well accepted __4__, although he lost some of them to one of his __5__. The real success of this company didn't come until Disney animated Mickey Mouse and gave the little mouse kind __6__. Walt Disney __7__ with cartoon movies with __8__ synchronized sound. This was proved to be a great success. The Academy of Motion Picture Arts and Sciences even set a new prize for movies of this kind—Academy Award for Best Cartoon in 1932. Besides this, Disney Company also built __9__ Disneyland parks which __10__ the children and their family members to enjoy the happiness of cartoon world. With audience of each age group, Disney Company has a brilliant future.

Ⅳ. Translate the following sentences into English.

1. 公司已经成功地与两家欧洲公司签约,成为他们在中国的批发商。(sign up)

2. 本产品有着柔软性和耐磨性的特点,能够满足消费者的要求。(feature)

3. 微软公司已经签合同为中国提供2,000台电脑及其配件。(contract to)

4. 电脑的应用已经彻底改变了商务活动。(revolutionize)

5. 一系列的投诉事件表明,公司的管理不能继续依赖原有的规章制度。(rely on; a series of)

Text B

The Dream Becomes a Business

Ford Motor Company entered the business world on June 16, 1903, when Henry Ford, a born mechanic, and 11 business associates signed the company's articles of incorporation. With $ 28,000 in cash, the founders gave birth to what was to become one of the world's largest corporations. Few companies are as closely identified with the history and development of industry and society throughout the 20th century as Ford Motor Company does.

As with most great enterprises, Ford Motor Company's beginnings were not so pleasant. The company had anxious moments in its early time. The earliest record of business is July 20, 1903, about one month after incorporation, to a Detroit physician. With the company's first sale came hope—a young Ford Motor Company had taken its first steps.

Perhaps Ford Motor Company's single greatest contribution to automotive manufacturing was the moving assembly line. Firstly used at the Highland Park plant (in Michigan, US) in 1913, the new technique allowed individual workers to stay in one place and perform the same task repeatedly. The line proved very efficient, helping the company far surpass the production levels of their competitors and making the vehicles more affordable.

When autos were firstly manufactured, they attracted the interest of the wealthy people. But for the mass public, they were too expensive. That was not what Henry Ford expected. He insisted that the company's future lay in the production of affordable cars for a mass market. Beginning in 1903, the company began using the first 19 letters of the alphabet to name new cars. In 1908, the Model T was born. 19 years and 15 million Model T's later, Ford Motor Company was a giant industrial corporation that had branches all over the world. In 1925, Ford Motor Company got the Lincoln Motor Company and in the 1930's, the Mercury division was created to establish a division centered on mid-priced cars. Ford Motor Company was growing.

In the 1950's, the company went public and, on Feb. 24, 1956, had about 350,000 new stockholders. Henry Ford Ⅱ's keen understanding of political and economic situation in the 1950's led to the global expansion of FMC in the 1960's, and the establishment of Ford of Europe in 1967. The company established its North American Automotive Operations in 1971, and thus connected U. S. , Canadian, and Mexican operations more than two decades ahead of the North American Free Trade Agreement.

Ford Motor Company started in the last century with a single man who wanted products that would meet the needs of people. Today, Ford Motor Company is a family of brands consisting of: Ford, Lincoln, Mercury, Mazda, Jaguar, Land Rover, Aston Martin, and Volvo. The company is beginning its second century of existence with a worldwide organization that keeps and expands Henry Ford's heritage by developing products that serve the varying and ever-changing needs of people in the global community.

Words & Expressions

1. associate/əˈsəuʃieit/n. a person united with another or others in an act, an enterprise, or a business 合伙人
2. article/ˈɑːtikl/n. a particular section or item of a series in a written document, as in a contract, constitution, or treaty 条款
3. incorporation/inˌkɔːpəˈreiʃən/n. becoming or forming a legal corporation 结合，合并；形成法人组织，组成公司(或社团)
4. enterprise/ˈentəpraiz/n. a business organization 企业；商业机构
5. identify/aiˈdentifai/v. recognize somebody or something as being the specific person or thing 确认,证明某人/某物；鉴别出某人或某物
6. assembly/əˈsembli/n. fitting together the parts of something 装配；安装
7. repeatedly/riˈpiːtidli/adv. more than once; again and again 再三；一再；多次
8. efficient/iˈfiʃənt/adj. acting or producing effectively with a minimum of waste, expense or unnecessary effort 高效的
9. surpass/səːˈpɑːs/v. be or go beyond, as in degree or quality; exceed 超越；胜过
10. affordable/əˈfɔːdəbl/adj. that can be afforded 买得起的
11. mass/mæs/adj. done or carried out on a large scale 大规模进行(完成)的
12. stockholder/ˈstɔkhəuldə(r)/n. one who owns a share or shares of stock in a company (also called stockowner) 股东
13. division/diˈviʒn/n. an area of government or corporate activity organized as an administrative or functional unit 政府或公司的一个部分
14. center/ˈsentə/v. to have a central theme or concern; be focused 具有中心主题；关注,聚焦
15. establishment/iˈstæbliʃmənt/n. the act of establishing 建立,设立；建立的行为

16. community/kəˈmjuːnəti/*n.* a group of people having common interests 有共同利益的一群人

17. heritage/ˈheritidʒ/*n.* something which is passed down over many years within a family or nation 遗产;继承物;传统

18. decade/ˈdekeid/*n.* a period of ten years 十年(期)

19. brand/brænd/*n.* name of a product 品牌

20. vary/ˈvɛəri/*v.* to undergo or show change 经受或表现出变化

21. give birth to   produce (a baby); establish (an organization) 生育;建立;造就

Notes

1. Ford Motor Company(福特公司): Founded in 1903, it is a multinational, one of the largest auto companies in the world. It is named after its founder Henry Ford, who was only an engineer. Now it has over 325,000 employees and 110 factories all over the world.

2. company, corporation and enterprise:
   The three of them all can be called "公司、企业" in Chinese.
   "Company" originally means a group of people united for business or commercial purpose. Now it refers to an organization that produces goods or services to the public.
   "Corporation" is preferred by Americans. It means companies that are incorporated(有限公司). Sometimes it also means "法人".
   "Enterprise" means a business organization. It is more used as "企业" in Chinese.

3. associate(合伙人): A person united with another or others in an act, an enterprise, or a business; a partner or colleague.

4. incorporation(组成公司): The activity of forming into a legal corporation.

5. production level(生产水平): The ability of producing of a producer.

6. Model T (T 型轿车): Model T is a model which was originated in 1908. After its launch, 15,000,000 Model Ts had been sold all over the world.

7. stockholder (股东): People who own a share or shares of stock in a company. Sometimes they are called stockowners.

8. Ford, Lincoln, Mercury, Mazda, Jaguar, Land Rover, Aston Martin, and Volvo: Some world famous brands of autos, in Chinese they are "福特","林肯","水星","马自达","捷豹","陆虎","阿斯顿·马丁","沃尔沃".

9. Henry Ford Ⅱ（小亨利·福特）：The eldest grandson of Henry Ford. He was president from 1945 until 1960 and chief executive officer from 1945 until 1979. He was chairman of the board of directors from 1960 until 1980, and remained as chairman of the finance committee from 1980 until his death in 1987. He did great contribution to FMC.

10. Ford of Europe（福特欧洲公司）：FMC had started to launch business in Europe in the end of 1920's and the beginning of 1930's. But after over three decades of development, an integrated Ford of Europe was not set up until in 1967, mainly on the base of the British and German Ford.

11. North American Free Trade Agreement（北美自由贸易协议）：Originally, in 1989, USA and Canada signed North America Free Trade Agreement. On August 12th, 1992, after 14 months of negotiation, Mexico became a member of North American Free Trade Agreement. The agreement became effective from January 1st, 1994 with the purpose to destruct the bulwark of free trade and encourage the flow of labor and merchandise among the members.

12. North American Automotive Operations（北美汽车公司）：FMC has two sections for his car business, namely NAAO（北美汽车公司）and IAO（国际汽车公司）.

Word Study

1. associate

v. ① to join as a partner, ally, or friend 合伙,合营

They associated after 7 weeks of negotiation.

经过七个礼拜的谈判后,他们合伙了。

② to connect or join together; combine 联合,结合

Do not associate the two components before you switch the power.

打开电源前,请勿将两部分接合。

③ to connect in the mind or imagination 联想

People tend to associate high quality with well known brands.

人们总是倾向于将好的质量和著名品牌联想到一起。

n. partners in a professional practice 合作伙伴

They are associates since they have signed the contract.

自从他们签订合同后,他们就是合作伙伴了。

adj. joined with another or others and having equal or nearly equal status 与别

人有联系的

an associate editor 副编辑

2. sign *n.*

① something which is seen and represents a generally-known meaning 符号

The color of red is the sign of gaining.

红色代表盈利。

② a movement of the body intended to express a particular meaning or command, etc. 信号

The manager gave his secretary a sign of dismiss.

经理示意他的秘书离开。

③ a notice giving some information 告示,标牌

There is a sign of "No Parking" over there.

那儿有"禁止停放"的标牌。

④ something that shows or points to the presence of or likely future existence, fact or condition 迹象;征兆

The economy is showing signs of improvement.

经济有好转的迹象。

3. vary

vt. to make or cause changes 改变

The board decided to vary the pattern of promotion in the next campaign.

董事会决定在下次促销活动中,改变促销的方式。

vi. to undergo or show changes 变化;不同

The price of gold may vary from 100 yuan per gram to 120 yuan throughout the whole year. 一年中,黄金价格变化可能从每克 100 元至每克 120 元变化。

variable *adj.* 可变的,变化不定的

The speed of the shipment could be variable due to the bad weather.

由于坏天气的影响,船运的速度可能有所变化。

various *adj.* 多种多样的

The business annalist has presented various possible results to us.

经济分析师给我们介绍了多种可能的结果。

variety *n.* 变化,多种多样

a variety of

The shop has a variety of toys.

商店有很多种玩具。

There is a great deal of variety in this job.

这个工作有很多变化。

Vocabulary Building

import and export company/corporation 进出口公司
consultation corporation 咨询公司
ocean shipping company 远洋运输公司
land agency 地产经纪公司
foreign contract company 对外承包公司
technology development company 技术开发公司
advertising agency 广告公司
service company 服务公司
trade fair 贸易交易会
chamber of commerce 商会
associate company 联营公司
family company 家族公司
holding company 股权公司
limited/liability company 有限(责任)公司
listed company 上市公司

Word Formation：Attitude and Locative Prefixes(态度和方位前缀)

Prefixes of Attitude	Meaning	Added to	Examples	Illustrative Sentences
co-	with, joint	verbs, nouns	cooperate, co-author, co-driver	The staff members have to cooperate to maximize the profit.
counter-	against, in opposition to	verbs, nouns	counteract, counterattack, counterpart	The Chairman called us to counteract the effect of the inflation.
anti-	against	nouns, adjectives, adverbs	anti-war, anti-social, anti-nuclear, anti-clockwise	It's anti-social of you not to come to the conference.

pro-	for, on the side of	nouns, adjectives	pro-government, pro-American	He supports the American government and purchases American products for he is very pro-American.
Locative Prefixes	**Meaning**	**Added to**	**Examples**	**Illustrative Sentences**
super-	over, above	nouns	superfine	We've declined your order of the superfine silk.
sub-	under, beneath	nouns, adjectives, verbs	subway, subconscious, subdivide, subsidiary	The question of finance is subsidiary to the question of whether the project will be approved.
inter-	between, among	adjectives, verbs, nouns	international, interact, Internet	An international conference will be held in Beijing.
trans-	across, from one place to another	adjectives, verbs	transaction, transfer	These transactions take on various forms.

Post-reading Activities

Ⅰ. True or False Questions.

1. Henry Ford, the founder of the giant, was quite wealthy when the company firstly opened for business.

2. The first cars of the brand of Ford were an immediate success once it launched in the market.

3. Henry Ford introduced a new way of car-manufacturing from his competitors.

4. FMC not only produces those mid-prized cars.

5. We can infer from the passage that the management of FMC had difficulty in following the global economic development.

6. FMC produces mainly the vehicles in the brand of Ford.

Ⅱ. **Fill in the blanks with the words or phrases given in the box. Change the forms if necessary.**

| incorporation | affordable | serve | expansion |
| identify with | center on | consist of | far surpass |

1. The United Kingdom _____ Great Britain and Northern Ireland.

2. Compared to those imported clothes, ordinary consumers prefer those marked "Made in China", for they are _____ .

3. Mrs. White can't come to the telephone —she's _____ a customer.

4. Haier is planning a(n) _____ to the West Europe.

5. The _____ of the four main giants electrical appliance (家用电器) caused great panic(恐慌) to those small companies.

6. The reformation plan _____ cutting cost and increasing credit of the banks.

7. Analysts generally _____ the reducing of the staff _____ the poor economic situation.

8. The great demand for mid-prized cars has already _____ the domestic supply.

Ⅲ. **Dictation.**

Ford Motor Company was originated by Henry Ford, an American ___1___, and other 11 business ___2___. He did not invent the first car, but he successfully mass-produced it. When cars were firstly produced, they were done by hand, and thus too expensive to those ordinary people. But in 1913, Ford ___3___ the first moving ___4___ to the car manufacturing industry, and that turned the price of cars down to being ___5___ to the ___6___ public. After several decades of development, Ford had successfully brought his company to a giant car ___7___. His ___8___ went to the ___9___ and the company had also opened its ___10___ all over the world. Now, FMC is playing the leading role in his sector.

Exercises

Ⅰ. **Structures: Passive Voice**(被动语态)

语态是一个语法范畴,它是表示主语和动词之间的主动或被动关系的动词形式。当主语是动作的执行者时,动词采用主动语态;如果主语是动作的承受者,那么动词就应当采用被动语态。被动语态的结构是:be + -ed。事实上被动语态可以有几种形式:will be done,be going to be done,be/get done,have been done,be being/getting done,等等。

Voice is a grammatical category. It is a form of the verb which shows whether the subject of a sentence acts or is acted on. When the subject is the agent or doer of an action, the verb takes the form of active voice; if, on the other hand, the subject is the recipient of the action, the verb takes the form of passive voice.

Look at the following examples:

1. These are all produced by a famous cartoon producer—Disney Company.

2. The first Disneyland was built in Los Angeles.

3. When autos were firstly manufactured, they attracted the interest of the wealthy people.

4. The Mercury division was created to establish a division centered on mid-priced cars.

From the examples, we can see that the structure of a passive voice should be: *be + -ed*. Actually, passive voice can appear in the following forms. They can be, for example, *will be done*, *be going to be done*, *be/get done*, *have been done*, *be being/getting done*, *etc.*

Now, read the following sentences and try to fill in the blanks with passive voice.

1. China _____ (regard) as the leading economic force of the 21st century.

2. The new economic community _____ (govern) by the board for more than 20 years.

3. That young man got _____ (fire) by his managing director after 2 days.

4. Our new office building _____ (paint) now, so we have to stay in the old one until it _____ (finish).

5. Every new product must _____ (test) before the producer launches(投放市场) it.

6. Our plan of incorporation _____ (discuss) in the meeting tomorrow.

7. Your order _____ (finish) in two weeks.

8. It _____ (say) that he _____ (promote) to the director of marketing department.

9. All that can _____ (do) _____ (do).

10. According to the statistics(数据) from IMF(国际货币基金组织), the average salary of that region _____ (raise) to 2 times it was 10 years ago.

Ⅱ. Vocabulary

Fill in the blanks with suitable words or phrases we have learned in this unit. Change the form if necessary.

1. This is an exclusive _____ , ie. nobody has the right to use the brand of Haier.

2. Customers do not have to pay _____ in our department—check and visa cards are both acceptable.

3. The _____ is crashing while the demand remains high. As a result, the price is rising.

4. The company is planning to open a _____ in Japan to expand to foreign market.

5. Bank of China is the first national commercial bank which _____ in foreign security market in China mainland.

6. During his _____ , Japan became an economic giant.

7. The law will _____ each private company to be free of tax in one year.

8. Whether we can get the package does not _____ the weather tomorrow.

9. Our new CEO who _____ from the failure in China promised that he would study the culture of a strange nation for the next attempt.

10. John is not the best choice for the position in our sales department—his _____ is too silent.

Ⅲ. Word Formation

1. Do not _____ (ideal) the situation; it can turn out to be even worse than we have imagined.

2. This new mechanism _____ (able) us to open the gate of the garage without getting out of the car.

3. The mass _____ (produce) of the same product lowers its price.

4. The _____ (manufacture) of each product is required to list its address and phone number over the package.

5. The company had some problems in product _____ (distribute) in the first quarters, and this caused a dash in its net profit.

6. He _____ (capital) the money his grandpa left him and opened a firm dealing with woolen fabrics.

7. The wine features for its soft and _____ (fruit) flavor.

8. The handle here is _____ (adjust) so that you can make the wheelchair fit

your size.

9. The _____ (modern) of industry is an important feature of a developed economy.

10. The supermarket has to be _____ (large) to fit the demand of those newly moved in residents.

Ⅳ. Translation

1. 统一的亚洲市场将在不久后形成。(come into being)

2. 世界贸易组织就是原来的关贸总协定。(be originally known as)

3. 新规定使得有孩子的员工可以更好地照顾家庭。(enable to)

4. 接待顾客时务必保证留下他们的电话号码。(see to it that)

5. 联合国在解决非洲的经济发展问题上应当起到领导作用。(play a leading role)

6. 不能简单地将利润与公司的规模相等同起来。(identify with)

7. 毫无疑问,我们将无法按时完成这项工作。(There is no doubt that...)

8. 本公司的董事会由 11 名成员组成。(consist of)

9. 新上任的董事长坚持认为,员工们不应当在上班时间打私人电话。(insist that)

10. 政府必将采取措施阻止通货膨胀。(take steps)

Ⅴ. Cloze

In 1965, Yale University undergraduate Frederick W. Smith wrote a term paper about the passenger route systems used by most airfreight shippers, which he viewed as economically inadequate (经济上不恰当的). He thought the shippers needed a system that was fast and __1__.

In August of 1971, Smith bought controlling interest in Arkansas Aviation Sales, located in(位于) Little Rock, Arkansas. While operating his new __2__, Smith __3__ the great difficulty in getting packages delivered __4__ two days. This dilemma(两难的局面) made him do the necessary research for resolving the bad __5__ system. __6__, the idea for Federal Express was born: a company that __7__ global business practices and now defines(定义) __8__ and reliability.

Federal Express was so-named due to the patriotic(爱国的) meaning related to the word "Federal", which suggested an interest in nationwide economic activity. At that time, Smith hoped to obtain a __9__ with the Federal Reserve Bank and, although the plan was refused, he believed the name was a good one for attracting public __10__ and keeping name recognition (认识,了解).

The company incorporated in June 1971 and began operations on April 17, 1973, with the launch of 14 small aircrafts from Memphis International Airport. On that night, Federal Express delivered 186 __11__ to 25 US __12__ from Rochester, New York, to Miami, Florida.

Company headquarters were moved to Memphis, Tennessee, a city selected for its geographical center to the original target market cities for small packages. In addition, the Memphis weather was so __13__ that the Memphis International Airport was always open __14__ business. The airport was also willing to improve itself for the __15__ .

1. A. reliable   B. quick   C. cheep   D. free
2. A. family   B. firm   C. factory   D. office
3. A. infer   B. refer   C. identified   D. finish
4. A. for   B. within   C. after   D. more than
5. A. posting   B. distribution C. acceptance   D. paying
6. A. But   B. Thus   C. However   D. And
7. A. reached   B. realized   C. did   D. revolutionized
8. A. price   B. speed   C. speedy   D. cheap
9. A. help   B. contract   C. file   D. information
10. A. happiness B. anger   C. blame   D. attention
11. A. packages   B. letters
    C. newspapers   D. suitcases
12. A. cities   B. nations   C. states   D. town
13. A. hot   B. good   C. strange   D. terrible
14. A. in   B. with   C. on   D. for
15. A. safety   B. packages   C. operation   D. Fedex

VI. Reading Comprehension

After two unsuccessful attempts to establish a company to manufacture automobiles, the Ford Motor Company was incorporated in 1903 with Henry Ford as vice-president and chief engineer. The company produced only a few cars a day at the Ford factory on Mack Avenue in Detroit. Groups of two or three men worked on each car from components made by other companies.

Henry Ford realized his dream of producing an automobile that was reasonably priced, reliable, and efficient with the introduction of the Model T in 1908. This vehicle initiated a new era in personal transportation. It was easy to operate, maintain, and handle on rough roads, immediately becoming a huge success.

By 1918, half of all cars in America were Model Ts. To meet the growing demand for the Model T, the company opened a large factory at Highland Park, Michigan, in 1910. Here, Henry Ford combined precision manufacturing, standardized and interchangeable parts, division of labor, and, in 1913, a continuous moving assembly line. Workers remained in place, adding one component to each automobile as it moved past them on the line. Delivery of parts by conveyor belt(传送带) to the workers was carefully timed to keep the assembly line moving smoothly and efficiently. The introduction of the moving assembly line revolutionized automobile production by significantly reducing assembly time per vehicle, thus lowering costs. Ford's production of Model Ts made his company the largest automobile manufacturer in the world.

1. From the text above, we can infer that in the year of 1906, Henry Ford was mainly in charge of _____ of Ford Company.

    A. advertising and selling

    B. selling and technical innovation

    C. incorporating and selling

    D. advertising and incorporating

2. What can the underlined word in Paragraph 2 most probably mean?

    A. sold   B. interested   C. invented   D. started

3. What is not mentioned as the characteristic of Model T?

    A. Easy to perform.   B. Easy to maintain.

    C. Easy to handle in country.   D. Easy to transport.

4. What was the original purpose of setting a new plant in Michigan?

    A. To popularize Model T.

    B. To introduce the new assembly line.

    C. To produce the cars affordable.

    D. To lower cost.

5. What is not Henry Ford's contribution to Henry Motor Company?

    A. Model T.

    B. Moving assembly line.

    C. Precision manufacturing, standardized and interchangeable parts for motors.

    D. Idea of producing affordable motors.

Ⅶ. Writing

(Ⅰ) Writing Basics

Sentence Building(2): Subordination

Sometimes, ideas in a sentence carry the same weight, which requires the use of coordination. However, in many cases, ideas are not of the same importance. To show clear relationship between the ideas, we need to use subordination. Subordination is a writing technique that enables you to stress the more important idea by putting the less important ones as the dependent elements.

Take a look at the following sentences to see how subordination works:

1. He smiled at me and passed the envelope to me. (Coordination is used here, because both ideas—his smiling and passing the envelope—are of the same importance.)

2. He smiled when he passed the envelope to me. (The subordination clause reduces the importance of his passing the envelope to me and showed how his passing the envelope and his smiling.)

Subordination can be achieved by using subordinate clauses.

There are three types of subordinate clauses: the adverb clause, the adjective clause and the noun clause.

Look at the following examples:

After the personnel manager read my application, she called me for an interview. (adverb clause)

Henry, *who is usually very serious*, told a joke. (adjective clause)

The fact *that the manager has asked Jim to handle the project* suggests he will get promotion. (noun clause)

Subordination can be achieved also by punctuation, for example:

The overseas cargo ship brought goods from all over the world: *spices*, *clothes*, *furniture*, *and heavy machinery*.

Subordination can also be used in many other forms. Try to read the following samples and notice the subordination in each sentence.

Beijing, *the capital of China*, is where the Summer Palace located. (subordinating by appositive)

Delayed by the terrible weather, we have to postpone the delivery. (subordinating by participle phrase)

The luggage and the passport checked, Jeffrey passed the custom. (subordinating by absolute phrase)

Besides all the above, we can also subordinate by gerunds(动名词), infinitives (不定式) or prepositional phrases.

Now, please try to combine the following sets of sentences in each group.

1. The chairman read about the notice over his table.

   He looked for his pen over the table.

2. Chinese New Year is celebrated by the Chinese, Koreans and the people in some other countries.

Chinese New Year is based on a lunar calendar.

_____

3. We were defeated by his company.

They had a better promoting campaign.

The main reason for the defeat was _____.

4. That was the only treasure he held.

He held the treasure that he had the quality of never giving up.

_____

5. Mr. Smith came to China only three years ago.

Mr. Smith is the new manager of the company.

_____

6. He also set up one of the biggest auto companies in the world.

He was remembered as the inventor of the assembly line.

_____

(Ⅱ) **Writing Assignment**

You are supposed to find the information on line and write a composition on the topic of "History of..." Write about 100 to 120 words about the history of a company or your college. Remember to list the key dates and events of the company or your college. The following sequencing words may be of some help: originally, then, secondly, later, finally, now.

Ⅷ. **Presentation(Speaking)**

Work in pairs and talk about the history of Haier Company, China. One focuses only on Chart A, and the other focuses only on Chart B. Now exchange your information about this company and note down what you hear from your partner. Finally, you can present the whole class of the full picture of Haier.

Chart A

the end of 1984	_____
the end of 1988	became the leader in fridge market
1990	passed UL of the USA
1991	Haier Group founded
_____	passed ISO 9001
1993	went public
1997	
1999	a plant was set up in America

Chart B

the end of 1984	almost bankrupt
	became the leader in fridge market
_____	_____
1990	
1991	Haier Group founded
1992	passed ISO 9001
	went public
_____	
1997	extended to other home appliances
1999	_____

Enjoy Your Time

A Red, Red Rose

by Robert Burns

O, my Luve's[1] like a red, red rose,

That's newly sprung in June.

O, my Luve's like the melodie[2],

That's sweetly played in tune.

As fair thou art, my bonnie[3] lass,

So deep in luve am I,

And I will luve thee still, my dear,

Till a'[4] the seas gang[5] dry!

Till a' the seas gang dry, my dear,

And the rocks melt wi'[6] the sun!

And I will luve thee still, my dear,

While the sands o' life shall run[7].

And fare thee weel[8], my only Luve!

And fare thee weel, a while!

And I will come again, my Luve,

Tho'[9] it were ten thousand mile!

Notes

Robert Burns (1759 – 1796), son of a poor peasant, was born in Scotland. He received only two and a half years of regular schooling. His poetry is famous for its beautiful lyricism（抒情语句）and sincerity of emotions, and is characterized by a profound sympathy for the pressed people.

1. Luve: love
2. melodie: melody
3. bonnie: pretty and healthy
4. a': all
5. gang: go
6. wi': with
7. While the sands o' life shall run: So long as I live. This refers to the sand-glass, a glass instrument used in ancient times for measuring time.
8. weel: well
9. tho': though

Unit 4

Business Communication

Learning Objectives

In this unit you will ◆understand the role of business communication;

◆know the reason of learning business communication;

◆and review the grammar item: Adverbial Clause (I).

Pre-reading Activities

New Words: semiconductor 半导体　cost-effective 有成本效益的　gather 聚会
single-hearted 真心诚意的　unified 统一的　self-glory 荣耀　progress 发展

Ⅰ. **Listen to the following short passage twice and fill in the blanks with the words you've heard.**

Yueshan-Phoenix Semiconductor Ltd. is a company ___1___ invested by Motorola Co. and Yueshan Radio Co. Ltd. , which was ___2___ in April 1996. However, only after a short ___3___ of less than three years, it is now regarded as the most ___4___ company of the Motorola Group in the world.

No matter how busy he is, every week the general manager will ___5___ some time to talk to the employees. Besides, an employee gathering is ___6___ regularly every month so that employees in the company can better ___7___ with each other among themselves. An arrangement like this makes all the ___8___ at the company work with single-hearted devotion. As a result, a sense of fondness and ___9___ for their work and a

unified concept of "self-glory with the progress of the company" have already taken
____10____ among the employees.

Ⅱ. **Discuss the following questions with your partner.**

1. Which do you think is the most effective communication channel in present business transaction? Why?

2. With new technology such as mobile phones and computers, people spend less time talking to each other directly. Do you think this is a good development? Give specific examples and reasons to support your opinion.

3. What do you think are some of the advantages/disadvantages of communicating in writing?

Text A

Business Communication

Business communication is a dynamic, multi-channeled process, which covers internal as well as external communication in a given organization. An organization refers to a certain number of persons who are able to communicate with each other and who are willing to make contributions for a common goal.

Business communication is defined as dynamic because it is always changing with the changing business and never remains static. For example, every day business people—from the CEO to employees—should take part in all kinds of business activities inside or outside the organization in an oral/written way, and communicate with different people for different reasons or purposes.

Being multi-channeled is another important feature of business communication. In their daily communication, business people get in touch with each other in a multi-channeled way. For example, sometimes they send either e-mails or faxes to each other. And sometimes they choose the form of telephone or video conference to discuss important issues. Still sometimes they have their activities recorded or produced on a tape or disk, so as to make it portable and convenient for promotions or for distribution. It won't be hard for us to find out what an active role business communication may play in our versatile business activities.

Internal communication refers to the communication taking place within a given organization. Internal communication can be subdivided into three kinds: downward communication (DC), upward communication (UC) and horizontal communication (HC). Downward communication refers to the communication from the management to the employees, which is a one-way communication. When DC is passed through an oral channel, part of the messages may get distorted or lost. What really matters for DC is clarity and accuracy. Although management is entitled to any channels for a DC, a face-to-face talk is often more preferable. One of the changes for DC now is coaching, which refers to a manager's help to develop his employees' abilities.

Upward communication refers to the communication in the opposite direction, which enables the management to hear the opinions or suggestions from their subordinates. Management should take some actions to encourage UC.

Horizontal communication refers to the communication between the employees who work at the same level. HC is often neglected by the management because of its informality.

External communication refers to the communication between the organization and the outside institutions and people, which involves a lot of activities. Advertising is a popular practice for many companies. Advertising does play an important role in building an image either for a product or for a company, which should be accompanied by good service. To make customers satisfied, the quality of the product and the service must match their expectations. Many companies are now moving towards this direction.

Corporate culture refers to the established values, beliefs and principles within a given organization, which enables the organization to move towards its goal. As corporate culture sets a framework for the organization's activities, it has a great impact on its internal communication. It is highly necessary for an organization to cultivate a good corporate culture so as to have a sound internal communication.

Formal communication (FC) refers to those communicative activities related to business in an oral or written way. FC asks for good preparation, which is often supported by facts and figures. In order to make FC an effective action, a manager should pay attention to the way the FC is conducted. Usually, the persuasive way works better than the directive one.

Informal communication (IFC), also called grapevine, exists in almost all organizations. Grapevine has a small number of activists guiding and influencing the IFC. Besides, grapevine has its members for the speedy transmission of information. The appropriate way for the management to go is to have more direct contacts with their employees, to listen to their opinions and suggestions, and to care about their welfare.

Words & Expressions

1. dynamic/dai'næmik/*adj.* having energy; of power that causes movement; of dynamics 动态的,动力的,动力学的

2. multi-channeled/ˌmʌlti'tʃænld/*adj.* of many channels 多渠道的

3. internal/in'tə:nl/*adj.* of or on the inside; within a particular country; domestic 内在的;国内的

4. external/ik'stə:nl/*adj.* on, of, or for the outside 外部的;[医]外用的 *n.* 外部,外面

5. static/'stætik/*adj.* not moving or changing; of or concerning objects at rest; of electricity not flowing in a current 静态的;静电的

6. portable/'pɔ:təbl/*adj.* that can be easily carried or moved; small and light 可携带的,轻便的

7. promotion/prə'məuʃn/*n.* raising of rank or position; advertising activity 促销,促进;晋升

8. distribution/ˌdistri'bju:ʃn/*n.* the act of giving things to a large group of people; the way in which people, buildings etc. are arranged over a large area 分发,发送

9. versatile/'və:sətail/*adj.* having many different kinds of skills or abilities; having many different uses 多才多艺的;多变的,多方面的,多用途的

10. subdivide/ˌsʌbdi'vaid/*v.* divide into even smaller parts 再分,细分

11. horizontal/ˌhɔri'zɔntl/*adj.* parallel to the horizon; flat 地平线的,水平的,平行的

12. distort/di'stɔ:t/*v.* give a false account of; pull, twist, out of the usual shape; make something look or sound unnatural 使变形;扭曲,歪曲(真理、事实等)

13. clarity/'klæriti/*n.* clearness 清楚,透明

14. accuracy/'ækjurəsi/*n.* being accurate; exactness 精确性,正确度

15. entitle/in'taitl/*vt.* give a right (to) 使有权利,给与权利

16. coach/kəutʃ/*v.* teach or train somebody esp. for an examination or a sporting contest 教导,训练

17. subordinate/sə'bɔ:dinət/*adj.* less important 次要的, 从属的, 下级的 *n.* someone of lower rank 下属 *v.* put in a subordinate position 服从

18. neglect/ni'glekt/*vt.* give no or not enough care or attention to (some body/ something); fail or forget to do something, esp. without care; leave undone

（what one ought to do）忽视，疏忽，不注意；漏做

19. informality/ˌinfɔːˈmæləti/*n.* the state or quality of being informal; an informal act 非正式

20. advertising/ˈædvəˌtaiziŋ/*n.* the business which concerns itself with making known to the public what is for sale and encouraging them to buy esp. by means of pictures in magazines, notices in newspapers and messages on television 广告业，广告 *adj.* 广告的

21. practice/ˈpræktis/*n.* regular or repeated doing of something, to gain skills; experience gained by this; actual doing of something; business of a doctor or lawyer; something regularly done 实行，实践，习惯，练习，实习，业务，惯例

22. image/ˈimidʒ/*n.* mental picture or idea; copy of the shape of a person or thing 图像，肖像，偶像，形象

23. accompany/əˈkʌmpəni/*vt.* escort; be present or occur with something; play an accompaniment for somebody 陪伴，伴随

24. corporate/ˈkɔːpərət/*adj.* of or belonging to a corporation; of, shared by members of a group of persons 公司的，法人的，共同的

25. framework/ˈfreimwəːk/*n.* main supporting parts of a building, vehicle, etc.; set of facts, ideas etc. from which more complicated ideas are developed 构架，框架，结构

26. cultivate/ˈkʌltiveit/*vt.* preparations for crops; improve or develop by careful attention, study, etc.; pay friendly attention to (people) 培养；耕作

27. sound/saund/*adj.* in good condition; without disease or damage; dependable; having the right opinions, based on reasons 健全的，可靠的，合理的

28. persuasive/pəˈsweisiv/*adj.* able to persuade others 有说服力的

29. grapevine/ˈgreipvain/*n.* a climbing plant on which grapes grow; unofficial way of spreading news 葡萄藤，葡萄树；传闻，小道新闻，谣言

30. transmission/trænzˈmiʃn/*n.* radio or TV broadcast; action or process of transmitting or being transmitted 播送，发射，传送，传输，转播

31. contact/ˈkɔntækt/*n.* the condition of meeting, touching or coming together with 接触，联系 *vt.* get in touch with (someone); reach (someone) by message, telephone, etc. 接触，联系

32. welfare/ˈwelfɛə(r)/*n.* comfort, health, and happiness; help with living conditions, social problems, etc. 福利

33. define. . . as. . . 把……定义为……;把……解释为……;与……交流

34. communicate with 与……交流

35. get in touch with 和……取得联系

36. play/take a role/part in. . . 在……中起作用,参加

37. refer to 查阅,提到,谈到,打听

38. take. . . action 采取行动

Notes

1. This text is selected and adapted from the book *Business Communications* published by Foreign Language Teaching and Research Press.

2. business communication:商务沟通; internal communication:内部沟通; upward communication:上行沟通; horizontal communication:平行沟通; downward communication:下行沟通; external communication:外部沟通; corporate culture:企业文化; formal communication:正式沟通; informal communication:非正式沟通

3. CEO(执行总裁,首席执行官): Chief Executive Officer. This is the senior manager who is responsible for overseeing the activities of an entire company. The CEO usually also holds a position on the board of directors, or also holds the title of president.

4. Business communication is a dynamic, multi-channeled process, which covers internal as well as external communication in a given organization. An organization refers to a certain number of persons who are able to communicate with each other and who are willing to make contributions for a common goal. 商务沟通是一个动态的、多渠道的过程,该过程包括组织内外的沟通。组织是指能够彼此沟通并愿为共同的目标作出贡献的某些人。

5. Still sometimes they have their activities recorded or produced on a tape or disk, so as to make it portable and convenient for promotions or for distribution. It won't be hard for us to find out what an active role business communication may play in our versatile business activities. 有时他们把活动记录在磁带或光盘上,以便促销时携带方便和分发。由此我们不难发现:商务沟通在我们变化万千的商务活动中起到了非常积极的作用。

   play a role/part in. . . 在……中起作用,参加

   She played the leading role in the school play.

   He has played an important part in carrying through the whole plan.

6. What really matters for DC is clarity and accuracy. Although management is

entitled to any channels for a DC, a face-to-face talk is often more preferable. One of the changes for DC now is coaching, which refers to a manager's help to develop his employees' abilities. 下行沟通的注意要点是信息的清晰性和精确性。尽管管理层可以就下行沟通选择任何渠道,但是面对面的谈话方式常作为首选渠道。下行沟通的变化之一是"教练法",是指经理帮助其员工开发其自身的能力。

be entitled to 给予……权利(资格);使……有资格(做某事)

You are not entitled to unemployment benefit if you have never worked.

Women are entitled to maternity leave.

You are not entitled to travel first class.

7. External communication refers to the communication between the organization and the outside institutions and people, which involves a lot of activities. Advertising is a popular practice for many companies. 外部沟通指的是企业与外部机构或人的沟通,该沟通涉及到很多活动。做广告是很多公司常见的做法。

8. FC asks for good preparation, which is often supported by facts and figures. In order to make FC an effective action, a manager should pay attention to the way the FC is conducted. Usually, the persuasive way works better than the directive one. 正式沟通要求认真准备,它常常需要事实和数字的支持。为保证正式沟通行为的有效性,经理应注意正式沟通实行时的方式。一般来说,说服性方式远比指令性方式更为有效。

9. Informal communication (IFC), also called grapevine, exists in almost all organizations. Grapevine has a small number of activists guiding and influencing the IFC. 非正式沟通(IFC),又称做"内部传递",在几乎所有的公司中都存在。"内部传递"中的积极分子为数很少,但他们引导和影响着非正式沟通。

Word Study

1. distribution *n.* the act of giving things to a large group of people; the way in which people, buildings etc. are arranged over a large area 分发,发送

They could not agree about the distribution of the profits.

他们不能赞同利益的分配。

Can you please tell me who is in charge of distribution?

你能告诉我谁来分配么?

distribute *v.* give or send out; spread through an area or range 分配,分布

This species of butterfly is widely distributed over our country.

这类蝴蝶在我国广泛分布。

They had distributed the lands among the peasants.

他们把地分给了农民。

2. neglect *vt.* give no or not enough care or attention to (some body/something); fail or forget to do something, esp. without care; leave undone (what one ought to do) 忽视，疏忽，不注意；漏做

He was dismissed for neglecting his duty.

他因为玩忽职守被解雇。

He was so busy that he neglected his health.

他太忙了以至于疏忽了他的健康。

n. neglecting or being neglected 忽视，忽略

These children were in a state of virtual neglect.

这些孩子实际上处于被忽视状态。

He has shown a persistent neglect of duty.

他总是疏于职守。

3. advertising *n.* the business which concerns itself with making known to the public what is for sale and encouraging them to buy esp. by means of pictures in magazines, notices in newspapers and messages on television 广告业，广告

adj. 广告的

The magazine contains a great deal of advertising.

这本杂志上有很多广告。

Advertising is often the most effective method of promotion.

广告常常是最有效的推销手段。

The advertising campaign didn't have much effect on sales.

这场广告大战对销售没有多大影响。

advertise *v.* make (something for sale) known to people, e.g. in a newspaper 做广告

If you want to sell your product, you must advertise it.

如果你想销售你的产品，你必须做广告。

The company is advertising for typists in the newspapers.

这个公司在报上登广告招聘打字员。

advertisement *n.* action of advertising 做广告；广告

I suggest that he put an advertisement in the local paper.

我建议他在当地报纸上登广告。

There are too many TV advertisements in between the program.

在节目之间广告太多。

ad *abbr.* (advertisement 的缩写) 广告

I got four replies to my ad about the bicycle for sale.

我刊登的卖自行车的广告有了 4 个回音。

4. persuasive *adj.* able to persuade others 有说服力的

Your argument seemed not very persuasive.

你的论点不是很有说服力。

persuade *v.* make (someone) do something by reasoning, arguing, begging, etc.

The salesman persuaded us to buy his product.

销售员说服我们买他的产品。

5. contact *n.* the condition of meeting, touching or coming together with 接触，联系

We have lost contact with him since he left last summer.

自从他去年夏天离开以后，我们和他失去了联系。

Have the children been in contact with the disease?

孩子们有没有和病菌接触？

vt. get in touch with (someone); reach (someone) by message, telephone, etc. 接触，联系

Where can I contact you tomorrow?

我明天在哪和你联系？

If the goods I ordered don't arrive tomorrow, I'll have to contact the supplier and chase them up.

如果我订的货物明天还不到，我将和供货商联系，催促他们快办。

Post-reading Activities

Ⅰ. Comprehension Questions.

1. Some people say that formal communication should be general, not specific. Some say that it should always be formal, otherwise it would not carry any weight. Still some say that FC should be static enough so as to avoid possible misunderstandings or dissatisfaction on the employees' side. What would you say on this point?

2. How significant is business communication to modern organizations? What do you think of the dynamic and multi-channeled nature of business communication?

3. Of the three kinds of internal communication, which is more important? Why?

4. What do you think of external communication? How important is it in the business industry from your experience?

5. What do you think of the corporate culture? What kind of role does it play in the internal communication of an organization?

6. What do you think of formal communication and informal communication? What should we pay attention to in our practice when using these two concepts?

7. After learning this text, what is your opinion on the relationship between business and communication?

8. If you were the CEO of an enterprise, what would you do to apply the theory of business communication in your organization?

II. **Fill in the blanks with the words or phrases given in the box. Change the forms if necessary.**

cultivate	persuasive	dynamic	subordinate	internal
take actions	have an impact on	promotion	accuracy	contact

1. The _____ developing economies of the world are ripe with potential.

2. I have found three telephone companies who can help us improve our _____ telephone system.

3. I have decided to accept a post that will give me greater possibility for _____ and an increase in my salary.

4. All holidays described in our brochure are advertised by us in good faith and every care is taken to ensure their _____.

5. In this situation, Party A has the right to take back the premises and _____ against Party B's breach.

6. Elections are not as important as some people think and they don't _____ as big _____ markets.

7. Your breach of our contract won't do any good to _____ our long-standing good business relation.

8. A business letter with particulars and specific facts is more impressive and _____.

9. We'll make _____ with the buyers to see if they are interested in our new products.

10. He treated his _____ like slaves.

III. **Fill in the blanks with suitable words to complete the summary of the text.**

The text first __1__ us the definition of business communication. We would like to define business communication as a __2__, multi-channeled process, which covers internal as ___3___ as external communication in a given organization. Business communication has ___4___ forms. It has included those essential elements like dynamic, multi-channeled ___5___, internal communication, ___6___ communication and organization. In order to have a ___7___ understanding on business communication, a brief introduction has been ___8___ in this text on those basic important concepts relating ___9___ it. At the last part of the text, the author explains corporate ___10___, formal communication and informal communication.

Ⅳ. **Translate the following sentences into English.**

1. 他从来不把自己标榜为最成功的商人。(define as)

2. 如果你失败三次,你便无权再尝试了。(be entitled to)

3. 如对召开一次交流会(seminar)的建议感兴趣,请与我们联系。(communicate with)

4. 我会与他联系,过一会儿给您回电话。(get in touch with)

5. 世贸组织在国际贸易关系方面扮演着重要的角色。(play a role in)

Text B

Effective Business Communication

Effective communication is becoming more critical for AB Company, a foreign-owned company dealing with fast-moving consumer products, which has expanded its business in China very quickly in the last five years. AB is a subsidiary of a well-established international company with the largest market share in the industry. For years, the company has been proud of its product's unique feature and quality. The brand also gained a reputation as an international brand closely related with worldwide sports activities. At the very beginning, all these advantages had contributed to the company's success in competing with other brands, and it soon became the No. 1 brand on the market. Recently the company encountered several aggressive competitors in China. One of the major reasons leading to AB Company's weakened competitiveness is its lower responsiveness to the changing market.

When the company was first established, there were only six salesmen, one marketing person, and one office supervisor reporting to the GM (general manager). The communication between the staff was quite direct and conducted mostly in an oral way. The salesmen reported to the GM any competitor's actions as soon as they had learned it from the market. The GM would discuss it with his staff and immediate responsive action would be taken. In addition, there was a weekly meeting for the whole staff. At the meeting, the GM usually assigned tasks, announced action plans, summarized sales performance, etc. Meanwhile, the staff would bring up their problems with their jobs, give comments for the sales policy, and raise questions about the assignments in a very open way. People in different functions also exchanged their respective viewpoints on a particular issue so as to have better co-ordination. Good communication within the organization helped the company to give quick response to the customers' needs and against the competitors' movements.

With its success in enlarging its market share and penetration into more local markets, the company soon established sales offices around the Eastern China regions. Most employees were hired and many of them were put in their local regions. As a result, the headquarters office in Shanghai also expanded and developed into a functional organization structure to centralize its control over the dispersed operations. The functions of marketing, finance, human resources and logistics all became specialized departments. Within some departments, several reporting levels evolve with the further expansion of the business.

Gradually, the company changed its way of communication with the organization. The GM and the department managers have now become frequent business travelers and seldom have time to sit together with the employees for a talk. Another factor of the change is the dispersed operation sites. It is expensive and time-consuming to have all the staff come over for a meeting whenever there is a release of policy. Thus, the face-to-face conversation stays only at a functional level. Mobile phone and e-mail system have become two main tools for communication in the company. People now rely more on mobile phones to keep close contacts with each other. Although the organization structure has become more complicated than before, the communication is no less fast and efficient with the help of mobile phone. E-mail is another effective tool for the expanded organization. With e-mail system, people interact with each other in a timely way.

Words & Expressions

1. critical/ˈkritikl/*adj.* decisive; of or at a crisis; crucial 紧要的，关键性的;重大的;急需的

2. subsidiary/səbˈsidiəri/*adj.* connected to but smaller, of less importance than something else 附属的;次要的;副的

3. compete/kəmˈpiːt/*v.* try to be more successful than another person or

organization 比赛，竞争

competitive *adj.* 竞争的　competitor *n.* 竞争者

4. encounter/in'kauntə/*v.* be faced with; meet unexpectedly 遭遇，遇到，相遇

5. responsive/ri'spɔnsiv/*adj.* answering readily with words or feelings 响应的，作出响应的;反应的;共鸣的;敏感的

   responsiveness *n.* 应答性，反应性

6. supervisor/'sju:pəvaizə/*n.* one who supervises 监督人

   supervise *v.* 监督，管理，指导

7. assign/ə'sain/*vt.* give as a share or duty; decide on name 分配，指派;布置

   assignment *n.* 分配，委派;任务，(课外)作业

8. respective/ri'spektiv/*adj.* for or of each one; particular and separate 分别的，各自的

9. viewpoint/'vju:point/*n.* a way of considering or judging a thing, person, event, etc. 观点

10. issue/'isju:/*n.* important topic for discussion; point in question 问题;争端;论点

11. co-ordination/ˌkəuɔ:di'neiʃn/*n.* the act of coordinating; the state of being coordinate; harmonious adjustment or interaction 协调

    coordinate *vt.* (使)协调

12. penetration/ˌpeni'treiʃn/*n.* (action or process of) penetrating; ability to think and understand quickly and deeply 穿过，渗透，突破

    penetrate *vt.* 穿透，渗透，看穿，洞察

13. centralize/'sentrəlaiz/*vt.* to draw to a central point; to bring under one control 集中，施行中央集权

14. disperse/di'spə:s/*v.* scatter in different directions (使)分散，(使)散开，疏散

15. logistics/lə'dʒistiks/*n.* detailed planning of an operation 后勤学;后勤

16. evolve/i'vɔlv/*v.* (cause to) develop naturally and (usu.) gradually; (of plants, animals, etc.) gradually develop from a simple form to a more complex one (使)发展，(使)演变;推断;推论

17. release/ri'li:s/*n.* make free; make public 释放;发布，公之于众

18. mobile/'məubail/*adj.* able to move 可移动的

19. complicated/'kɔmplikeitid/*adj.* involving a lot of different parts, in a way that is difficult to understand 复杂的，难解的

20. interact/ˌintər'ækt/*vi.* have an effect on each other 互相作用，互相影响

Notes

1. market share(市场占有率;市场份额):It is the ratio of sales of a brand to the total sales of that product-type in a defined area (country, continent, etc). Market share can also be defined as the ratio of sales of a company's entire product line to the total sales of all related companies. Market share is usually presented as a percentage, although sometimes a raw number(原始数字) of sales or units is provided. If the total raw number is also provided, you can calculate the market share percentage by dividing the brand's number by the total number, and multiplying the result by 100.

2. A company is usually organized in the following way:

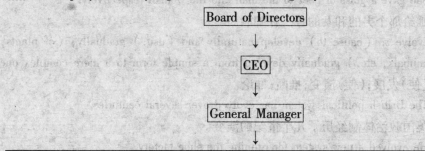

3. AB is a subsidiary of a well-established international company with the largest market share in the industry. AB 公司是一家享有声誉的跨国公司的子公司, 在同行业里占有最大的市场份额。

4. When the company was first established, there were only six salesmen, one marketing person, and one office supervisor reporting to the GM (general manager). 公司刚成立时仅有六个销售员、一个营销主管以及一个办公室主任(负责向总经理汇报有关情况)。

5. Within some departments, several reporting levels evolve with the further expansion of the business. 在一些部门里,若干级汇报层也随着业务的扩展而发展。

6. Thus, the face-to-face conversation stays only at a functional level. 因此,面对面的谈话只能是在职能部门层次进行。

Word Study

1. respective *adj.* for or of each one; particular and separate 分别的,各自的

My husband and I are each going to visit our respective mothers.

① respective 后面一般跟复数名词。

They went back to their respective houses after work.

下班后他们各自回自己的家。

② 注意区分词形相似的词,如 respective, respectable, respectful。

It's not respectable to get drunk in the street.

在街上喝醉酒是不体面的。

We should be respectful of the old.

我们应该尊重老年人。

respectively *adv.* 各自地;分别地

She gave a glass of beer to the man and the woman respectively.

她给那个男的和女的各一杯啤酒。

2. evolve *v.* (cause to) develop naturally and (usu.) gradually; (of plants, animals, etc.) gradually develop from a simple form to a more complex one (使)发展;(使)演变;推断;推论

The British political system has evolved over several centuries.

英国政治体制经历了几个世纪的演变。

He evolved a new system for running the shoe factory.

他发展出一种新的经营鞋厂的体制。

3. issue

n. ① an important topic for discussion; point in question 问题;争端;论点

An increase in global temperature makes the greenhouse effect an international issue which needs worldwide study and response.

全球气温升高使得温室效应成为一个需要世界性研究和反应的世界问题。

The United Nations' move(决议) should help a peaceful solution to Korean nuclear issue. 联合国决议寻求和平方法解决朝核问题。

② distribution of books, newspapers, etc. 发行;发行物;(报刊)期号

I read a piece of surprising news in today's issue of *The Times*.

我从今天的《泰晤士报》中读到了一个令人惊奇的消息。

There is an issue of 1,000,000 copies of the book *My Life* by Bill Clinton.

比尔·克林顿出版的《我的自述》发行达百万册。

issue of shares/bonds/currency 发行股票/证券/货币

v. ① to bring out 发行;发布

A newly founded corporation might issue and sell 50,000 shares of common stock. 一个新成立的公司可能发行和销售 5 万股普通股。

The government issued a report on London's traffic.

政府发布了伦敦交通的报告。

② to supply or provide officially 发放；开立(单据)

The government issued winter clothing to the refugees.

政府向难民发放过冬衣服。

The buyer requests his bank to issue a letter of credit in favor of the seller.

买方要求银行开出以卖方为受益人的信用证。

4. release *v.*

① to set free; allow to come out 释放；解放；放行

The hunter released the bear from the trap.

猎人从陷阱中将熊放出来。

The robber was released on bail.

盗贼被保释。

② to allow (news, books, etc.) to be shown publicly 发表；发行

The local government refused to release the figures for the number of unemployed women.

当地政府拒绝公布未就业女性的数字。

③ to free...from 免除(债务)

The company was finally released from debt.

这个公司最后被免除了债务。

Vocabulary Building

department manager 部门经理	sales manager 销售部经理
contractor 承包商	wholesaler 批发商
retailer; retail merchant 零售商	broker 经纪人
customer; client 顾客	commission agent 代理商
stockholder; shareholder 股东	exclusive agent 包销商
middleman; intermediary 中间商	exporter 出口商
importer 进口商	manufacturer 制造商
trade negotiator 贸易谈判人员	commercial secretary 商务秘书

Word Formation: Prefixes of Time and Order, Number Prefixes(时序前缀)

Prefixes of Time and Order	Meaning	Added to	Examples	Illustrative Sentences
fore-	before	verbs, nouns	foretell, forecast, forewarn, foresight, foreknowledge	The dealer forecasts a fall in the stock market. We had no foreknowledge of what he might say.
pre-	before	nouns, adjectives	pre-school, pre-war, precondition, premarital	Economic growth is a precondition of human advance.
post-	after	nouns, adjectives	post-war, postelection, postgraduate, post-modern, post-industrial	Many students want to go overseas to pursue their postgraduate studies.
ex-	former	nouns	ex-president, ex-wife, ex-husband	Men on average want their ex-wives to keep more joint possessions when getting divorced.
re-	again, back	verbs, nouns	resell, rebuild, restaff, resettlement, reelection	In rebuilding an urban area, resettling the former residents is often a difficult task.

Post-reading Activities

Ⅰ. True or false questions.

1. Effective communication is becoming more critical for AB Company, for the main reason leading to AB Company's weakened competitiveness is its lower responsiveness to the changing market.

2. AB Company, with less effective business communication, has expanded its business in China very quickly in the last five years.

3. When the company was first established, good communication within the company is another major reason leading to its success.

4. With its success in enlarging its market share and penetration into more local markets in China, AB Company set up the headquarters office in Shanghai.

5. Mobile phone and e-mail system have become two main tools for communication in the company so a face-to-face talk to solve a problem is not necessary.

6. Although the organization structure has become more complicated than before, the communication is not fast and efficient with the help of mobile phone and e-mail.

7. How to create a more effective communication environment has become a challenge for AB Company to keep its leading status in the industry.

Ⅱ. Fill in the blanks with the words or phrases given in the box. Change the forms if necessary.

deal with	critical	contribute to	response	gain a reputation
co-ordination	bring up	disperse	evolve	release

1. Groups of police were _____ all along the street where the Queen was to pass.

2. Don't _____ this news to the public until we give you the go-ahead.

3. That is why we _____ in our last letter the question of currency(货币) in L/C for your consideration and advice.

4. Our products _____ an outstanding _____ in many countries.

5. They have helped the _____ of commodity circulation(商品流通) in the mountainous areas and increased competitiveness of local goods.

6. Up to now, the Sales Manager, John Martin, _____ the advertising.

7. We are at a _____ time in the history of our firm.

8. Trade _____ from the exchange of goods.

9. They have been several _____ to our advertisement.

10. The frank exchange of views _____ better understanding.

Ⅲ. **Dictation.**

Exercises

Ⅰ. **Adverbial Clauses**（Ⅰ）

Adverbial clauses are phrases that function as an adverb in a sentence. Adverbial clauses can be used to show time（temporal clauses）, place, concession（让步）, purpose, result, condition, cause（causal clauses）, comparison, or manner, etc.

An adverbial clause may begin with or be introduced by a subordinating conjunction（从属连词）—a word like when, because, if, so that, whatever, provided, lest, and although etc. It is very important to learn to use these subordinating conjunctions.

1. Clause of Time

   While the teacher was explaining the text, the students were listening attentively and taking notes.

   I will wait until the doctor comes.

2. Clause of Place

   Wherever you go in China, you will receive a warm welcome.

   Just stay where you are.

3. Clause of Reason

   John didn't come to my birthday party because he had a meeting to attend.

   As the weather was fine, I opened all the windows.

4. Clause of Purpose

   They set out early（so）that they might arrive in time.

   We must handle the goods with care for fear that they（should）be damaged.

   The teacher spoke slowly and in simple English so that the students could understand her.

5. Clause of Result

   We worked fast and well so that we overfulfilled our production plan.

   He was so tired that he couldn't go any further.

6. Clause of Manner

   You may do as you please.

He smiled as if nothing happened.

7. Clause of Concession

He has never been absent from class though he is very busy.

However hard I try, I can't pronounce that word properly.

I managed to attend the meeting even if I had a lot of work to do.

Little as the profit is, we'll trade in it.

8. Clause of Condition

We can lower our price provided you increase your quantity to 10,000 dozen.

Suppose/ Supposing he doesn't come, what shall we do?

He is sure to come unless he has some urgent business.

9. Clause of Comparison

Guilin is as beautiful as Hangzhou.

Canada is a little bigger than the United States.

The sooner, the better.

Fill in the blanks with proper subordinators (than, if, even if, when, so... that, as, since, because, before, wherever, etc.).

1. It's half a year _____ I met you last.

2. We are prepared to do extensive advertising _____ business is possible.

3. Please make out the contract _____ I told you.

4. _____ there is some difference in price, you will have no difficulty in pushing the sale of the goods.

5. He worked _____ late _____ he couldn't get up early the next day.

6. It won't be long _____ you have our order.

7. Is this style more attractive _____ that one?

8. Please get in touch with Mr. Zhang _____ you are in need of this article.

9. _____ your prices are reasonable, we shall let you have our specific inquiry.

10. I hope you will ship the goods in time _____ we are in urgent need of them.

II. Vocabulary

| as well as   make contribution   for... purpose   refer to   lead to   relate to |
| subdivide into   develop into   in an oral or written way   market share |

1. Did you come to London for the purpose of seeing your family, or _____ business _____ ?

2. We are producing carpets of modern designs _____ traditional designs.

3. The sales manager _____ notable _____ to the development and expansion of the company.

4. Both "can" and "could" in this sentence _____ a future possibility.

5. This letter _____ the sale of the house.

6. As far as its form is concerned, downward communication can be carried out _____ (like memos, bulletins, reports, news letters, etc.) or _____ (like telephone talks, presentations, speeches, video conferences, etc.).

7. We believe this first shipment _____ further business.

8. A builder bought the farm, _____ it _____ lots, and built homes on them.

9. How shall we increase our _____ in South America in view of American competition?

10. The small river port _____ one of our great cities.

Ⅲ. Word Formation

Fill in the blank with the proper form of the word given in the parentheses.

1. We hope we'll keep frequent _____ (communicate) with the manufacturers.

2. Horizontal communication is often neglected by the management because of its _____ (informal).

3. Would it be _____ (prefer) to leave tomorrow?

4. We have every effort to _____ (persuasive) our client to accept your offer.

5. We hope this new office will serve to _____ (promotion) our already excellent business relations.

6. You must work out your fact-finding report with great _____ (accurate).

7. We have _____ (distribution) the samples to our customers for their research, but the samples you sent us is not sufficient for tests.

8. Your prompt _____ (responsive) to our request will be highly appreciated.

9. We are ready to _____ (competition) with any producers.

10. The manual gives very _____ (complicate) instructions.

Ⅳ. Translation

1. 卖方的答复指的是我们 CU-1379 号订货单。(refer to)

2. 中国公司与美国公司有很多业务交往。(have contact with)

3. 他对他的损失满不在乎。(care about)

4. 这甚至牵涉到我们在欧洲的利益。(involve)

5. 我们必须研究日本市场的特点。(feature)

6. 在你方上海的代表帮助下,我们一个星期之内就得到了许可证。(with the help of)

7. 进口商品打入市场的势头正在削弱。(penetration)

8. 我丈夫和我各自去看自己的母亲。(respective)

9. 我们的产品须与其他产品竞争。(compete with)

10. 我们曾访问过你们的国家,在那里意外地遇到一些客户。(encounter)

V. Cloze

It is a typical day at the office—a senior manager is away when an urgent letter arrives from one of her clients. Meanwhile someone has ... Example... that the wrong price list has been sent out and half of the last ___1___ has been returned because the addresses are out of date. After a lot of time and effort has been ___2___ sorting out all these problems, someone asks ___3___ the new computer system didn't ___4___ all of these from happening. Unfortunately, such problems are ___5___.

One form which used to have serious computer problems is Brinkman Lewis, a professional services firm. David Callaghan, a partner at the firm, ___6___ "The initial problem for us was that we had all this information on computers around the office but didn't know what to ___7___ with it."

Finally, Brinkman Lewis decided to ___8___ a network linking all the machines in the office. ___9___ than simply asking one of the senior managers to ___10___ responsibility for information technology, the firm brought in ___11___ Zoe Edlington to plan the development of its network. She began by upgrading the ___12___ telephone system so it could be integrated with the computers to provide closer links between the ___13___ of the firm. She then began finding other ways in which the information already on the network could be ___14___ more effectively.

The strategy worked. The company soon realized that there could be a market for such a ___15___, and before long Zoe Edlington was head of the firm's new network consultancy business.

1. A. campaign   B. postage   C. mail shot   D. launch

2. A. spent   B. lost   C. taken   D. employed

3. A. where   B. what   C. when   D. why

4. A. avoid   B. prevent   C. block   D. frustrate

5. A. common   B. average   C. traditional   D. general

6. A. convinces   B. discusses   C. refers   D. explains

7. A. make   B. try   C. have   D. do

8. A. manufacture   B. found

    C. introduce   D. make

9. A. Rather   B. Other   C. Instead   D. Opposite

10. A. confirm   B. manage   C. exercise   D. accept

11. A. agent   B. specialist   C. master   D. authority

12. A. former   B. once   C. existing   D. ongoing

13. A. members B. colleagues   C. workmates   D. subscribers

14. A. used   B. worked   C. practiced   D. operated

15. A. result   B. clarification C. solution   D. decision

VI. Reading Comprehension

"The organizational weaknesses that entrepreneurs have to deal with every day would cause the managers of a mature company to panic," Andrew Bidden wrote recently in *Boston Business Review*. This seems to suggest that the leaders of entrepreneurial or small businesses must be unlike other managers, or the problems faced by such leaders must be the subject of a specialized body of wisdom, or possibly both. Unfortunately, neither is true. Not much worth reading about managing the entrepreneurial or small business has been written, and the leaders of such businesses are made of flesh and blood, like the rest of us.

Furthermore, little has been done to address the aspects of entrepreneurial or small businesses that are so difficult to deal with and so different from the challenges faced by management in big business. In part this is because those involved in gathering expertise about business and in selling advice to businesses have historically been more interested in the needs of big business. In part, in the UK at least, it is also because small businesses have always preferred to adapt to changing circumstances.

The organizational problems of entrepreneurial or small businesses are thus forced upon the individuals who lead them. Even more so than for bigger businesses, the old saying is true—that people, particularly those who make the important decisions, are business' most important asset. The research that does exist shows that neither money nor the ability to access more of it is the major factor determining growth. The main reason why an entrepreneurial business stops growing is the lack of management and leadership resource available to the business when it matters. Give an entrepreneur an experienced, skilled team and he or she will find the funds every time. Getting the team, though, is the difficult bit. Part of the problem for entrepreneurs is the speed of change that affects their businesses. They have to cope with continuous changes yet have always been suspicious about the latest "management solution". They regard the many offerings from business schools as out of date even before they leave the planning board and have little faith in the recommendations of consultants when they arrive in the hands of young, inexperienced graduates. But such impatience with "management solutions" does not mean that problems can be left to solve themselves. However, the leaders of growing businesses are still left with the problem of who to turn to for advice.

The answer is horribly simple: leaders of small businesses can ask each other. The collective knowledge of a group of leaders can prove enormously helpful in solving the specific problems of individuals. One leader's problems have certainly been solved already by someone else. There is an organization called KITE which enables those responsible for small businesses to meet. Its members, all of whom are chief executives, go through a demanding selection process, and then join a small group of other chief executives. They come from a range of business sectors and each offers a different corporate history. Each group is led by a "moderator", an independently selected businessman or woman who has been specially trained to head the group. Each member takes it in turn to host a meeting at his or her business premises and, most important of all, group discussions are kept strictly confidential. This encourages a free sharing of problems and increases the possibility of solutions being discovered.

1. What does the writer say about entrepreneurs in the first paragraph?
   A. It is wrong to assume that they are different from other managers.
   B. The problems they have to cope with are specific to small businesses.
   C. They find it difficult to attract staff with sufficient expertise.
   D. They could learn from the organizational skills of managers in large companies.

2. According to the second paragraph, what has led to a lack of support for entrepreneurs?
   A. Entrepreneurs have always preferred to act independently.
   B. The requirements of big businesses have always taken priority.
   C. It is difficult to find solutions to the problems faced by entrepreneurs.
   D. Entrepreneurs are reluctant to provide information about their businesses.

3. What does the writer say about the expansion of small businesses?
   A. Many small businesses do not produce enough profits to finance growth.
   B. Many employees in small businesses have problems working as part of a team.
   C. Being able to recruit the right people is the most important factor affecting growth.
   D. Leaders of small businesses lack the experience to make their companies a

success.

4. What does the writer say is an additional problem for entrepreneurs?

    A. They rely on management systems that are out of date.

    B. They will not adopt measures that provide long-term solutions.

    C. They have little confidence in the business advice that is available.

    D. They do not take market changes into account when drawing up business plans.

5. What does the writer say the members of the KITE organization provide?

    A. Advice on how to select suitable staff.

    B. A means of contacting potential clients.

    C. A simple checklist for analyzing problems.

    D. Direct experience of a number of industries.

6. The writer says that KITE groups are likely to succeed because _____.

    A. members are able to elect their leader

    B. the leaders have received extensive training

    C. members are encouraged to adopt a critical approach

    D. information is not passed on to non-members

VII. Writing

(I) Writing Basics: Sentence Building(3): Variety

Variety is essential to good writing. It will be difficult to interest the reader if all the sentences in a composition are of the same structure or of the same length. There are a number of ways to achieve variety including coordination and subordination we have learned in the last two units. In this unit we will learn how to begin a sentence and how to vary the length of a sentence.

Most English sentences begin with a subject. We can also begin a sentence in the following ways:

With adjectives: Kind and pretty, she is liked by many young men. (c.f. She is kind and pretty and is liked by many young men.)

With a prepositional phrase: Over the years, we have tasted many hardships.

With an adverb: Reluctantly the child turned off TV and went to bed.

With an adverbial clause: As I looked back over the work I had done I feel so surprised that I had made great progress.

With an infinitive phrase: To make me feel at ease, she invited me with much food.

With an appositive: Aristotle, the ancient Greek philosopher, thought that the mind was based in the heart.

With a noun clause: That he died in the car accident shocked us all.

Sentence length is also important to achieve variety. Short sentences and long sentences can avoid the monotony and make the composition more interesting and pleasant. For example: The traveller came up to an old grey building and climbed the stairs leading to the second floor. He stopped in front of a room with the number 5 painted on its door, took out an old envelope from his black handbag, checked the address written on it and put it back in his bag. Then he rang the bell.

Now will you try to combine the following short sentences into one sentence using whatever way you like? But pay attention to the variation of the beginning of the sentence.

1. The house is old and dilapidated.

   The house is situated in a deserted lane.

   The house makes a dismal picture.

2. The girl was singing merrily.

   The girl was singing on her way home.

   The girl was singing an American song.

3. The tourists were caught in the rain and soaked through.

   They hurried back to the hotel.

4. The Wuyi Mountains are noted as the most picturesque area in southeast China.

   The mountains extended more than 500 kilometers along the border of Fujian and Jiangxi.

5. He is an honest man.

   They all know that.

6. The story has a sad ending.

   The ending of the story impressed me deeply.

(Ⅱ) **Writing Assignment**

Being a good and effective listener is the key to communicating with people and keeping successful relationships. But how can we be a good listener or even a professional listener? Different people have different opinions and experience. You are supposed to write an article of 150 words on the topic **"How to Be a Good Listener"**? Each paragraph of your article could begin with the following topic sentences:

Listening is likely the most frequently required communication skill.

Poor listening can cause many problems.

Effective listening not only requires skills but also efforts.

VIII. Presentation(Speaking)

Work in pairs and in this part you are asked to give a short talk on a business topic. You have to choose one of the topics from the two below. You have time to prepare your ideas. Go to the library or visit the Internet to find out your topic by referring to some materials or books. Write down the information you have found and give a presentation next time. You may refer to the following expressions:

A WHAT IS IMPORTANT WHEN...?
   WORKING ON A TASK WITH OTHERS
   · COOPERATION
   · COMMUNICATE WITH EACH OTHER
   · WORK HARD

B WHAT IS IMPORTANT WHEN...?
   GIVING A SHORT PRESENTATION
   · THE STRUCTURE
   · VOICE
   · EYE CONTACT

Enjoy Your Time

1. There's one language used in every country. People who use it are young and old, short and tall, thin and fat. It's everybody's second language. It's easy to understand, though you can't hear it. Do you know what it is?

2. My first is in "snow", but not in "ice",
   My second is in "rose", and also in "rice",
   My third is not in "pencil", but in "paper".
   My whole is a place where there is a lot of water.

Examination One (Unit 1 – Unit 4)

Ⅰ. **Make a guess of the underlined words or phrases in the following statements and tick off the best choice that has the closest meaning.** (1 × 15 = 15 **points**)

1. He was a <u>prestidigitator</u> who makes the children happy by pulling rabbits out of hats, making fire from the mouth, and other similar tricks.

   A. magician   B. teacher

   C. doctor   D. businessman

2. Mother was tall, fat and middle-aged. The headmaster of the school was an older woman, almost as <u>plump</u> as mother, and much shorter.

   A. beautiful   B. slim   C. fat   D. tall

3. In the past, the company seemed to run in an orderly way. Now, however, everything seems to be in a state of <u>turmoil</u>.

   A. peace   B. confusion   C. success   D. safety

4. Before the main business of a conference begins, the chairman usually makes a short <u>preliminary</u> speech. In other words, he says a few things by way of introduction.

   A. introductory   B. concluding

   C. important   D. short

5. Since I could not afford to buy the real painting of the famous painter, I bought a <u>replica</u>. An inexperienced eye could not tell the difference.

   A. false   B. copy   C. true   D. similarity

6. If you are capable of working twelve hours a day without a rest, and if you can engage in physical exercise for hours without seeming to get tired, then you are <u>indefatigable</u>.

   A. tiresome   B. tireless   C. strong   D. healthy

7. There is no cure for Alzheimer's. But a drug called <u>ARICEPT</u> has been used by millions of people to help their symptoms.

   A. a medicine to cure Alzheimer's

   B. a medicine to delay signs of aging

   C. a medicine to reduce the symptoms of Alzheimer's

   D. a medicine to cure brain damages

8. Finally although some social science majors may still find it more difficult than

their technically trained classmates to <u>land</u> the first job, recent graduates report that they don't regret their choice of study.

    A. keep for some time   B. successfully get

    C. immediately start   D. lose regretfully

9. Today young couples who are just starting their households often spend lots of their money on <u>appliances</u>, for instance, washing machines, refrigerators and color televisions.

    A. electric equipments   B. furniture

    C. cooking equipments   D. daily goods

10. They will <u>be on the night shift</u>—from midnight to 6 a.m.—next week.

    A. work at daytime   B. work from day to night

    C. work at night   D. work without rest

11. American businessmen expect employees to be <u>punctual</u>. They do not expect that the workers will come late.

    A. on time   B. loyal   C. hard working D. clever

12. Should the government <u>regulate</u> the cost of resources such as oil and gas? Some people do not believe that government control is the solution to the problem of the rising cost of fuel.

    A. announce   B. control   C. know   D. publish

13. One of the <u>predominant</u> concerns today is the future of our natural resources. This issue is of greatest importance because it is becoming clear to many people that our present resources will not last forever.

    A. first   B. final   C. little   D. important

14. Cleaning up waterways is an <u>enormous</u> task. The job is so large, in fact, that the government may not be able to save some of the rivers and lakes which have been polluted.

    A. simple   B. little   C. very great   D. hard

15. We were told that our's was the most <u>spacious</u> room in the hotel. That was why we had to pay so much for it.

    A. quite large   B. beautiful

    C. magnificent   D. modern

Ⅱ. **Complete the following statements by ticking off the best choice.** (1 × 15 = 15
   points)

1. When does the new law become _____ ?

   A. effective   B. efficient   C. affection   D. affective

2. According to a recent _____ , 30% of employees wanted to change their
   present jobs.

   A. statistics   B. research   C. survey   D. speech

3. You will see this product _____ wherever you go.

   A. to be advertised   B. advertised

   C. advertise   D. advertising

4. We must try to _____ the best of our moral values for our children and
   grandchildren.

   A. predict   B. prescribe   C. purchase   D. preserve

5. Clark felt that his _____ in one of the most dramatic medical experiments of
   all time was worth the suffering he has experienced.

   A. application   B. appreciation

   C. presentation   D. participation

6. Damage to the goods was _____ at $ 1,000.

   A. assessed   B. applied   C. advanced   D. assured

7. They often _____ this product with poor quality.

   A. connect   B. apply   C. associate   D. relate

8. The medicine is out of date and it's without any _____ .

   A. effect   B. influence   C. progress   D. impression

9. Microsoft _____ Windows and made the computer widely used.

   A. came across   B. came up

   C. came up with   D. came to

10. Would you be able to _____ within six weeks of receipt of the order? Our
    customers are in urgent need of them.

    A. deliver   B. place   C. design   D. check

11. Manufacturing and banking are the chief _____ of the country.

    A. enterprises   B. part

    C. companies   D. corporations

12. The manager asked a lawyer to take _____ action against that company.

    A. certain   B. affective   C. legal   D. strong

13. The _____ price our customers can accept is $ 150 per set.

A. minimum   B. largest   C. high   D. maximum

14. The _____ IT has brought about the development of science and technology.

    A. advanced   B. experienced
    C. new   D. out-of-date

15. He is always late for work, and his boss was finally _____ and laid him off.

    A. impossible   B. unbearable
    C. tolerable   D. bad

Ⅲ. Fill in the blanks with the words or phrases given in the box. Change the forms if necessary. (1 × 10 = 10 **points**)

distribute	afford	efficient	maximum	assure
contract	deliver	apply to	keep pace with	identify

1. We wish to appoint you as our exclusive _____ for our hardware in Los Angeles.

2. We always honour our _____ and keep our words.

3. We can _____ one hundred and fifty yuan for a piece but no more.

4. The new tax law does not _____ joint ventures signed before its promulgation.

5. I can _____ you that the prices we offer you are very favorable.

6. As we are heavily committed with orders, we can only _____ half of the quantity in May and the other half in June.

7. We should speed up the production so as to _____ the growing demand.

8. We understand quite well that you have increased your production to the _____.

9. The report criticized the _____ of the sales staff.

10. The buyer buys from the seller all products _____ as follows.

Ⅳ. Cloze (1 × 15 = 15 **points**)

A big part of __1__ success is learning to manage your emotions. We all have times when we are anxious, angry or even burnt-out. Learning to be aware of our feelings, __2__ the surrounding situation, will allow us to develop alternative responses and redirect our emotions in positive, constructive ways.

All of us face moments when we __3__ anxiety on the job. The important thing is to know what's making you uncomfortable and turn it into an opportunity to learn.

When something does not go as you __4__ and you feel anxious or disappointed, it helps to understand that these feelings are hard to be prevented. The most experienced professional still feel anxious __5__. The technique is to keep it __6__ control. You have to decide to take each day as it comes. Do your planning, be careful of your own job, produce the best quality product or service you can, and __7__ will come.

One technique, which may help keep you calm in your work, is to develop __8__ method to your job. Put things in order according to its importance and do first things first. Use checklists. This will allow you to __9__ more time and energy to the most important items.

If you start to feel any of the symptoms(症状) of burn-out-over tiredness, lack of interest, a unclear sense of uselessness—immediately take corrective action. It's not __10__ for professionals to get near the range of burn-out. Many are serious about their job and put it long, hard hours to be successful. The fact is, after a certain point, one loses his sharpness. The harder you work, __11__ you get.

Burn-out is a workplace depression, so learn to recognize the symptoms and take the necessary preventative actions:

First, __12__ on your actual hours, but increase the intensity(强度) of your attention, so those hours will be more __13__.

Take a vacation, even if it's only a long weekend or, an afternoon off.

One of the best things to lower your pressure is exercise. Plan to take a walk __14__ once a day, even if it's during lunch.

Get out and meet new people; learn new things.

In the end, remember that you are __15__ your emotions. Although you cannot control every event in your workplace, you can control your own feelings and actions. That's as much as anyone can ask and as much as anyone needs to succeed.

1. A. get   B. achieving   C. have   D. having
2. A. also   B. the same as C. as well as   D. the same to
3. A. experience   B. enjoy   C. expect   D. take
4. A. wish to   B. hope   C. expect   D. get
5. A. at times   B. all the time C. at a time   D. in time
6. A. on   B. under   C. up   D. at
7. A. happiness   B. money   C. success   D. trouble
8. A. systematic   B. tight   C. loose   D. great
9. A. put   B. invest   C. use   D. devote
10. A. usual   B. uncommon   C. common   D. great

11. A. the less   B. less   C. more   D. the more
12. A. cut back   B. increase   C. cut   D. reduce
13. A. important   B. useless   C. powerful   D. productive
14. A. at least   B. at most   C. often   D. more than
15. A. in the charge of   B. control
    C. in charge of   D. having

V. Reading Comprehension (2 × 10 = 20 points)

(A)

Employee loyalty is on the rise, according to a recent survey of U. S. workers earlier this year, and the surveyor, Walker Information, said that is good news for their employers, but they still have a way to go to build a truly loyal work force that can lower costs.

The survey of 2,500 employees finds that 34 percent of those surveyed are both committed to their employers and planning to stay at least two years. That's up from 30 percent in a 2003 survey and only 24 percent in 2001.

Loyal employees are also far more likely to perform beyond their job's minimum requirements, according to the firm. But only 55 percent of those surveyed said companies treat employees well, and only 41 percent felt their employer views staff as its most important asset. Those measures that lead to employee loyalty need to improve, according to Walker.

The survey characterized 31 percent of respondents as "high risk" and looking to leave their employer, although that is down from 34 percent in the 2003 survey.

Ethical behavior by employers is also important to building employee loyalty, according to the firm's survey.

Chris Woolard said that being able to build loyalty and reduce turnover is a financial advantage for companies. He said some businesses that have been hit by high turnover rate have done the most to improve employee ties, with loyalty among health care workers climbing to 39 percent in the most recent survey, up from 31 percent in 2003. Information technology saw the biggest jump, with 36 percent feeling truly loyal, up from only 19 percent in 2003, when employees were far more likely to report they were ready to jump at the next best offer.

1. According to the survey, which analysis is false?

   A. According to the recent survey, 34 percent of those surveyed are both committed to their employers and planning to stay at least two years.

   B. The loyalty rate is 30 percent in a 2003 survey.

   C. The loyalty rate is the lowest in 2001.

   D. The loyalty rate of employees has been raised 6% compared to that in 2001.

2. For the employers, _____ .

   A. nothing needs to be done at present, for the employees are satisfied already

   B. building loyalty and reducing turnover is a financial advantage for companies

   C. building loyalty is no good, and they can hire new ones if they are dissatisfied

   D. ethical behavior by employers is of little importance to building employee loyalty

3. The Walker Information suggests that _____ .

   A. those measures that lead to employee loyalty need to improve

   B. loyal employees are far more likely to perform beyond their job's minimum requirements

   C. ethical behavior by employers is also important to building employee loyalty

   D. all of the above

4. Which is correct according to the passage?

   A. The recent survey is done on 2 300 employees.

   B. Those surveyed who are both committed to their employers and planning to stay at least two years have risen 3 percent as compared with that in 2003.

   C. Less than half of those surveyed said companies treat employees well.

   D. About 40 percent of those surveyed felt their employer views staff as its most important asset.

5. What can't be concluded from the text?

   A. The employee loyalty reaches the highest.

   B. Though the employee loyalty is on the rise, the employers should still be careful.

   C. Most of the employees are satisfied with their present working conditions.

   D. The employee loyalty is closely connected with a company's turnover.

(B)

ITV, the biggest commercial broadcaster in Britain and a subject of frequent takeover speculation, said Wednesday that it had rejected an approach from a group of buyout firms, under which a former head of the British Broadcasting Corp. would take over as chief executive of ITV.

However, the buyout firms hinted that they might come back with a revised offer.

ITV provided no details of the bid(投标), but a person briefed the investment group would invest £ 1. 3 billion, or more into ITV, acquiring a 48 percent share. Existing shareholders would be left with 52 percent ownership.

Under the proposal that was presented to ITV, Greg Dyke, a former director general of the BBC and currently an adviser to Apax, would become chief executive of ITV, taking the place of Charles Allen. Dyke stepped down from his BBC role in 2004 after that broadcaster was criticized for its report on the government's case for joining the war in Iraq.

ITV gets most of its revenue from advertising. The company's flagship(旗舰) channel, ITV1, has suffered in recent years as viewers have changed to new, digital channels or the Internet; advertising revenue at ITV1 fell 3. 3 percent last year, though ITV's overall ad revenue rose 2. 7 percent.

Big U. S. media companies, including Time Warner, were cited as possible suitors.

Shares of ITV rose 9. 4 percent, to close at 128 pence Wednesday for a market value of £ 5. 2 billion. ITV's bonds plunged on concern that debtholders would suffer from the way the bid was structured. The ITV board "all concluded that the proposal could not be in the best interests of all shareholders and accordingly rejected it. "

6. What does the word "reject" mean according to the text?

    A. accept   B. refuse   C. thank   D. take

7. Which information about ITV is false?

    A. ITV is the biggest commercial broadcaster in Britain.

    B. It is now facing a lot of difficulties.

    C. It has been a subject of frequent takeover speculation.

    D. ITV gets most of its revenue from government's support.

8. Why has it become the target of takeover speculation?

    A. The company's in trouble recently.

    B. The company's flagship channel, ITV1, has suffered in recent years as viewers have changed to new, digital channels or the Internet.

    C. Advertising revenue at ITV1 fell 3. 3 percent last year.

    D. All of above.

9. At the beginning of the material, why did it reject an approach from a group of buyout firms?

A. ITV's bonds plunged on concern that debtholders would suffer from the way the bid was structured.

B. The ITV board "all concluded that the proposal could not be in the best interests of all shareholders and accordingly rejected it."

C. ITV could go through the problem by itself.

D. Both A and B.

10. What do you know about Greg Dyke?

    A. Greg Dyke had been the director general of the BBC.

    B. He left BBC because he was criticized for his reporting on the government's case for joining the war in Iraq.

    C. He is currently an adviser to Apax, and he would become chief executive of ITV if the buyout is possible.

    D. All of the above.

VI. Translate the following Chinese sentences into English. ($2 \times 5 = 10$ points)

1. 那里存货很多,市场不佳。

2. 我们感谢你们的提议,并希望下次可进一步协助你们,为你方来信所列其他商品找到买主。

3. 这家公司在几个城市里设有分公司。

4. 国际贸易产生于国际分工。

5. 请寄来价目表,以便我们能充分研究开展业务的可能性。

VII. Write a short passage of no less than 100 words according to the sentences given below. (15 points)

Private Cars

Should the development of private cars be encouraged or limited in China? To judge this issue, we should look at different aspects.

First of all, the private car is a symbol of freedom.

However, too many private cars can be harmful. _____

_____

_____

_____

It seems to me that China, at its present stage of development, should _____

_____

_____

_____

Unit 5

Product Description and Development

Pre-reading Activities

New Words: ear-ring carat gem accessory visible

I. **Listen to the following short passage twice and fill in the blanks with the words you've heard.**

The best thing about these diamond ear-rings is that they can be __1__ every single day to show them off. The diamonds have a total carat weight of 1/3 carats. The smooth finish of the __2__ and the light-reflecting cut of the gems make the pair immediately __3__. This is an essential __4__ that can be worn frequently and with almost anything—it is certain to be a __5__.

These are fine __6__ diamonds, with special light. They are near-colorless, with a __7__ color rating of H-I, and __8__ white to the eye. The __9__ rating of these diamonds is SI1/2, which are not __10__ to the unaided eye.

II. **What do you think is the most important for a company if it wants to sell its products? Tell us your reasons.**

Text A

Product Strategy Issues in China

There are three strategic product issues facing Chinese manufacturers. The first is quality. The second is product specialization. The third is product innovation. Quality improvement can make China more competitive in the market for standard products, like refrigerators, cell phones and TVs. Product specialization can get China into the high performance segment of product categories. This means higher prices and better margins.

The third strategy is product innovation, which enables China to not only get the highest prices and margins from early adopters of advanced technology, but also position companies for market dominance. Chinese executives have been wrestling to break the general impression that "Made in China" means low quality and low price. In order to succeed in the Chinese market against foreign competitors, as well as to win market share for value-added brands in global markets, companies must be able to match the quality of foreign products.

When Haier Chief Executive Zhang Ruimin decided the direction of the company, he moved with a passion for quality. When a customer complained about a broken refrigerator, he walked through the factory and found 76 defective appliances. He piled them up and handed sledgehammers to the workers who assembled them. At his suggestion, they all set upon the fridges, reducing them to junk. That act of destruction impressed on employees that poor quality would no longer be acceptable.

This strict means paid off Haier. It now has 62 distributors and 30,000 sales outlets in the markets of many developed countries and regions. In the period of World Trade Organization entry, Zhang believes that Chinese companies will not be able to dominate the Chinese market unless they succeed in capturing market share in the markets of developed countries and regions. The quality strategy is not just for export purposes, but also for success and profitability in the domestic market.

Lack of improved technology can be costly to Chinese companies. While Chinese manufacturers dominated the VCD market, they were slow to develop DVD products. As a result, Panasonic, Phillips, Sony and Pioneer captured the DVD market. Chinese companies are just shaving off small pieces with copy products and unreasonable price cuts. It will be hard to drive foreign brands from DVD control.

Some companies are trying to move up the value chain in terms of technology. The

Konka Group has 25 per cent of the Chinese television market, selling 4. 7 million sets in 1998. In spite of the fact that foreign brands are reaching 40 per cent to 50 per cent of the domestic market, and that foreign technology is considered to be superior, Konka is planning to introduce high definition TV in the US market. It will offer large clear HDTV at half the price of foreign brands. As technology improves and competitive prices fall, Konka feels that it can keep an obvious price difference for the consumers at a profit to the company rather than being satisfied to remain in the conventional TV segment, it is seeking the higher margins of new technology.

It is making a leap forward in consumer electronics through technology. With foreign TV companies seen on store shelves by half the domestic market, Chinese manufacturers are certain that their national future requires technological innovation. The era of dominating market share through price-cutting is coming to a close. General manager for sales at Panda firmly states, "Without technical support and highly competitive products, the industry is filled with difficulties and threats."

There are now five state-level research and development (R&D) institutes leading innovation. Skyworth has put public a "Green TV" and Xiahua launched a variable frequency TV. Price cutting wins a greater share of low-end markets, while new products and technology offensives always win at the high end where brand value and long-term advantages are created. Phillips and Sharp used China as the first market to launch new and most advanced TV models, like plasma panel TVs. Focused R&D and product introduction strategies can bring China's companies into this game.

Words & Expressions

1. specification/ˌspesifiˈkeiʃən/*n.* a detailed instruction about how something should be designed or made 规格
2. innovation/ˌinəuˈveiʃən/*n.* the instruction of new ideas or methods 革新, 创新
3. refrigerator/riˈfridʒəˌreitə/*n.* a special cupboard kept cold by electricity, in which you store food and drink, also called fridge 冰箱
4. cell phone—a telephone that you can carry around with you, that works from a system that uses a network of radio stations to pass on signals（利用无线电通讯网的）移动电话
5. segment/ˈsegmənt/*n.* a part of something that is in some way different from or affected differently from the whole 部分
6. margin/ˈmɑːdʒin/*n.* the difference between the cost and the selling price of

commodities（成本与售价间的）差额,利润,赚头

7. dominance/'dɔmɪnəns/*n.* the fact of being more powerful, more important, or more noticeable than other people or things 优势,显要,突出

8. wrestle/'resl/*v.* try to deal with or find a solution to a difficult problem 努力解决,绞尽脑汁

9. impression/im'preʃən/*n.* the opinion or feeling you have about someone or something because of the way they seem（对人、事的）印象,感想

10. value-added/ˌvælju'ædid/*adj.* extra value that a product gains 增值的

11. passion/'pæʃən/*n.* a very strong, deeply felt emotion, especially of the sexual love, of anger, or of belief in an idea or principle 强烈的感情,激情

12. defective/di'fektiv/*adj.* not made properly, or not working properly 有问题的,有毛病的,有缺陷的

13. appliance/ə'plaiəns/*n.* a piece of electrical equipment such as a cooker or washing machine, used in people's homes 家用电器,家用电子设备

14. sledgehammer/'sledʒˌhæmə/*n.* a large, heavy hammer 大锤

15. assemble/ə'sembl/*v.* to put all the parts of something together 组合,装配

16. reduce/ri'djuːs/*v.* bring sb/sth into a specified state or condition（与 to 连用）变为,化为

17. junk/dʒʌŋk/*n.* old or unwanted objects that have no use or value 废旧杂物

18. distributor/di'stribjutə/*n.* a company or person that supplies shops and companies with goods 销售者,批发商,分销商

19. outlet/'autlet/*n.* a shop, company or organization through which products are sold 批发商店,经销公司（机构）

20. capture/'kæptʃə/*v.* to get something that previously belonged to one of your competitors 夺得,抢占

21. profitability/ˌprɔfitə'biliti/*n.* the state of producing a profit, or the degree to which a business or activity is profitable 获利（状况）,盈利（程度）

22. costly/'kɔstli/*adj.* something that is costly causes a lot of problems or trouble 代价高的,损失大的

23. superior/suː'piəriə/*adj.* a word meaning of very good quality, used especially in advertising 质量上乘的,优质的

24. conventional/kən'venʃənl/*adj.* a conventional object or way of doing something is of a type that has been used or available for a long time and is considered the usual type 按惯例的,因袭的,传统的

25. leap/liːp/*n.* vigorous jump 跳跃

by/in leaps and bounds 迅速地,突飞猛进地

26. launch/lɔ:ntʃ/*v.* to make a new product, book etc. available for sale for the first time 把(新产品、新书等)投放市场,推出,发行

27. low-end *adj.* 低档的,生产低档产品的

28. focused/'fəukəst/*adj.* paying careful attention to what you are doing, in a way that shows you are determined to succeed 集中注意力的,聚精会神的

29. set upon   to make people or animals attack someone 唆使(人或动物)攻击 (某人)

30. pay off   if a plan or something that you try to do pays off, it is successful (计划等)取得成功

31. domestic market 国内市场

32. lack of   not having something, or not having enough of it 没有,不足,缺乏

Notes

1. This text is selected and adapted from CNNMoney. com.

2. market share(市场份额,市场占有率): The proportion of the total demand (for a product) that is supplied by a particular manufacturer or brand.

3. high definition: Type of digital television system offering a significantly greater number of scanning lines, and therefore a clearer picture, than that provided by conventional systems. Typically, HDTV has about twice the horizontal(水平的) and vertical(垂直的) resolution of current 525-line or 625-line standards; a frame rate of at least 24 Hz; and a picture aspect ratio of 9:16 instead of the current 3:4.

4. plasma panel: A type of flat-panel display that works by sandwiching(夹入) a neon(氖)/xenon(氙) gas mixture between two sealed glass plates with parallel electrodes(电极) deposited on their surfaces. The plates are sealed so that the electrodes form right angles, creating pixels(像素). When a voltage(电压) pulse passes between two electrodes, the gas breaks down and produces weakly ionized(电离的) plasma, which emits UV(紫外的) radiation(放射线). The UV radiation activates(刺激) color phosphorous(磷) and visible light is emitted from each pixel. Today, plasma displays are becoming more and more popular. Compared to conventional CRT displays, plasma displays are about one-tenth the thickness—around 4, and one-sixth the weight—under 67 pounds for a 40 display. They use over 16 million colors and have a 160 degree-viewing angle.

Word Study

1. assemble *v.*

   ① to put all the parts of something together 组合,装配

   ② if a group of people assemble in one place, they all go there together 集合,聚集

   All the people assembled at Mary's house. 所有的人都聚集在玛丽的屋子里。

   assemble in the school hall 在学校礼堂集合

   assembly line *n.* a system for making things in a factory in which the products move past a line of workers who each make or check one part 装配线,流水作业线

2. reduce *v.*

   ① bring sb/sth into a specified state or condition (与 to 连用)变为,化为

   reduce the rocks to dust 把石块碎成粉末

   reduce sth to rubble/ashes 把某物(尤指建筑物)夷为废墟/化为灰烬等

   ② to make something smaller or less in size, amount, or price 缩小,减少,降低(尺寸、数量或价格)

   We were hoping that they would reduce the rent a little.

   我们希望他们会把租金降低一点。

3. distributor *n.* a company or person that supplies shops and companies with goods 销售者,批发商,分销商

   distribute *v.* (尤指有计划地)分发,分配,分送

   He is distributing leaflets to passersby. 他向行人分发传单。

   distribute sth among sb

   distribute books among the students 把书分给学生

4. capture *v.*

   ① to get something that previously belonged to one of your competitors 夺得,抢占

   Japanese firms have captured over 60% of the electronics market.

   日本公司已经抢占了超过60%的电子市场。

   ② to catch someone in order to make him prisoner 俘虏,逮捕

   The criminal was captured when trying to escape from the city.

   罪犯在企图逃离这座城市时被捕获。

   ③ succeed in representing (sb/sth) in a picture, on films, etc. 记录;以影片、文字等保存原状

The state visit by the premier captured the headlines of all newspapers.
总理的国事访问各报都用大标题登出。

In his traveling report, he tried to capture the beauty of the Great Waterfalls. 他努力在他的这篇游记中记录下大瀑布的美。

Post-reading Activities

I. Comprehension Questions.

1. What are the three things that face Chinese manufacturers?

2. What is the benefit of quality?

3. What is the benefit of product specialization?

4. What is the benefit of product innovation?

5. What is the general image of "Made in China"?

6. What did Haier Chief Executive Zhang Ruimin do to achieve quality? Why did he think quality is so important?

7. What did Konka do to improve technology?

8. What did other famous TV manufacturers do to win the market?

II. Fill in the blanks with the words or phrases given in the box. Change the forms if necessary.

profit	superior	focus	dominate	impression
distribute	outlet	digital	defective	launch

1. Benetton has retail _____ in every major European city.

2. The _____ each day from the store is usually around $ 500.

3. The company _____ everyday goods to the local stores.

4. This western restaurant is _____ to the one we went to last week.

5. All the cars are tested for _____ before they leave the factory.

6. We're _____ with the standard of the products.

7. He has a large amount of money and _____ the factory economically.

8. _____ cameras have more functions than common cameras.

9. The company is going to _____ its new products next month.

10. Haier has been successful by _____ on the quality of its products.

III. Summary of the Text.

Chinese manufacturers are __1__ three strategies. The first is quality, which can make them more __2__ in the market. "Made in China" has the general __3__ of low quality and low price. To __4__ in __5__ market, companies must be able to match those foreign products.

Next comes product __6__. This can earn better __7__ for them.

The third strategy is product __8__. Lack of __9__ technology can be costly to Chinese companies. Therefore, many companies are making improvement in this field. For instance, Konka is to __10__ HDTV in the US market.

Ⅳ. **Translate the following sentences into English.**

1. 父亲向我强调努力工作的重要意义。(impress)
2. 那家制鞋厂商有几家代销店。(outlet)
3. 中国拥有广阔的国内市场。(domestic market)
4. 高清晰电视吸引了众多的消费者。(high definition, popular)
5. 生产商都希望占有最大的市场份额。(capture, market share)

Text B

Panasonic Launches World's Most Advanced 58-inch HD Plasma TV

Continuing its commitment to providing the most technologically superior HD plasma televisions for every room size and viewing environment, Panasonic, world leader in plasma manufacturing and sales, has once again raised the bar on HDTV performance with the release of two 58-inch, 1366 × 768-pixel resolution models capable of displaying nearly 29 billion colors.

Scheduled to ship in early summer, both models feature Panasonic's technology for single remote/one-button control of TV, DVD recorders and home theater systems, and incorporate an integrated SD Memory Card slot for instant, cableless viewing of digital images and slide shows.

"The new 58-inch plasma is the perfect complement to and rounds out Panasonic's existing line by providing a screen size that fits nicely between our 50-inch and our soon to be delivered 65-inch 1080p plasma," said Andrew Nelkin, Vice President of Panasonic's Display Group.

"We exceeded all our expectations in 2005," Nelkin continued. "It was an extraordinary year in which Panasonic made great gains in technology, sales, and industry recognition. This past year saw Panasonic's plasmas rated at the top of a number of media best-of-the-year awards, and we fully expect to repeat those results this year."

"Now that we've increased the number of our panel's displayable colors and upped our maximum contrast range, we feel very confident of keeping our top ranking with both HDTV plasma buyers and the consumer electronics media. "

"We believe that products facilitating the coming Digital Lifestyle must be designed from a human engineering as well as an electronic engineering point of view," Nelkin added.

"Take our new EZ-Sync. At first glance, it might look like just another so-called universal remote. But universal remotes are really not 'universal' at all. What they do is combine a bunch of incompatible controllers into one case. Playing a DVD with a DTS soundtrack with a universal remote requires pushing just as many buttons as using three separate remotes. "

"With EZ-Sync, you press one button and the TV turns on, the DVD player turns on, and the home theater surround sound system turns on and automatically selects the right inputs and settings to use for the DVD. "

Nelkin added that such features as built-in memory card slots, single-cable connection to such components as DVD recorders and Media Center PCs and integrated Cable card ports were all part of Panasonic's goal of making "the digital experience easier and more enjoyable".

"Our customers are in the process of learning how to create a host of new experiences using Panasonic plasma TVs with the increasing number of services and applications newly available for their enjoyment," Nelkin said. "This is not just the domain of the technically literate early adopters anymore. Increasingly, it has become the general public's market—a user group of families, young singles, and retired couples who have come to appreciate the benefits and enjoyment inherent in the plasma-centric Digital Lifestyle.

With this in mind, Panasonic's 2006 Plasma TV models were designed with great attention to reducing and, in many cases getting rid of, the whole idea of a learning curve.

Words & Expressions

1. commitment/kə'mitmənt/n. a promise to do something or to behave in a particular way 承诺
2. release/ri'li:s/v. to let news or official information be known and printed 发布, 公开发表
3. pixel/'piksəl/n. any one of the individual dots on a computer screen which

119

together make up the whole display 像素，像点

4. resolution/ˌrezəˈluːʃən/*n.* the power of a television, camera, microscope etc. to give a clear picture of things, or a measure of this （电视、照相机、显微镜的）清晰度；分辨率

5. ship/ʃip/*v.* to deliver goods or make them available for people to buy 发货，供货，使（商品）上市

6. remote/riˈməut/*adj.* far away in space or time 遥远的

7. incorporate/inˈkɔːpəreit/*v.* to include something as part of a group, system, plan, etc. 把（某物）并入，包含，吸收

8. integrated/ˈintəˌgreitid/*adj.* an integrated system, institution etc. combines many different groups, ideas, or parts in a way that works well （各组成部分）相互协调的，综合的

9. slot/slɔt/*n.* a long narrow hole made in a surface, especially for putting something into （可放进东西的）狭长窄孔，投币口

10. digital/ˈdidʒitl/*adj.* using a system in which information is represented in the form of changing electrical signals 数字的，数码的

11. slide/slaid/*n.* a small piece of film in a frame that shows a picture on a screen when you shine light through it 幻灯片

12. complement/ˈkɔmplimənt/*n.* someone or something that emphasizes the good quality of another person or thing 突出某人优点的人，衬托（物），补足物

13. deliver/diˈlivə/*v.* to take goods, letters etc. to the place where they are addressed to 把（货物、信件等）送往（某处）

14. exceed/ikˈsiːd/*v.* to be more than a number or amount, especially a fixed number 超出，超过

15. extraordinary/ikˈstrɔːdənəri/*adj.* very much better, more beautiful, or more impressive than usual 非凡的，出色的

16. contrast/kənˈtræst/*n.* a difference between people, ideas, or things etc. that are compared 差异，差别（＋between）

17. confident/ˈkɔnfidənt/*adj.* sure that you can do something or deal with a situation successfully 自信的，有信心的

18. facilitate/fəˈsiliteit/*v.* (formal) to make it easier for a process or activity to happen （正式）使容易，使便利，有助于

19. lifestyle/ˈlaifˌstail/*n.* the way someone lives, including the place they live in, the things they own, the kind of job they do, and the activities they enjoy 生活方式

20. at first glance   when you first look at something 乍一看,最初看到时

21. universal/ˌjuːniˈvɜːsəl/*adj.* involving or understood by everyone in the world 普遍的,一般的

22. bunch/bʌntʃ/*n.* something fastened together 束,串

23. incompatible/ˌinkəmˈpætəbl/*adj.* two things that are incompatible are of different types so that they cannot be used together 不相配的,不兼容的

24. surround/səˈraund/*n.* an area around the edge of something, especially one that is decorated or made of a different material 围绕物,(尤指)围饰

25. automatically/ˌɔːtəˈmætikli/*adv.* by the action of a machine, without a person making it work 自动地

26. input/ˈinˌput/*n.* information that is put into a computer（输入计算机的）信息

27. built-in/ˈbiltˈin/*adj.* forming a part of something that cannot be separated from it 作为固定装置而建造的,装在结构里的,固定的,内在的

28. a host of   a large number of 大量,许多

29. domain/dəˈmein/*n.* an area of activity, interest, or knowledge（活动、兴趣、知识的）领域,范畴,范围

30. literate/ˈlitərit/*adj.* able to read and write 能读写的,识字的

31. appreciate/əˈpriːʃieit/*v.* to understand how good or useful someone or something is 欣赏,赏识,鉴赏

32. inherent/inˈhiərənt/*adj.* a quality that is inherent in something is a natural part of it and cannot be separated from it 内在的,固有的

33. curve/kɜːv/*n.* a line which gradually bends like part of a circle 曲线,弧线

Notes

1. This text is selected from: http://www.panasonic.com.

2. Panasonic: Best known by its Panasonic brand name, Matsushita Electric Industrial Co., Ltd. is a worldwide leader in the development and manufacture of electronic products for a wide range of consumer, business, and industrial needs. Based in Osaka, Japan, the company recorded consolidated net sales of US $ 76.02 billion for the year ended March 31, 2006. The company's shares are listed on the Tokyo, Osaka, Nagoya, New York (NYSE: MC), Euronext Amsterdam and Frankfurt stock exchanges. For more information on the company and the Panasonic brand, visit the company's website at http://www.panasonic.net.

Word Study

1. incorporate *v.* to include something as part of a group, system, plan, etc. 把（某物）并入，包含，吸收

   incorporate sth into/in 把某物包含在内

   We've incorporated many environmentally-friendly features into the design of the building.

   我们在这座建筑的设计中加进了许多环保特点。

2. deliver *v.* to take goods, letters etc. to the place where they are addressed to 把（货物、信件等）送往（某处）

   deliver sth to; have sth delivered

   deliver sb from danger 救某人脱险

   deliver sth to sb 把某物交付给某人

   deliver a message 带信，传话

   Could you deliver the letter to the accounts department?

   你能把这封信送到会计部么？

   Some new books have been delivered to the school.

   一些新书已被送到学校。

   delivery *n.* 送货，送信，交付

   There is no delivery of letters on Sundays. 星期日不送信。

3. facilitate *v.* (formal) to make it easier for a process or activity to happen（正式）使容易，使便利，有助于

   The broken lock facilitated my entrance into the empty house.

   坏了的门锁使我毫不费力地进入那所空房子。

   The new underground railway will facilitate the journey to all parts of the city.

   新的地下铁路将为去城市各处提供方便。

   Tractors and other agricultural machines greatly facilitate farming.

   拖拉机及其他农业机械大大方便了农业耕作。

4. appreciate *v.*

   ① to understand how good or useful someone or something is 欣赏，赏识，鉴赏

   Do you appreciate good wine? 你会鉴赏好酒吗？

   I think that young children often appreciate modern pictures better than anyone else. 我认为小孩对现代图画往往比任何人都更有鉴赏力。

   ② to be grateful for something that someone has done 感激

I would appreciate it if... 如果……我将不胜感激

I appreciate your help. 我感谢你的帮助。

We greatly appreciate your timely help.

我们非常感谢你们的及时帮助。

③ to gradually become more valuable over a period of time 增值

This land has appreciated in value. 这块土地增值了。

Vocabulary Building

best/top seller 畅销商品	quality goods 精品
slow seller/slow-selling goods 滞销品	popular and inexpensive goods 大路货
inferior/substandard goods 次品	semi-finished/semi-manufactured goods 半成品
end/finish product 成品	smuggled/contraband goods 走私品
bargain-priced goods 特价商品	products suited to popular tastes 产品对路
product positioning 产品定位	a highly sophisticated product 尖端产品
cost performance 性价比	three guarantees（产品）三包
company/corporate image 企业形象	

Word Formation：Conversion Prefixes（转换前缀）and Other Prefixes

Conversion Prefixes	Meaning	Added to	To Form	Examples	Illustrative Sentences
be-	causing a condition to exist, covering or affecting	nouns, adjective, verbs	transitive verbs, adjectives	befriend, belittle, befall, bespectacled, becloud	They befriended me when I first arrived in London as a student. He tends to belittle her efforts.
en-, em-	causing to become, providing with	nouns, adjectives	verbs	endanger, empower, enrich, enlarge	The development of oil fields enriched the Arab nations.
a-	on, in, to, into	verbs	adjectives, adverbs	asleep, awash, afloat	Prices for goods afloat（在途货物）rose to $ 20 per 100 kilos.

Other Prefixes

Prefixes	Meaning	Added to	Examples	Illustrative Sentences
auto-	self	nouns, adjectives	autobiography, automatic, autocrat, autogamy, automation, automobile	Something is wrong with our automatic telling machine.
neo-	new, revived	nouns, adjectives	neo-classicism, neo-Nazi, neo-liberal, neoconservative, neo-realism, neo-economist	His systematic research on China's situation started from 1985 as a pioneer of this field, and is esteemed as a "neo-economist" home and abroad.
pan-	all, world-wide	adjectives	pan-Africanism, pan-Arabism, pan-African, pan-American	The Pan-American Games are a multi-sport event, held every four years between competitors from all nations of the Americas.
semi-	half	nouns, adjectives	semiconductor, semi-conscious, semicircle, semidarkness, semimanufacture, semi-final, semi-automatic	We must introduce foreign funds and advanced technology to export more finished-goods instead of semimanufactures.
therm(o)-	heat	nouns	thermochemistry, thermometer	This paper is about how energy works and focuses on how the thermometer works.
vice-	deputy	nouns	vice-chairman, vice-president, vice-premier	Mr. Smith has been appointed Vice-president.

Post-reading Activities

I. True or False Questions.

1. The new HDTV has a screen size of 65-inch.

2. Panasonic has won a number of awards for its plasmas.

3. The new HDTV has only increased the displayable colors as compared with the existing ones.

4. The new EZ-Sync has provided one-button control of TV, DVD recorders and home theater systems. Once you turn on TV, you will turn on DVD and other equipment.

5. The new HDTV can only be used by those educated people.

II. Fill in the blanks with the words or phrases given in the box. Change the forms if necessary.

| incorporate exceed confident integrated universal deliver |

1. Personal computers are of _____ interest; everyone is learning how to use them.

2. We will _____ your suggestion in the new plan.

3. The teachers are trying to _____ all the children into society.

4. This month's amount of deposits in the bank _____ last month's by fifteen percent.

5. You don't have to go out into the rain since the store _____ free of charge.

6. Peter is _____ of winning the post as the assistant to the managing director.

III. Dictation.

After winning a number of best-of-the-year __1__, Panasonic, the world leader in __2__ manufacturing has displayed its HD plasma TV of 50-inch. This new TV has provided one __3__ control of TV, DVD, and home __4__ systems, which makes "the __5__ experience easier and more __6__. It has a __7__ memory card slot and __8__ viewing of slide shows. It can be __9__ to anyone to enjoy a new __10__ —young singles, and retired couples etc. Panasonic is confident about its future in the TV industry.

Exercises

Ⅰ. Structures: Adverbial Clauses

1. The WTO cannot live up to its name _____ it does not include a country that is home to one fifth of mankind.
   A. as long as   B. while
   C. if   D. even though

2. She found her calculator _____ she lost it.
   A. where   B. when   C. in which   D. that

3. The man will have to wait all day _____ the doctor works faster.
   A. if   B. unless   C. whether   D. that

4. —Did you remember to give Mary the money you owed her?
   —Yes, I gave it to her _____ I saw her.
   A. while   B. the moment   C. suddenly   D. once

5. John shut everybody out of the kitchen _____ he could prepare his grand surprise for the party.
   A. which   B. when   C. so that   D. as if

6. As far as I am concerned, education is about learning and the more you learn,
   _____ .
   A. the more for life are you equipped
   B. the more equipped for life you are
   C. the more life you are equipped for
   D. you are equipped the more for life

7. He was about to tell me the secret _____ someone patted him on the shoulder.
   A. as   B. until   C. while   D. when

8. _____ , I have never seen anyone who's as capable as John.
   A. As long as I have traveled
   B. Now that I have traveled too much
   C. Much as I have traveled
   D. As I have traveled too much

9. The famous scientist grew up _____ he was born and in 1930 he came to Shanghai.
   A. when   B. whenever   C. where   D. wherever

10. You will succeed in the end _____ you give halfway.

    A. even if   B. as though   C. as long as   D. unless

Ⅱ. Vocabulary

appreciate	commitment	lack	impression	extraordinary
remote	automatically	lifestyle	literate	distributor

1. It's our _____ to bring you the top service.

2. You can use _____ controls to turn on or turn off electric appliances while lying on bed.

3. We _____ your efforts for the development of the company.

4. He is always _____ of courage in case of difficulties.

5. Information age will greatly change the _____ of human beings.

6. During the economic depression, his _____ wisdom has saved the company.

7. Just key in the numbers, the computer will show you the answers _____.

8. To suit the development of science and technology, our government is making great efforts to get rid of the _____.

9. He left a bad _____ on his colleagues on the first day.

10. Big companies have some _____ to push the sales of its products.

Ⅲ. Translation

1. 去年史密斯公司与别家合并了。(incorporate)

2. 要是你再合作些,事情就会变得更容易。(facilitate)

3. 质量上乘的商品总是受欢迎的。(superior)

4. 由于修建了新公路,这一地区的房屋都涨价了。(appreciate)

5. 经过改革,该公司取得了突飞猛进的发展。(by leaps and bounds)

6. 产品在流水线上经过组装后上市。(assembly line, assemble)

7. 她对自己的职业有种强烈的感情。(passion)

8. 这种软件和微软计算机 Windows 98 是不兼容的。(compatible)

9. 新的产品是对旧产品技术上的弥补。(complement)

10. 如果你能光临,我将不胜感激。(appreciate)

Ⅳ. Blank Filling

Foreign automakers with joint ventures in China are seeing their profits f 1 in the world's third largest car market, with some losses due to h 2 price wars.

Volkswagen's are ventures with China's top two vehicle m 3 , Shanghai Automotive Industry Corp (SAIC) and First Automobile Works Corp (FAW), suffered their s __4__ declines last year. P __5__ at Shanghai's Volkswagen dropped to 700 million yuan from 3. 7 billion yuan in 2004. FAW Volkswagen reported 235 million yuan in profits in 2005, down from 2. 5 billion yuan the year before.

Shanghai GM recorded 5. 1 billion yuan in profits last year, d __6__ almost 60 percent from 2004. The venture is still the most profitable Sino-foreign vehicle joint venture in China.

Car prices have gone down over the past several years due to increasingly stiff c __7__ . BMW, for example, cut prices of its Chinese produced 5 Series sedans by as much as 100,000 yuan last year.

Foreign manufacturers are doing everything they can to c __8__ costs as a m __9__ of coping with falling profits and losses. Volkswagen announced last year that it p __10__ to cut costs by 40 percent by 2008 by using more Chinese-made parts and improving management. The German company has also cancelled plans to increase capacity to 1. 6 million cars per year by 2008 due to bad sales.

V. Word Formation: Prefixes and Suffixes

"-less" can be added to many nouns or verbs to form adjectives or adverbs, to show: 1) without something; 2) never end doing something; 3) unable to be treated in a particular way. Use the correct forms of the words in the bold face to fill the blanks.

1. The operation didn't cause her any **pain**. It was _____ .

2. She always loses **hope** in her life, and thinks that she's _____ .

3. When she was asked to take **care** of the patient, she was so _____ that she made a lot of mistakes.

4. He was _____ and never **feared** anything. Eventually, he was successful.

5. The couple have no **child** all their life. They are _____ .

6. There's no **end** to study. You should study _____ .

7. He is never **tired** of helping others. He is a _____ helper.

8. On _____ occasions, you can only **count** on yourself. Therefore, you should be confident of yourself.

9. During the revolution, many people died _____ . People didn't know their **names**.

10. The _____ king even has no **power** to deal with state affairs.

VI. Reading Comprehension

Most companies trying to get a <u>foothold</u> in China's competitive telecoms market would find reason to celebrate if they land a US $ 600 million order. But Carl Henic

Svanberg, president and CEO of Swedish mobile telecoms equipment manufacturer Ericsson, is not exactly jumping for joy.

In August 2003 the company announced it had get a US $ 600 million purchase order from China Mobile subsidiary Guangdong Mobile.

Just days before he flew to China, Svanberg told the Swedish media that Ericsson would be profitable by late 2003.

He pulled it off, but the pressure was on to keep continuing profitability. The first deal with Guangdong Mobile was followed by another US $ 200 million agreement two months later, but the situation was tense because profit margins were quickly dropping. Even the head of Ericsson said the firm had no revenues growth in 2004.

"It's become much more difficult for equipment makers to keep high profitability. They need to sell more but the market has slowed down. "

On the other hand, cost advantages and improved technological capabilities have helped domestic firms push many foreign companies out of the market. "We used to use foreign telecoms equipment because there was not much choice, but now we are replacing them with domestic products. "

The upcoming launch of 3G (third generation) mobile communication services in China is expected to push telecoms spending higher and significantly drive investment in optical networks. Domestic firms are expected to expand their dominance of the industry, which could possibly force foreign manufacturers out of the market, analysts say.

1. What did Svanberg think of the agreement with Guangdong Mobile at the beginning?
   A. He was very happy because he thought Ericsson would be profitable very soon.
   B. He thought he should keep cool even after the signing of the agreement.
   C. He didn't say anything for it.
   D. He didn't know what would happen in the future.

2. Why is Svanberg unhappy of the US $ 600 million order?
   A. Because he thinks the order is not big enough.
   B. Because the order hasn't brought about expected profits for the Ericsson.
   C. Because the profits go up only a little.
   D. Because other equipment makers earn more than his company.

3. What about the condition of Ericsson after the cooperation with China Mobile?
   A. The profits grow greatly.

B. The profits grow steadily.

C. There's no growth of profit margins in 2004.

D. There are no profits at all.

4. Why foreign investors find it hard to make a profit in the Chinese market?

A. The market is slowing down.

B. Domestic products begin to take place of the foreign ones.

C. Both A and B.

D. The Chinese consumers do not like foreign products.

5. What changes will take place after the launch of 3G mobile communication services in China?

A. More and more foreign companies will capture the market share.

B. This is a great chance for the domestic companies.

C. The domestic companies will be greatly hurt.

D. Both the domestic and foreign companies will get higher profits.

6. What's the meaning of "foothold" in Paragraph 1?

A. 立足点　　B. 统治地位　　　C. 优势　　　　D. 脚步

Ⅶ. Writing

(1) Writing Basics

Paragraph Structures: Topic Sentence, Supporting Sentence and Concluding Sentence.

Ⅰ. Topic Sentence

The topic sentence does the following tasks:

a. It names the topic in the paragraph, telling the reader what the paragraph is about.

b. It contains a controlling idea that limits the paragraph to a special part of the topic. A controlling idea is a key word or phrase that expresses the basic point of a paragraph.

c. It tells the reader what to expect in the paragraph.

d. It usually is the most general and most important statement in the paragraph.

F.g.: *Going to college requires much more self-reliance than going to high school.*

The topic in the sentence is "going to college". The basic idea is expressed in the word "requires much more self-reliance than going to high school." The reader expects to see the contrast in the rest of the paragraph.

Ⅱ. Supporting Sentence

They explain and back up the main idea—proving the reader with special evidences and reasons. They present facts, figures, thoughts, observations, examples and personal experience. The supporting sentences help to illustrate your point and help the reader understand what you mean. When you provide adequate information, the central idea of your paragraph becomes clear and meaningful.

III. Concluding Sentence

You repeat the basic idea of the topic sentence but in different words. This helps to achieve emphasis and remind the reader of what the paragraph is about, especially when the paragraph is a long one.

Exercise:

1. Underline the topic sentence of the following paragraph.

Mary has a plan for doing well in her classes this term. She is not going to miss any classes, and she is going to take notes of all the lessons. She has formed a study group with her classmates. Finally, she has blocked out three hours a day on weekdays to study.

2. Develop a topic sentence for the topic below and work out at least five facts that support the topic sentence.

Topic: My teacher Ms. Lee

Topic sentence: ＿＿＿＿＿＿＿＿＿＿＿＿＿＿＿＿＿＿＿＿＿＿

Support: 1. ＿＿＿＿＿＿＿＿＿＿＿＿＿＿＿＿＿＿＿＿＿＿

2. ＿＿＿＿＿＿＿＿＿＿＿＿＿＿＿＿＿＿＿＿＿＿

3. ＿＿＿＿＿＿＿＿＿＿＿＿＿＿＿＿＿＿＿＿＿＿

4. ＿＿＿＿＿＿＿＿＿＿＿＿＿＿＿＿＿＿＿＿＿＿

5. ＿＿＿＿＿＿＿＿＿＿＿＿＿＿＿＿＿＿＿＿＿＿

3. Underline the concluding sentences of the paragraph below.

The sky is clear blue. Sparrows chirp in the early mornings. The fruit trees are beginning to bloom. The hills are turning green, and purple and yellow wildflowers are appearing in the fields, the snow on top of Camel Mountain has all melted. It must finally be spring.

(2) Writing Assignment

Choose one of the products which you are familiar with, then write a product description about 100—150 words, your essay should include the following points:

1. the name, the producer, the price level of the product;

2. its function or how to use it;

3. the benefits and advantages of the product.

VIII. Presentation (Speaking)

What kind of trade and business opportunities with those foreign investors have in China? Try to list at least three parts, and show your reasons.

IX. Case Study

Read the case below, and say what kind of measures does Singapore Airlines take to attract customers? Do you think it is effective or not?

Singapore Airlines recently introduced Live Text News so that customers can keep abreast of current events and information.

Available to Singapore Airlines customers in all classes, this latest product can be accessed for free on KrisWorld, the airline's in-flight entertainment system. The content covers several categories including world news, business, technology, sports, entertainment and weather. The information is obtained from an extensive list of news sources, including Associated Press, Financial Times, Wall Street Journal and Dow Jones.

Enjoy Your Time

1. What's too much for one, just right for two, but nothing at all for three?
2. What person tries to make you smile most of the time?
3. What never asks any questions but always gets answers?
4. What starts with a T, ends with a T, and is full of T?

Unit 6

Job Interviewing

Learning Objectives

In this unit you will
◆ understand several types of interviews;
◆ learn how to interview for success;
◆ and review the grammar item: relative clause.

Pre-reading Activities

New Words: crucial   downturn   burden

Ⅰ. **Listen to the following short passage twice and fill in the blanks with the words you've heard.**

According to experts, it takes an __1__ of 10 interviews to get one job offer. If you hope to have several __2__ to choose from, you can expect to go __3__ 20 to 30 interviews during your job search. Because __4__ takes time, start seeking jobs well in advance of the date you want to start work. Some students start their job __5__ as much as nine months before __6__. Early planning is even more crucial during downturns in the __7__, because many employers become more __8__ when times are tough. Moreover, many corporations __9__ their campus visits and campus hiring programs during bad times, so more of the job search burden __10__ on you.

Ⅱ. **What's important in job hunting? Choose from the list below, discuss with your classmates and tell why.**

Salary ☐   Work hours ☐   Responsibility ☐

Company's location ☐   Nice colleagues ☐

Text A

Interviews

Selecting the most qualified people available for a position is a major managerial responsibility. Many screening tools are used in employee selection, including application forms and aptitude and personality tests, but the most common is the interview.

Supervisors and team members most often get involved in the selection process at the stage of employment interviews. These interviews bring together job applicants and representatives of the employers to obtain information and evaluate the applicant's qualifications. While the applicant is providing information, he or she is also forming opinion about what it is like to work for the organization. Most organizations use interviewing as part of the selection process.

The ability to match competent applicants with the correct job leads to the success of an organization. Making good hiring decisions also reduces the cost of turnover, which can be significant. The US Department of Labor estimates that it costs a company one-third of a new hire's annual salary to replace an employee. More than 75 percent of turnover can be traced back to poor interviewing and hiring practices, according to a Harvard Business School study. Managers have a responsibility to both the organization and the applicant to see that an applicant-job match exists.

An interview may be nondirective or structured. In a **nondirective interview**, the interviewer has great discretion in choosing questions to ask each candidate. For example, the interviewer might ask, "What is your greatest accomplishment in your current position?" The candidate's reply might suggest to the interviewer what other questions to ask. Often, these interviews include open-ended questions about the candidate's strength, weaknesses, career goals, and work experience. Because nondirective interviews give the interviewer wide latitude, their reliability is not great.

To manage the risk of a nondirective interview, many organizations substitute the use of a **structured interview**, which establishes a set of questions for the interviewers to ask. Ideally, these questions are related to the requirements set out in the job description. The interviewer asks questions from the list and is supposed to avoid asking questions that are not on the list. Some interviewers object to being limited in this way, but a list of well-written questions can provide more valid and reliable results.

Some of the best results of interviewing come from the use of **situational interviews.** In this type of structured interview, the interviewer describes a situation likely to arise on the job, then asks the candidate what he or she would do in that situation. Situational interviews have been shown to have high validity in predicting job performance. A variation is the **behavior description interview** (BDI), in which the interviewer asks the candidate to describe how he or she handled a type of situation in the past. Questions about the candidates' actual experiences tend to have the highest validity.

The common setup for either a nondirective or structured interview is for an individual (an HR professional or the supervisor for the vacant position) to interview each candidate face to face. However, variations on this approach are possible. In a **panel interview**, several members of the organization meet to interview each candidate. A panel interview gives the candidate a chance to meet more people and see how people interact in that organization. It provides the organization with the judgments of more than one person, to reduce the effect of personal biases in selection decisions. At the other extreme, some organizations conduct interviews without any interviewers; they use a computerized interviewing process. The candidate sits at a computer and enters replies to the questions presented by the computer. Such a format eliminates a lot of personal biases—along with the opportunity to see how people interact. Therefore, **computer interviews** are useful for gathering objective data, rather than assessing people's skills.

Interviews can give insights into candidates' personalities and interpersonal styles. While research shows that the interview is low in both reliability and validity, no adequate replacement exists. It is the only technique that gives managers the chance to personally evaluate the candidate and to pursue questioning in a way that tests cannot.

Words & Expressions

1. qualified/ˈkwɔliˌfaid/*adj.* with the right education and experience 有资格的
2. available/əˈveiləbl/*adj.* (of things) that can be used or obtained; (of people) free to be seen, talked to, etc. (指物)可用的或可得到的；(指人)可会见的,可与之交谈的等
3. managerial/ˌmænəˈdʒiəriəl/*adj.* of managers or management 管理的；经理的
4. responsibility/riˌspɔnsəˈbiliti/*n.* being responsible or accountable 责任；负责；义务
5. aptitude/ˈæptitjuːd/*n.* an inherent ability (to do a task) 天资

6. applicant/'æplikənt/ *n.* person who applies 申请人

7. representative/ˌrepriˈzentətive/ *n.* a person who acts on behalf of another 代表;代理人

8. evaluate/iˈvæljueit/ *v.* find out or form an idea of the amount of somebody/something; assess 评价;评估　evaluation *n.*

9. qualification/ˌkɔlifiˈkeiʃən/ *n.* required education, ability or experience 资格

10. competent/'kɔmpitənt/ *adj.* (of people) having the necessary ability, skill, knowledge, etc. 有能力的,有知识的

11. turnover/'təːnˌəuvə(r)/ *n.* the rate at which employees join and leave a company 人员更替比例;营业额,成交量

12. significant/sigˈnifikənt/ *adj.* important; considerable 重要的;可观的

13. estimate/'estimeit/ *v.* calculate roughly the cost, size, value, etc. of sth 估计;估算

14. annual/'ænjuəl/ *adj.* yearly 每年的;年度的

15. discretion/diˈskreʃən/ *n.* the ability to decide what is most suitable to be done 判断力,辨别力

16. accomplishment/əˈkɔmpliʃmənt/ *n.* thing achieved 成就;成绩

17. current/'kʌrənt/ *adj.* in the present time; happening now 通行的;通用的;现时的;当前的

18. open-ended/ˌəupənˈendid/ *adj.* without any limits, restrictions or aims set in advance 无限制的;无结论的;广泛的

19. latitude/'lætitjuːd/ *n.* freedom to behave and hold opinions without restriction (行动、意见的)自由

20. reliability/riˌlaiəˈbiliti/ *n.* state or quality of being reliable 可靠性

21. substitute/'sʌbstitjuːt/ *v.* to put sth or sb in place of another 代替;替代

22. establish/iˈstæbliʃ/ *v.* to set up 建立;设立　establishment *n.*

23. valid/'vælid/ *adj.* legally usable or acceptable 〈法〉有效的;得到认可的

24. reliable/riˈlaiəbəl/ *adj.* dependable 可信赖的;可靠的

25. predict/priˈdikt/ *v.* say in advance that (sth) will happen; forecast 预言(某事物)将发生;预报;预告

26. variation/ˌvɛəriˈeiʃən/ *n.* (an example or degree of) the action of varying 变化(程度);变动

27. vacant/'veikənt/ *adj.* not filled or occupied 空缺的;未被占用的

28. panel/'pænl/ *n.* a group of people who with skills or specialist knowledge who have been chosen to give advice or opinions on a particular subject 由选定人

员组成的专门小组;专题讨论小组

29. extreme/ik'stri:m/*n.* greatest or highest degree; either end of anything 最大程度;极端

30. conduct/kən'dʌkt/*v.* direct (sth); control; manage 指挥(某事物);操纵;管理

31. format/'fɔːmæt/*n.* the general arrangement, plan, design, etc. of sth 总体安排、计划、设计等

32. eliminate/i'limineit/*v.* remove (esp. somebody/something that is not wanted or needed) 消除;排除　elimination *n.*

33. interpersonal/ˌintə'pɜːsənəl/*adj.* existing or done between two people 人际的

34. be supposed to do　be expected or required to do sth 被期望或被要求做某事

35. provide... with　make sth available for sb to use by giving, lending or supplying it 为某人提供某物

Notes

1. This text is selected and adapted from *Fundamentals of Human Resource Management* by Raymond A. Noe etc.

2. application form(申请表): A pre-printed form to make a request for a job.

3. aptitude test(智力测试): Tests that assess how well a person can learn or acquire skills and abilities.

4. personality test(个性测试): An employment test which measures personality traits such as extroversion and adjustment. Research supports their validity for appropriate job situations, especially for individuals who score high on conscientiousness, extroversion, and agreeableness.

5. open-ended question(开放式问题): An open-ended question has virtually no restriction on the type of response that is received.

6. selection process(选才程序): Through selection process, organizations make decisions about who will or will be allowed to join the organization. Selection begins with the candidates identified through recruitment and attempts to reduce their number to the individuals best qualified to perform the available jobs. At the end of the process, the selected individuals are placed in jobs with the organization.

7. It is the only technique that gives managers the chance to personally evaluate the

candidate and to pursue questioning in a way that tests cannot. "it"引导的强调句用来对句中某一成分加以强调,其结构为:It is(was)+强调部分+that(who)。在正式英语中,无论强调什么部分,都要求用连接词 that,在一般情况下,如果被强调的主语是人,则也可用 who。当被强调部分是状语时,只能用 that,不要用 when,where,how 等。动词"be"的时态可以随着 that 从句时态的不同而变化。例如,我们可以分别对下句中成分进行强调:

The financial director was responsible for the firm's budgets last year.

It was **the financial director** that/who was responsible for the firm's budgets last year.

It was **the firm's budgets** that the financial director was responsible for last year.

It was **last year** that the financial director was responsible for the firm's budgets.

Word Study

1. estimate

v. ① calculate roughly the cost, size, value, etc. of sth 估计(成本、规模、价值等);估算

We estimated that it would take two years to complete the job.

我们估计需花两年的时间完成这项工作。

② calculate the probable price of (a specified job) 估算(某项工作的)费用

We asked our builder to estimate for the repair of the ceiling.

我们要承建商对修理天花板的费用作出估价。

You must ask three companies to estimate for the job.

你必须请三家公司对此项工作的费用作出估算。

n. ① a calculation of the cost, size, value, etc. of something 估计、估算

I can give you a rough estimate of the number of staff needed to work on the project. 我可以粗略估算一下从事这项工程所需的工作人员数量。

I suspect that £ 30,000 for the work is a conservative estimate.

我想花费3万英镑完成这项工作是一个保守的估算。

Your estimate was far more than we want to pay.

你们的估算远远超出我们的支付能力。

② statement of the price a builder, etc. will probably charge for doing specified work (营造商等对承建工程的)报价

We got estimates from three different contractors before accepting the lowest.

我们得到三个承包商的报价后,接受了价钱最低的。

③ judgment of the character or qualities of somebody/something [对某人(事物)性格或质量的]判断

I don't know her well enough to form an estimate of her abilities.

我对她不太了解,无法对她的能力作出判断。

2. substitute

v. ① to put sth or sb in place of another 代替;替代

substitute somebody/something for somebody/something

We must substitute a new chair for the broken one.

我们必须用新椅子来代替破椅子。

② substitute for somebody/something act or serve as a substitute 取代

Honey can substitute for sugar in this recipe.

在这个食谱中,可用蜂蜜代替食糖。

n. person or thing that replaces, acts for or serves as sb or sth else 代替者;代用品

The manager was unable to attend but sent his deputy as a substitute.

经理不能出席,派了个副手代表他。

比较:replace...with...

We've replaced the old adding machine with a computer.

我们用电脑代替了旧的加法机。

3. predict *v.* say in advance that (sth) will happen; forecast 预报;预告

She predicted that the improvement would continue.

她预测情况将继续好转。

The earthquake had been predicted several months before.

这次地震早在几个月以前就发布了预报。

prediction *n.* 预告;预测

Do you take seriously his prediction of a government defeat?

他预料政府要受挫,你认为这话靠得住吗?

4. conduct *v.*

① direct (sth); control; manage 操纵;管理;经营

conduct business, a meeting, negotiations 经营生意、主持会议、主持谈判

She was appointed to conduct the advertising campaign.

她被委派主持宣传活动。

② lead or guide (somebody/something) 领导;引导

A guide conducted the visitors round the museum.

导游带领游客参观博物馆。

I asked the attendant to conduct him to the door.

我让服务员领他到门口。

5. establish *v.*

① to set up 建立；设立

establish a company 创设公司

establish sales territories 开拓销售地区

The company was established in 1850. 这家公司成立于1850年。

A solid relationship and a mutual trust were established very early between them. 他们之间很早就建立了牢固的关系并相互信任。

② place sb/oneself in a position 使任职、安置

establish sb/oneself in sth/as sth

He established himself as governor of the province.

他当上了省长。

She has now firmly established in business as an art dealer.

她已稳固地奠定了艺术品商的地位。

③ prove；show sth to be true 证实

The police can't establish where he was at the time.

警方无法确定当时他在哪里。

Post-reading Activities.

Ⅰ. Comprehension Questions.

1. What is the purpose of an interview?

2. How many kinds of interviews are mentioned in the text? What are they?

3. What is the definition of a situational interview?

4. Which interview is comparatively valid according to the text?

5. Do you agree that the interview is low in both reliability and validity? Why or why not?

Ⅱ. Fill in the blanks with the words or phrases given in the box. Change the forms if necessary.

> available   turnover   responsibility   current   vacant   valid
> predict   provide...with   be supposed to   get involved in

1. The company has a very high _____ of staff, perhaps the wages are low.

2. Can you give me a list of _____ prices of your new products?

3. It is impossible to _____ who will win in the present price war.

4. You will be informed when the book becomes _____.

5. The manufactures disclaim all _____ for damages caused by misuse.

6. All prices and promotional offers are _____ until 30th, September.

7. He _____ a costly and time-consuming business.

8. He got a promotion for the high sales volume this month. The firm has _____ him _____ a car.

9. You _____ pay the bill by Friday. Otherwise, you will be fined.

10. One of the positions is _____ at present.

Ⅲ. **Fill in the blanks with suitable words to complete the summary of the text.**

Interview is the most __1__ approach __2__ selecting the most qualified people available for a position. The manager's __3__ to match competent applicants __4__ the correct job leads to the __5__ of an organization. So it's important to understand __6__ interviews. An interview may be nondirective or __7__. The latter __8__ of situational interview and behavior description interview. Besides, panel interview and __9__ interview are also mentioned in the text. All in all, interviews can give __10__ into candidates' personalities and interpersonal styles.

Ⅳ. **Translate the following sentences into English.**

1. 由于非典(SARS),最近药品的价格呈上涨趋势。(tend to)

2. 他的讲话使我们对通货膨胀(inflation)的问题有了深入的了解。(give insight into)

3. 我强烈反对出任该公司纯粹是名义上的(nominal)经理。(object to)

4. 为了避免歇业,业主们应该准备一份好的企业计划。(avoid doing sth)

5. 她在一封长信里阐明了辞职的原因。(set out)

Text B

Interviewing for Success

The way to handle the actual interview depends on where you stand in the interview process.

If you are being interviewed for the first time, your main objective is to differentiate yourself from the many other candidates who are also being screened. Say you've signed up to talk with a recruit on campus, who may talk with 10 or 15 applicants during the course of the day. Without resorting to gimmicks, you need to call attention to one key aspect of your background so that the recruit can say, "Oh yes, I remember Jones—the one who sold used Toyotas in Detroit. " Just be sure the trait you accentuate is relevant to the job in question. In addition, you'll want to be prepared in case an employer such as Microsoft expects you to demonstrate a particular skill (such as problem solving).

If you progress to the initial selection interview, you should broaden your sales pitch. Instead of telegraphing the "headline", give the interviewer the whole story. Touch at least briefly on all your strengths, but explain three or four of your best qualifications in depth. At the same time, probe for information that will help you evaluate the position objectively. As important as it is to get an offer, it's also important to learn whether the job is right for you.

If you're asked back for a final visit, your chances of being offered a position are quite good. At this point, you'll talk to a person who has the authority to make the offer and negotiate terms. This individual may already have concluded that you have the right background for the job, so she or he will be concerned with sizing up your personality. In fact, both you and the employer need to find out whether there is a good psychological fit. Be honest about your motivations and values. If the interview goes well, your objective should be to clinch the deal on the best possible terms.

Regardless of where you are in the interview process, every interview will proceed through three stages: the warm-up, the question-and-answer session, and the close.

Of the three stages, the warm-up is the most important, even though it may account for only a small fraction of the time you spend in the interview. Psychologists say that 50 percent of the interviewer's decision is made within the first 30 to 60 seconds, and another 25 percent is made within 15 minutes. If you get off to a bad start, it's difficult to turn the interview around.

Questions and answers will consume the greatest part of the interview. During this phase, the interviewer will ask you about your qualifications and discuss many of the points mentioned in your résumé. You'll also be asked whether you have any questions of your own. Remember, let the interviewer lead the conversation, and never answer a question before he or she finished asking it. The last few words of the question might surprisingly alter how you should respond.

Like the opening, the end of the interview is more important than its duration would indicate. In the last few minutes, you need to evaluate how well you've done and to correct any misconceptions the interviewer might have. The closing is memorable. Always remember to thank the interviewer for her time.

Words & Expressions

1. process/ˈprəuses/ *n.* the method used to make something 流程;程序
2. recruit/riˈkruːt/ *n.* the person who finds a new member 招聘人员
3. gimmick/ˈgimik/ *n.* something unusual or amusing 花招;手法
4. aspect/ˈæspekt/ *n.* particular part or feature of sth being considered 方面
5. trait/treit/ *n.* element in sb's personality; distinguishing characteristic 人的个性;显著的特点
6. accentuate/əkˈsentʃuˌeit/ *v.* make sth very noticeable or prominent 突出;强调
7. demonstrate/ˈdemənˌstreit/ *v.* show sth clearly by giving proof or evidence 示范操作;示威;证明;表明 demonstration *n.* 示范;示威游行
8. pitch/pitʃ/ *n.* (in music) set in a certain key(音乐)定调
9. headline/ˈhedlain/ *n.* line of words in large type at the top of a page 页首的大字标题
10. authority/ɔːˈθɔriti/ *n.* power to give orders and make others obey 权力;权威
11. psychological/ˌsaikəˈlɔdʒikəl/ *adj.* of or affecting the mind 心理的;精神上的
12. motivation/ˌməutiˈveiʃən/ *n.* state of being motivated, inspiration 激励;动机
13. proceed/prəˈsiːd/ *v.* go on a further or the next stage 继续进行
14. fraction/ˈfrækʃən/ *n.* small part, bit or proportion of sth 小部分;一点儿
15. psychologist/saiˈkɔlədʒist/ *n.* expert in psychology 心理学家
16. consume/kənˈsjuːm/ *v.* use (sth) up 用尽;消耗
17. résumé/ˌrezjuˈmei/ *n.* 【AmE】 an account of a person's qualifications, interests and work experience, usually sent with an application for a job (Latin: curriculum vitae) 简历
18. alter/ˈɔːltə(r)/ *v.* to (cause to) become different (使) 改变
19. duration/djuˈreiʃən/ *n.* the time during which something exists or lasts 持续;持续时间
20. indicate/ˈindiˌkeit/ *v.* state sth briefly or indirectly 表明;暗示 indication *n.*
21. misconception/ˌmiskənˈsepʃən/ *n.* understanding wrongly 误解
22. differentiate...from show sth to be different 区分;区别
23. resort to make use of sth for help 凭借;求助
24. be relevant to connected with the subject 与……有关的

25. in addition—as an extra person, thing or circumstance 除……之外

26. be concerned with—be about sth 与某事物有关

Notes

1. This text is selected and adapted from *Business Communication Today* by Courtland L. Bovée & John V. Thill.

2. résumé(个人简历): A résumé is a structured, written summary of a person's education, employment background, and job qualifications. A résumé is a form of advertising, designed to stimulate an employer's interest in meeting the candidate. A good résumé inspires the prospective employer to pick up the phone and ask the candidate to come in for an interview.

3. If you're asked back for a final visit, your chances of being offered a position are quite good.

   The chances... are(that)... 常用在口语里,意为"很可能……"

   Chances are (that) they'll be out when we call.

   If approved, the chances are that most of us will get more pay.

   The chances of winning the competition are true.

Word Study

1. process

   n. ① the method used to make something 流程;程序

   Unloading the cargo was a slow process.

   卸货的过程很缓慢。

   Reforming the education system will be a difficult process.

   改革教育制度将是一个艰难的过程。

   ② method 方法;(尤指)工艺流程

   The company has developed a new fruit preservation process.

   公司已开发出新的水果保鲜法。

   What process do you use to dry the paint so quickly?

   你用什么方法使油漆干得这么快?

   v. to treat by a particular process 处理

   It will take about two weeks for your order to be processed.

   处理你的订货大约需要两星期。

   The computer will take about an hour to process the data.

这台电脑要花大约 1 小时来处理这些数据。

2. demonstrate

vt. to explain and show how something works or is done 示范操作

The salesman demonstrated the use of the photocopier.

推销员示范复印机的使用方法。

vi. to put on a show of protest against, or support for, something 示威

demonstrate against/for something 为反对/争取某事举行示威

Workers demonstrated against the low pay offer.

工人举行示威反对工资报酬低。

Workers demonstrated for higher wages.

工人举行示威要求提高工资。

demonstration *n.*

① 示范；演示

give a demonstration of something 做示范

It's easier to learn by demonstration than by reading a manual.

示范操作比说明书容易理解。

The system manager gave a demonstration of the new computer system.

系统部经理做了一次新电脑系统的操作示范。

② 示威游行；集会

Steel workers held a demonstration against proposed job losses.

钢铁工人举行示威反对裁员建议。

3. proceed *v.*

① go to a further or the next stage, go on 继续进行

Let us proceed to the next item on the agenda.

让我们继续进行下一个议程吧。

Having said how much she liked it, she then proceeded to criticize the way I'd done it.

她先表明她非常喜欢这个,然后批评我方法不当。

② proceed with sth: begin or continue (sth) 开始或继续做某事

Please proceed with your report. 请继续作你的报告吧。

Shall we proceed with the planned investment? 我们着手进行有计划的投资,好吗?

③ proceed from sth: arise or originate from sth 由某物引起;源于某事物

the evils that proceed from war 邪恶由战争引起

4. consume v.

① use (sth) up 用尽；消耗

The car consumes a lot of fuel.

这辆汽车很费汽油。

Paperwork consumed much of the secretary's time.

文书工作花费了秘书许多时间。

② destroy somebody/something by fire, decay, etc. (因火烧、衰败等)毁掉

The fire quickly consumed the wooden hut.

火焰很快吞噬了那所小木屋。

5. indicate v.

① suggest the possibility or probability of 表明；暗示

Evidence indicates that the experiments were unsuccessful.

有证据表明那些实验没有成功。

A red sky at night indicated fine weather the following day.

晚上天边红预示明朝天气好。

② state sth briefly or indirectly(简要或间接)表示某事物

The minister has indicated that he may resign next year.

那大臣已示意他明年可能辞职。

She has not indicated how she proposes to react.

她未表示打算做何回应。

③ show the need for, call for 显示需要(某事物)

With the government's failure to solve the problem of unemployment, a fresh approach is indicated.

鉴于政府未能处理好失业问题，有必要采取新的措施。

indication n. 象征；预示

There are some indications that interest rates will soon fall.

有迹象表明利率不久将下调。

The situation shows no indication of improvement.

形势没有好转的迹象。

Vocabulary Building

engineer 工程师	executive 主任
assistant 助理	supervisor 主管;总监
architect 建筑师	cashier 出纳员
president 董事长;总裁	director 董事
personnel manager 人事部经理	administrative assistant 行政助理
marketing representative 销售代表	receptionist 接待员
trade finance executive 贸易财务主管	accounting staff 会计部职员

Word Formation Noun Suffixes（名词后缀）

Noun suffixes	Meaning	Added to	Examples	Illustrative Sentences
-age,-ance (-ence), -ment,-y	action or state of	verbs	passage, assistance, allowance, dependence, management, delivery	Businesses must have good human resource management practices so as not to lose talented employees.
-sion (-ssion), -tion (-ation), -(t)ure	action or condition of	verbs	expansion, provision, admission, organization, exposure, departure	The World Trade Organization came into being in 1995.
-ship	state of being; status; office	nouns	membership, friendship, ownership	All members have joined the system as a result of negotiation and therefore membership means a balance of rights and duties.
-ness, -ity	quality, state or character of	adjectives	happiness, awareness, ability, possibility	His success in business brought happiness to his parents.
-hood	state or condition of	nouns, adjectives	falsehood, childhood, neighborhood	The scene reminded Mary of her childhood.
-al,-ance,-ant/ -ent,-er/-or, -ress,-ee,-eer	person or thing that does	verbs	arrival, performance, assistant, beginner, survivor, actress, employee, mountaineer	What kinds of employees are needed for the E-era?

-er, -or	person concerned with, person belonging to	nouns	philosopher, banker, New Yorker, villager	A banker is the owner, director or manager of a bank.

Post-reading Activities

Ⅰ. True or False Questions.

1. The text illustrates some approaches to interviewing for success.

2. If you're asked back for a final visit, you'll definitely be employed.

3. Three stages are mentioned in a typical interview according to the text.

4. If you get off to a good start, you are possibly to be successful in the interview.

5. During the question-and-answer session, the interviewee can keep asking and answering questions without any consideration for the interviewer.

6. The end of the interview is not as important as the warm-up stage.

Ⅱ. Fill in the blanks with the words or phrases given in the box. Change the forms if necessary.

> motivation   indicate   demonstrate   negotiate
> consume   resort to   so that   be relevant to

1. For _____ to take place, workers must believe that effort on their part will lead to rewards.

2. We have decided to _____ with the employers about our wage claim.

3. He soon _____ his fortune, that is, spent the money wastefully.

4. They _____ the product with latest-technology during the Commodity Fair in Guangzhou.

5. She shook her head to _____ that she was unsatisfied with the applicant.

6. Income tax rates _____ one's annual income.

7. We shall have to _____ the law of supply and demand for a final resolution.

8. The store sold their goods at cost price _____ they could clear old stock.

Ⅲ. Dictation.

The way to handle the actual interview ___1___ where you stand in the interview process. If you are being interviewed for the first time, your ___2___ is to differentiate yourself from many other ___3___ who are also being screened. If you progress to the initial selection interview, you should __4__ . If you're asked back for a final visit, your chances of being offered a __5__ are quite good. __6__ will proceed through three stages. The warm-up is the most important, even though it may __7__ only a small fraction of the time you spend in the interview. Questions and answers will __8__ . But remember, let the interviewer lead the conversation, and never __9__ him or her. The closing is __10__ .

Exercises

Ⅰ. **Structures: Relative Clause**（关系从句）

关系从句也叫定语从句，一般放在它所修饰的名（代）词之后，这种名（代）词就是先行词。引导关系从句的关联词为关系代词和关系副词。关系代词在关系从句中可作主语、宾语、定语等；关系副词在从句中可作状语。关系从句有限制性关系从句和非限制性关系从句之分。

A. There are two types of relative clause in English: Identifying relative clauses and non-identifying relative clauses.

1. **Identifying relative clauses**: identify a person or thing in the same sentence. Notice the lack of commas:

—You seem a bit upset. Why is that?

—Well, you see, I applied for a job that I saw advertised last month.

—But you didn't get it?

—No, I phoned first and then I wrote a long letter. And the letter that I got back was just a photocopy! It said that the job that I wanted had already been given to someone inside the company.

—But you thought it was still vacant?

—Yes, the person who spoke to me on the phone told me the post was vacant.

—How annoying!

Instead of that we can use which, and instead of who we can use that.

If, and only if, the subordinate clause has a subject within it, we can omit who or that.

—Is everything OK with our order?

—No, the documents (that/which) you mailed to us last week haven't arrived.

—Can I discuss the matter with someone else, please?

—No, I'm afraid the person who/that knows about this is not available right now.

2. **Non-identifying relative clauses**: give more information about a known person

or thing. They are more common in writing than in speech. Notice the use of commas.

Alex Brown, who wrote to you about this, is no longer with your firm. Getting a good job, which everyone has a right to, is not easy. The application form, which is enclosed with this letter, must be returned to us by April 24.

B. Fill the gaps in these sentences with a suitable relative pronoun. Add any commas that are missing.

1. The person _____ impressed me most was Mr Wright.

2. Mr Wright _____ application form we received yesterday is a very promising candidate.

3. His CV _____ you showed me yesterday is more impressive.

4. He has excellent references from his present employers _____ are software engineers.

5. He was working in Norwich _____ they have their headquarters.

6. His qualifications _____ you commented on are excellent.

7. The personnel officer _____ interviewed him says that he's available at once.

8. The thing _____ impressed her most is her personality.

9. Mr Gray _____ you spoke to yesterday is our Personnel Manager.

10. Please telephone Ms Kurtz _____ extension number is 666.

II. Vocabulary

depend on	touch on	sign up	find out	differentiate... from
in depth	trace back to	lead to	size up	clinch the deal

1. Most developing countries _____ primary commodities(初级产品) for more than seventy percent of their exports.

2. The price of the product was hardly _____ in their negotiation.

3. Tom's constant carelessness in his work _____ his lay-off.

4. He was _____ as a sales manager by a company last week.

5. Her fear of investing in a new car can be _____ a childhood accident.

6. They try to study _____ the decisive factors in gaining the market share.

7. The interviewer and the interviewee _____ each other _____ at their first meeting.

8. I don't know what is the best method of payment, but I'll soon _____ .

9. Can you _____ one variety _____ the other?

10. I tried to negotiate a discount of 7% off the list price, and finally we _____ .

Ⅲ. Word Formation

Fill in each blank with the proper form of the word given in the brackets.

1. Do you have the right _____ (qualified) for the job?

2. It's not _____ (reliability) to judge a man only by his looks.

3. The _____ (establish) of legal minimum pay is one of the objectives.

4. Please fill in an _____ (applicant) form for a job.

5. His parents give him so much money that he's got no _____ (motivate) to get a job.

6. The situation shows no _____ (indicate) of improvement.

7. We need to _____ (negotiation) the terms and conditions of the contract.

8. Although the price is a little bit high, it is still _____ (accept).

9. Camera film shouldn't be exposed to _____ (extreme) hot or cold temperature.

10. There is an increasing demand for young men whose educational background is either technical or _____ (profession).

Ⅳ. Translation

1. 如果你面试开端良好,那么你很有可能获得那份职位。(chances of sth/doing sth)

2. 如果贵公司认为我的资格和经历合适的话,任何时候我会来面试。(available)

3. 这家公司总是以合理的价格提供给顾客合适的产品。(provide...with)

4. 她需要一份工作以便能维持她的生计。(so that)

5. 为降低职工流动率,那家公司不得不改变奖金(bonus)分配方案。(turnover)

6. 他做这工作不称职。(qualified)

7. 我们需要洽谈合同的具体条款及条件。(negotiate)

8. 估计我们今年亏损约五千美元。(estimate)

9. 今秋她把全部心思花在制订商务计划上。(consume)

10. 他很少有进一步晋升的机会。(have opportunity for)

Ⅴ. Cloze

Organizations and their employees must constantly expand their knowledge, skills, and behavior __1__ meet customer needs and compete in today's __2__ and rapidly changing business environment. In this climate, organizations are placing greater emphasis __3__ training and development.

We support a development for all our employees. Courses are divided __4__ two categories: technical training and personal development.

In the first year of training, staff follow a structured personal development program, __5__ is designed to teach the skills needed __6__ succeed in the commercial world: communication and business awareness, for example. __7__ the same time, technical training courses teach the skills needed for a particular job, __8__ as product design techniques.

In addition to training, there is __9__ regular individual supervision. __10__ recruits have a training manager, who guides their individual development.

Practical experience is gained in the company while __11__ on a variety of team projects. These projects __12__ last for a few months or for several years.

The company provides a friendly atmosphere, which we have managed to maintain __13__ the pressures of rapid growth. This continuing growth contributes __14__ a stimulating, exciting workplace, and creates excellent prospects for the individual at all levels __15__ the organization.

1. A. in   B. about   C. to   D. of
2. A. demanded   B. demanding   C. demands   D. demand
3. A. on   B. to   C. at   D. in
4. A. into   B. from   C. by   D. onto
5. A. who   B. which   C. where   D. what
6. A. for   B. to   C. of   D. in
7. A. At   B. In   C. During   D. After
8. A. so   B. like   C. such   D. that
9. A. also   B. too   C. and   D. about
10. A. Every   B. All   C. Whole   D. Each
11. A. work   B. worked   C. working   D. worked
12. A. may   B. ought   C. need   D. must
13. A. however   B. despite   C. although   D. if
14. A. through   B. across   C. towards   D. forward
15. A. between   B. under   C. within   D. among

Ⅵ. Reading Comprehension.

Staff Recruitment(员工招聘)

1. Job Vacancies(职位空缺)

There have been 20 job vacancies in the past year. 15 of these have been due to retirement and 5 were new posts. All the new posts were in the Information Systems

Division, but the other vacancies were spread evenly across the company.

2. Recruitment

Most of the vacancies were filled quickly, normally within four weeks of the post becoming available. There were some problems with the new jobs, as there are few qualified staff in this field and it is not as easy to promote employees who are already within the firm.

3. Methods of Recruiting Staff

There are two main methods for filling job vacancies—internal advertising and external advertising. All jobs in the company are initially advertised internally (in the company's staff newsletter) so that existing employees have the opportunity to apply for them first. 12 of the jobs this year brought applications from current employees, but only six of these were interviewed and only two were finally given new positions. None of the jobs was automatically filled by existing employees, so they were all advertised externally as well.

External recruitment has generally proved the most successful. This is done through a number of different methods. For temporary of casual staff, we sometimes take people on the recommendation of existing employees. For permanent staff, the more routine, lower level jobs are advertised in the local newspaper, higher level managerial positions are advertised in national newspapers and professional (e. g. legal and financial) posts in national business magazines. For specialist, technical jobs we put an advert in the most suitable trade or technical journal. Finally, secretarial and other office staff are normally provided through local job agencies where the agency does the recruiting for us.

This year, apart from the two internal appointments, 11 staff were recruited through local advertising, two through national papers, two through technical journals and three came from job agencies.

1. Where have the new posts been created in the company?

    A. In all parts of the company.

    B. In the Information Systems Division.

    C. In five new departments.

    D. In three new departments.

2. Why was it harder to fill the new jobs?

    A. They were not advertised for four weeks.

    B. All the suitable staff had already been promoted.

    C. There aren't many people with the right qualifications.

D. All of the above.

3. How many of the company's vacancies were filled by existing company staff?

   A. 2.   B. 6.   C. 12.   D. 8.

4. Which form of recruitment filled the largest number of vacancies?

   A. Advertising in local papers.

   B. Advertising in technical journals.

   C. Recruiting through job agencies.

   D. Advertising on TV.

5. According to the text, how does a company recruit a computer service technician?

   A. Advertising in trade journals.

   B. Advertising in local newspapers.

   C. Advertising in national newspapers.

   D. Advertising in magazines.

6. According to the text, how does a company recruit a secretary for the Sales Department?

   A. Personal recommendation by author member of staff.

   B. Recruitment through job agencies.

   C. Advertisement in national business magazines.

   D. Advertisement in the Internet.

Ⅶ. Writing

(Ⅰ) Writing Basics

Types of paragraphs: Opening, Body and Concluding Paragraphs

A composition consists of several paragraphs, each of which has one central thought. They must be arranged in some kind of order, so that one paragraph leads naturally to another to form an organic whole. Most, if not all, essays are made of an opening, a body, and a concluding paragraph.

The opening paragraph (the introduction) rouses the reader's interest in and secures his attention to the subject matter of the essay or provides necessary background information. The body (the middle) gives a clear and logical presentation of the facts and ideas the writer intends to put forth. The concluding paragraph (the end) winds up the essay often with an emphatic and forceful statement to influence the reader's final impression of the essay and shows the implication or consequences of the argument.

Please read Text A again and try to tell the opening, body and concluding paragraphs.

(Ⅱ) Writing Assignment

You are supposed to write a composition on the topic **My Viewpoints on Job Interviewing.** Write tips as much as you can and base your composition on the following outline.

1. Before the job interview;
2. During the job interview;
3. After the job interview.

Ⅷ. Presentation

Suppose you are a human resource professional at a large retail chain. You need to teach as well as learn effective interviewing skills. You also want to improve the quality of organization's interviewing so that interviews provide valid information. Your ideas may refer to the following ways to conduct interviews: (1) Decide what you are looking for; (2) Plan the interview; (3) Put the applicant at ease; (4) Work from a list, etc. Explain your ideas and give a presentation next time.

Enjoy Your Time

A Birthday

My heart is like a singing bird

Whose nest is in a watered shoot;

My heart is like an apple-tree

Whose boughs are bent with thickset fruit;

My heart is like a rainbow shell

That paddles in a halcyon sea;

My heart is gladder than all these

Because my love is come to me.

Unit 7

Joint Ventures

Learning Objectives

In this unit you will ◆understand the nature of joint ventures;

◆know the reason of learning joint ventures;

◆and review the grammar item: noun clause.

Pre-reading Activities

> **New Words**: manufacture   competitive   expansion
> routinely   evaluate   violation   antitrust

I. Listen to the following short passage twice and fill in the blanks with the words you've heard.

Joint ventures have __1__ for centuries. In the United States, their use __2__ with the railroads in the late 1800s. Throughout the middle part of the __3__ century they were common in the manufacturing sector. By the late 1980s, joint ventures increasingly __4__ in the service industries as businesses looked for new, competitive strategies. This expansion of joint ventures was particularly __5__ to regulators and lawmakers.

The chief __6__ with joint ventures is that they can restrict competition, especially when they are formed by businesses that are __7__ competitors or potential competitors. Another concern is that joint ventures can __8__ the entry of others into a __9__ market. Regulators in the Department of Justice and the Federal Trade Commission routinely evaluate joint ventures for violations of antitrust law; in ___10___, injured private parties may bring antitrust suits.

Ⅱ. **Which topics are you interested in？Choose from the list below, discuss with your classmates and tell the why.**

My favorite movie ☐   My best birthday present ☐

A most unforgettable failure ☐   My best friend ☐

My first volunteer experience ☐   My first part-time job ☐

My favorite English song ☐

Text A

Boost Your Business Now with Joint Ventures

Years ago, a husband and wife team, Jon and Leah Miner, partnered their small, unknown company with the likes of 3M & Disney. These joint ventures created a new technology of scratch & sniff stickers of Disney characters. The end result of this partnership was the birth of a multi-million dollar business, Mello Smello. Here is a brief introduction about how joint ventures create big boosts in business.

A joint venture or strategic alliance is a form of partnership where businesses come together to share knowledge, markets and profits. Joint ventures can take on various forms. Small companies can band together to take on the giants of their industry. Big companies can form alliances with quicker and nimbler small businesses. And small companies have the opportunity to forge strategic alliances with big name companies for expanded geographic reach.

According to Commonwealth Alliance Program, businesses anticipate strategic alliances to account for 25% of all revenue by 2005, a total of 40 trillion dollars. No small business today can afford to ignore the rewards of joint venturing. First of all, joint ventures will definitely help small businesses shorten their learning curve. In another word, small businesses will build more knowledge to expand into key markets, to develop new products, and to improve productivity, which used to be time-consuming and costly. Small businesses gain lead time, share expertise, and lower costs by forming joint ventures. Secondly, through joint ventures, all small businesses will enhance their company credibility. All businesses especially start-ups struggle with building acceptance within their market and customer base. A key alliance with a larger known branded company can dramatically improve your credibility in the eyes of your customers.

Another point that can't be ignored is that joint ventures can create new profit channels: Your business has limited resources and capital for growth. By formulating a joint venture with a solid partner, your company expands its sales force and distribution channel for low cost. Then, the last factor to make small businesses to win out is that joint ventures may build competitor barriers: A strategic alliance with several key players can erect impenetrable walls, keeping out competitors and maintaining high profit margins. Once these ties are in place, it is difficult for competitors to unravel these relationships.

Were you a CEO of a small business, you'd better not to rush into a joint venture without understanding the key concepts of strategic alliances and partnership ventures. Poorly executed and badly planned joint ventures are doomed from the start. Although the costs of forming alliances are inexpensive, the cost of not planning out the partnership is far greater in lost profits and failed relations. So, the first step for small businesses is to set clear goals from the beginning about what you want to accomplish. Has it reduced product costs, expanded sales, or market credibility? Your partner's goals may be different but complementary to yours. Then, with a crystallized goal in your mind, you need to find a possible partner. The best partnership is based on a mutual win-win relationship. Take the time to locate a company with an honest interest in joint ventures and a similar corporate culture. If your small business is focused on long-term customer relations and your strategic partner cares about gaining market share quickly, then your two cultures may clash. After that, you got to map out your negotiation tactics and understand the legal aspects of the deal. When all these things are settled, the real work takes place, as a good alliance is like a marriage, which is built on communication, trust and understanding.

Joint ventures and strategic alliances can be a positive outcome for all parties involved. Take the time to understand the process and your small business will be well positioned into the future.

Words & Expressions

1. partner/ˈpɑːtnə/n. either of two people sharing an activity, such as dancing together or playing together 伙伴，搭档
2. partnership/ˈpɑːtnəʃip/n. state of being a partner or partners, esp. in business 合伙人身份，合股，合伙经营

3. boost/buːst/*vt.* to increase the strength or value of (sth); help or encourage (somebody/something) 增强，提高(某事物)的价值；促进 *n.* increase; help; encouragement 促进,增强

4. strategic/strə'tiːdʒik/*adj.* ① of or relating to strategy 战略的；与战略有关的；② important or essential in relation to a plan of action 重大的,关键的

5. alliance/ə'laiəns/*n.* a close association of nations or other groups, formed to advance common interests or causes 联盟,同盟；联姻；结盟

6. take on to fight with 对付；与(对手)较量

7. nimble/'nimbl/*adj.* quick, light, or agile in movement or action; deft 灵敏的,轻快的

8. forge/fɔːdʒ/*n.* a furnace or hearth where metals are heated or wrought 锻铁炉 *vt.* to form (metal, for example) by heating in a forge and beating or hammering into shape 打(铁),锻制

9. geographic/ˌdʒiə'græfik/*adj.* of or relating to geography 地理学的

10. anticipate/æn'tisipeit/*vt.* ① to feel or realize beforehand; foresee 预感,预料；② to look forward to, especially with pleasure; expect 期望；期待

11. revenue/'revinjuː/*n.* the income of a government from all sources appropriated for the payment of the public expenses 收入；收益

12. ignore/ig'nɔː/*vt.* to refuse to pay attention to; disregard 不顾；拒绝注视(某事物)

13. trillion/'triljən/*n.* 万亿

14. productivity/ˌprɔdʌk'tiviti/*n.* ① the quality of being productive 生产力；② (Economics) the rate at which goods or services are produced especially output per unit of labor【经济学】生产率

15. time-consuming/taim kən,sjuːmiŋ/*adj.* taking up much time 耗时的

16. expertise/ˌekspə'tiːz/*n.* ① expert advice or opinion 专家鉴定；专家的意见或观点；② skill or knowledge in a particular area 专门知识

17. enhance/in'hɑːns/*vt.* to make greater, as in value, beauty, or reputation; augment 提高,增进；在价值、美、声望上增强；加强

18. credibility/ˌkredi'biliti/*n.* the quality, capability, or power to elicit belief 可信性；使人信任的本质、能力

19. formulate/'fɔːmjuleit/*vt.* ① to state as or reduce to a formula 使公式化；② to devise or invent 规划或构想

20. barrier/'bæriə/*n.* ① a structure, such as a fence, built to bar passage 栅栏,挡板,壁垒,关卡；② something immaterial that obstructs or impedes 非物质

的妨碍或阻碍物

21. erect/i'rekt/*adj.* being in a vertical, upright position 竖直的,直立的

22. impenetrable/im'penitrəbl/*adj.* ① impossible to penetrate or enter 不能穿过或进入的;② impossible to understand; incomprehensible 不能理解的;令人费解的

23. maintain/mein'tein/*vt.* ① to keep up or carry on; continue 维持或保持;继续;② to keep in an existing state; preserve or retain 坚持 保持;③ to keep in a condition of good repair or efficiency 保养

24. unravel/ʌn'rævəl/*vt.* ① to undo or ravel the knitted fabric of 拆散;② to separate (entangled threads) 分开

25. doom/duːm/*n.* ① a decision or judgment, especially an official condemnation to a severe penalty 判决;② fate, especially a tragic or ruinous one 命运,尤指厄运或劫数

26. complementary/ˌkɔmplə'mentəri/*adj.* ① forming or serving as a complement; completing 补充的;② supplying mutual needs or offsetting mutual lacks 互补的

27. mutual/'mjuːtʃuəl/*adj.* ① having the same relationship each to the other 彼此相关的;相互之间有共同关系的;② directed and received in equal amount; reciprocal 相互的,彼此的

28. win-win/win-win/*adj.* to be in a state that both sides get desired results 双赢的

29. clash/klæʃ/*vt.* ① to collide with a loud, harsh, usually metallic noise 发出撞击声;碰撞;② to come into conflict; be in opposition 冲突;抵触

30. negotiation/niˌɡəuʃi'eiʃən/*n.* the act or process of negotiating 谈判

31. involve/in'vɔlv/*vt.* ① to contain as a part; include 含有,包括;含有……为一部分;② to engage as a participant; embroil 使牵涉,卷入;使某人卷进来

32. dramatically/drə'mætikəli/*adv.* 戏剧地,引人注目地

33. map out to plan carefully (详细地)制定;筹划

▌Notes

1. Mello Smello: It is a private company, and its' headquarter is located on 3440 Winnetka Ave. N, Minneapolis MN 55427, United States.

2. scratch & sniff stickers: 摩擦生香技术(把有气味的化学品装入一刮即破的微小气囊中。制药公司也使用微型胶囊来制作缓释药片);嗅觉尖刀
   The basic idea behind scratch-and-sniff is to take the aroma-generating chemical and encapsulate it in gelatin or plastic spheres that are incredibly small—on the

order of a few microns in diameter. When you scratch the sticker, you rupture some of these spheres and release the smell. The smell is essentially held in millions of tiny bottles, and you break a few of the bottles every time you scratch the sticker. The tiny bottles preserve the fragrance for years.

3. CEO(首席执行官): This is the senior manager who is responsible for overseeing the activities of an entire company. The CEO(chief executive officer) usually also holds a position on the board of directors, or also holds the title of president.

4. A joint venture or strategic alliance is a form of partnership where businesses come together to share knowledge, markets and profits. 合资企业(企业战略联盟)是一种合作经营关系,合作的企业通过这种合作关系互享商务信息、市场和利润。

5. In another word, small businesses will build more knowledge to expand into key markets, to develop new products, and to improve productivity, which used to be time-consuming and costly. 换而言之,小企业将积累更多的信息,以进一步开拓其主要市场,加速新产品的研发,同时提高自身的生产力。而这一切,在结盟之前将耗掉小企业的大量时间和研发成本。

6. If your small business is focused on long-term customer relations and your strategic partner cares about gaining market share quickly, then your two cultures may clash. 如果你的小企业重在培养长期的客户关系,而你的战略伙伴却更看重快速获得市场份额,那么你们两种企业文化就会发生冲突。

Word Study

1. boost *vt.*

① to raise or lift by pushing up from behind or below 向上推,提升

If you boost me up a little bit, I can just reach the window.

假如你托我一把,我正好可以够到窗户。

② to increase; raise 增加;拔高

The management has made a series of plans to boost production by 25% next year. 管理层作了一系列的计划,期待来年增产25%。

③ to stir up enthusiasm for; promote vigorously; encourage 促进,改善,激励

The general believes that his soldiers need a big victory to boost their spirits.

将军认为他的士兵们急需一场大胜来鼓舞士气。

2. anticipate *vt.*

① to think likely to happen; expect (+*v.* -ing/that) 预期,期望

We anticipate meeting a certain amount of resistance to our plan.

我们预料我们的计划会遇到一些人的反对。

② to guess or imagine in advance (what will happen) and take the necessary action in order to be ready 预料到(会发生某事)而做好准备,预防

I tried to anticipate the kind of questions they were likely to ask me at the interview.

我设法预测一下他们在面试时可能向我提出的问题。

③ to do something before (someone else) 抢在他人之前,先于……而行动

We anticipated our competitors by getting our book into the shops first.

我们抢在竞争对手之前先把书送往书店出售。

3. maintain vt.

① to continue to have, do, etc., as before; keep up 维持,保持

I hope you will maintain your recent improvement.

我希望你能保持最近取得的进步。

② to keep up (something) in good condition by making repairs to it and taking care of it 维修,保养

It is more important to maintain the railway lines than to build them well.

保养好铁路线比建设好更重要。

③ to support with money 赡养

That old man is too poor to maintain his own family.

那个老头太穷了,无法养活家人。

4. formulate vt.

① to express in an exact way; frame 准确的阐述(表达,说明)

You should formulate your reply to the interviewers if you really want to take this post.

如果你真的想得到这个职位,你就应该把你的回答向面试者表达清楚。

② to invent and prepare (a plan, suggestion, etc.) 规划(制度);构想出(计划,建议)

The local government is formulating a new policy on housing prices.

地方政府正在制定一项关于房价的新政策。

5. involve vt.

① (in, with) to cause (someone or oneself) to become connected or concerned 使(别人或自己)卷入,使介入

Don't get yourself involved in that gambling scandal!

别卷入那起赌博丑闻之中!

② (*v.* -ing) to have as a necessary part or result；entail 包含；需要；使成为必要部分（必然结果）

The job involves traveling abroad for three months each year.

这份工作需要每年到国外出差三个月。

③ (of a situation or action) to have as the people or things taking part （情况，行动）牵涉,涉及

The world basketball championship involving hundreds of excellent players is going to be held in Japan next month.

全世界数百名优秀篮球运动员参加的世界篮球锦标赛下个月将在日本举行。

Post-reading Activities

I. Comprehension Questions.

1. What is the definition of joint venture according to the passage?

2. Could you name some big joint ventures either in your city or in some other cities?

3. What rewards will small businesses get if they join the big joint ventures?

4. For small businesses, how to find suitable joint ventures for the expected extension of their own business?

5. What risks will small businesses meet with while looking for their ideal partners?

II. Fill in the blanks with the words or phrases given in the box. Change the forms if necessary.

maintain	boost		anticipate	revenue	involve
in the eyes of	formulate. . . with		map out	in place	take on

1. _____ most students, their new English teacher looks more like their friend than a teacher.

2. As the _____ growth rate of 4. 5% had failed, the share price of Ford motors dropped by 2. 5% in the end of 1998.

3. By _____ a strong business tie _____ a KFC branch in the downtown, farmers have sold out more potatoes in the past two years.

4. A lot of famous footballers were _____ in that infamous football scandal.

5. Our plant has planned to _____ our production by 30% next year.

6. Lanny _____ a strange expression when she heard that one of her best friends had gone abroad.

7. Part of Mary's job is to _____ good relations with her company's suppliers.

8. From next week the new regulations will be _____, so all the staff should be well prepared for it.

9. The Greens are _____ where to go for their summer vacation.

10. The government of Iran was short of money because of falling oil _____.

Ⅲ. **Complete the sentences with the proper forms of the words given in parentheses.**

1. She has gone into _____ (partner) with some local enterprises.

2. The fast economic development of this town in recent decade has greatly _____ (boost) the growth of tourism.

3. A new _____ (strategic) will be possibly helpful if we want to create a better working environment for the workers.

4. Are you _____ (anticipate) any trouble when the factory opens again?

5. Good secretarial skills will _____ (enhancement) your chances of getting a post in the office.

6. If we don't keep our promises, we will lose our _____ (incredible) with the public.

7. The newspaper is having _____ (distribute) problem, and in some parts of the country people are unable to buy it.

8. These two types of teaching materials can _____ (complementary) each other quite well.

9. As the spokesman said, that was a _____ (negotiate) contract because some experts believed that the high payment would put the local government under immense economic pressure.

10. That famous footballer claimed that he was not _____ (involve) in that football scandal.

Ⅳ. **Fill in the blanks with suitable words to complete the summary of the text.**

This text mainly tells what is joint venture and __1__ small businesses can boost their business by cooperating with big joint ventures. According to the given definition, a joint venture is __2__ where businesses come together to share knowledge, __3__ and profits. So, it is naturally expected that small businesses can shorten their learning period and meanwhile enhance their company __4__. Besides that, big joint ventures can also create new __5__ channels and raise competitiveness for small businesses. In spite of all these advantages, small businesses should be more careful while looking for their possible __6__, otherwise, they will inevitably suffer more from their haste.

Ⅴ. **Translate the following sentences into English.**

1. 根据最新的调查,中国已经在最近的十年里建立了上万家合资企业。 (according to)

2. 随着新的银行法的颁布,外资银行将很难进入中国的电信领域。(keep out)

3. 要是心中有明确的目标,你就会通过自己的努力一步一步实现它。(with a crystallized goal in one's mind)

4. 我们两家公司的互相信赖是建立在长期的良好合作的基础之上的。(be based on)

5. 经理要求所有的员工将注意力集中在他们手头的工作上。(focus on)

Text B

China's Policy Direction of Absorption of Foreign Investment

With China's rapid development now, measures should be taken to further improve the soft environment for foreign investment, explore actively new methods for absorbing foreign capital, put emphasis on absorbing advanced technology, modern management and special talents, and actively absorb foreign capital to invest in industries of new and advanced technology, encourage world-known corporations to set up district headquarters, research and development centers; speed up the development of supporting industries and push on the service trade field to open up to foreign countries step by step.

In that case, better improving the political and legal environment for foreign investment, and further improving legal administration level seem quite urgent for China now. According to our commissions for joining WTO and the requirement for our opening-up process, we will further improve the legal system of absorbing foreign investment, and try to create a better environment for foreign investment. We will further simplify the examination and approval procedures for foreign investment and adopt an internationally accepted examination and approval system, creating a good administrative environment for foreign investment.

Besides that, maintaining and improving an open and fair market environment poses another focus for our government. We should combine this with the current work of standardizing the order of market economy; prohibit firmly the improper collecting fees from foreign companies as well as improper inspection and fine of them. We should also enhance the lawful measures to protect the intellectual property right and take strong actions against illegal piracy, therefore, establish an open, unified and fair market environment, render a quick service to the complaining of foreign-funded and protect the legal rights of foreign merchants according to law.

Meanwhile, China needs to further open the field of service industry. In accordance with China's self-development and Commitment to the WTO, we will further open this field, perfect rules and regulations for service industry and formulate a united and standard system for accession into the market of foreign investment service. We will encourage the import of modern service concepts and advanced management experiences, technology and modes of modern market operation, improve structure of service industry in China.

And the least thing not to mention is to encourage foreign businessmen to invest in the new high-tech industry, the basic industry, and supporting industry. We will continue to encourage foreign investors to introduce and develop new technology and to invest in technology-intensive project, and with this national tendency, more Chinese enterprises will leap greatly on their own way of technology development. Apart from that, the relevant regulations of setting pioneering investment enterprise should also be improved in order to better the conditions of setting and developing high-tech corporations. We should attract foreigners to invest in supporting industry, push domestic small and medium-sized enterprises to enforce cooperation with foreign companies and introduce the advanced and applicable technology to match the large foreign-funded enterprises, thus to enter the production and sales network of multinational companies.

Words & Expressions

1. explore/ik'splɔː/*vt.* to investigate systematically; examine 钻研；系统地研究；调查
2. absorb/əb'sɔːb/*vt.* ① to take (something) in through or as through pores or interstices 吸收；② to occupy the full attention, interest, or time of; engross 引人注意，使着迷；占据……的全部注意力、兴趣或时间；使全神贯注
3. administration/ədˌminiˈstreiʃən/*n.* the act of granting certain powers or the authority to carry out a particular task or duty 委任；委托
4. commission/kəˈmiʃən/*n.* ① action, task or piece of work given to sb to do 委

托,授权;② payment to sb for selling goods which increases with the quantity of goods sold 佣金

5. opening-up/ˌəupəniŋˈʌp/ n. in a state of being made to develop 开放;开发

6. simplify/ˈsimpliˌfai/ vt. ① to make simple or simpler 使变得简单或更简单;② to reduce in complexity or extent 使简化

7. approval/əˈpruːvəl/ n. the act of approving 同意;批准的行为

8. adopt/əˈdɔpt/ vt. ① to take into one's family through legal means and raise as one's own child 收养,过继;② to take and follow (a course of action, for example) by choice or assent 采用

9. administrative/ədˈministrətiv/ adj. of or concerning administration 行政的;管理的

10. pose/pəuz/ vt. ① to assume or hold a particular position or posture, as in sitting for a portrait 摆姿势;② to affect a particular mental attitude 装腔作势

11. standardize/ˈstændədaiz/ vt. to cause to conform to a standard 使……按照标准

12. improper/imˈprɔpə/ adj. ① not suited to circumstances or needs; unsuitable 不适当的,不妥当的;不合适的;② not in keeping with conventional mores; indecorous 不合宜的; 和传统的规范不相符的;不体面的

13. illegal/iˈliːgəl/ adj. prohibited by law 违法的,非法的;为法律所禁止的

14. piracy/ˈpaiərəsi/ n. ① robbery committed at sea 海盗行为,海上劫掠;② a similar act of robbery 抢劫行为;③ the unauthorized use or reproduction of copyrighted or patented material 剽窃行为,侵犯专利行为

15. self-development n. 自我发展

16. accession/ækˈseʃən/ n. the attainment of a dignity or rank 就职,就任

17. high-tech/ˌhaiˈtek/ adj. high technology 高科技的

18. technology-intensive adj. 技术密集型的

19. tendency/ˈtendənsi/ n. ① movement or prevailing movement in a given direction 趋势;② a predisposition to think, act, behave, or proceed in a particular way 思想、行为、举止的一种倾向,或以一种特殊方式进行

20. medium-sized adj. 中型的, 普通型的

21. enforce/inˈfɔːs/ vt. ① to compel observance of or obedience to 强制服从或遵守;② to impose (a kind of behavior, for example); compel 强求,强制,强加(比如说一种行为)

22. cooperation/kəuˌɔpəˈreiʃən/ n. ① the act or practice of cooperating 合作;合作的行为或实践;② the association of persons or businesses for common, usually economic, benefit 合作性团体

23. applicable/'æplikəbl/ *adj.* that can be applied; appropriate 可应用的；适当的

24. multinational/ˌmʌlti'næʃənəl/ *adj.* having operations, subsidiaries, or investments in more than two countries 多国的

25. put emphasis on sth give great attention to sth 强调；重视

26. prohibit... from... —prevent... from... 阻止

Notes

1. WTO(世界贸易组织): The World Trade Organization (WTO) is created in 1 January, 1995, after the Uruguay Round negotiations (1986—1994), headquartered in Geneva, Switzerland, with 149 countries. It is the only global international organization dealing with the rules of trade between nations. At its heart are the WTO agreements, negotiated and signed by the bulk of the world's trading nations and ratified in their parliaments. The goal is to help producers of goods and services, exporters, and importers conduct their business.

2. With China's rapid development now, measures should be taken to further improve the soft environment for foreign investment, explore actively new methods for absorbing foreign capital, put emphasis on absorbing advanced technology, modern management and special talents, and actively absorb foreign capital to invest in industries of new and advanced technology, encourage world-known corporations to set up district headquarters, research and development centers; speed up the development of supporting industries and push on the service trade field to open up to foreign countries step by step. 随着中国经济的快速发展，政府需要进一步采取措施改善外商投资的软环境，积极开拓吸引外资的新渠道，重视高新技术、现代管理和特殊人才的吸收，并积极引导外资投资于高新技术产业，鼓励世界知名企业在中国设立地区总部和研发中心，加速支撑行业的快速发展，并进一步推动服务行业逐渐向外商开放。

3. In accordance with China's self-development and Commitment to the WTO, we will further open this field, perfect rules and regulations for service industry and formulate a united and standard system for accession into the market of foreign investment service. 根据中国的自身发展及其对世贸组织的承诺，我们将进一步开放服务行业，完善服务业的规章制度，为外资进入这一行业的服务制订统一和规范的程序。

Word Study

1. absorb *vt.*

   ① to take (something) in through or as through pores or interstices 吸收(尤指液体)

   It is too difficult for the students to absorb all the language points within just two days! 学生们要在短短两天内吸收所有的语言点实在太难了。

   ② (in) to completely fill the attention of; engross 吸引(注意);使专心,使全神贯注

   The little boy was so absorbed in his toys that he didn't hear the bell.

   那个小男孩正专心玩他的玩具,根本没听到铃声。

   ③ (into) (of a country or organization) to make (a smaller country or organization) into a part of itself; gain control over 并入,吞并

   IBM has gradually absorbed its smaller rivals in the recent decade.

   IBM 公司在过去十年里逐渐吞并了一些小的竞争对手。

2. simplify *vt.*

   ① to make simple or simpler 使变得简单或更简单

   It would be better for you to simplify your instructions to the children.

   把你给孩子们的讲解说得简单一点会更好。

   ② to reduce in complexity or extent 使简化

   Some plots of the original novel have been simplified so that the readers can better understand it.

   原著小说中的一些情节已经简化过了,这样读者能更好地理解这些剧情。

3. adopt *vt.*

   ① to take into one's family through legal means and raise as one's own child 收养,过继

   Mr. Robert has decided to adopt Jerry, one of his best friend's sons.

   罗伯特先生决定收养杰瑞,他是罗伯特一个好朋友的儿子。

   ② to take and follow (a course of action, for example) by choice or assent 采用,采纳

   The engineer was very disappointed, as his boss didn't adopt his new production suggestion.

   这位工程师很失望,因为他的老板没有采纳他新的生产建议。

   ③ to begin to have (a quality or appearance) 采取

All the governments have unanimously agreed to adopt a tough approach to the terrorists. 所有政府一致同意对恐怖分子采取强硬手段。

4. pose

vi. ① (for) to (cause to) sit or stand in a particular position, esp. in order to be photographed, painted, etc. (尤指为拍照或画像)摆好姿势

Our foreign visitors all posed in front of the museum for a photograph.

我们的外国游客们都在博物馆前摆好姿势合影留念。

② (derog) to behave unnaturally or pretend to be clever, more artistic, etc. than one really is, in order to attract interest or admiration [贬]装腔作势

John's new wife always poses before his distinguished guests.

约翰的新婚妻子总在他的一些尊贵的客人面前装腔作势。

vt. to be the cause of (something difficult to deal with); present 造成,形成 (难局)

Pollution poses a threat to the continued existence of this species.

污染对这一物种的继续生存造成了威胁。

5. enforce *vt.*

① to cause (a rule or law) to be obeyed or carried out effectively 执行,实施 (法律),使生效

It is quite difficult for the government to enforce the newly adopted regulations.

政府要实施那些新规定颇有难度。

② (on, upon) to make (something) happen, esp. by threats or force 强迫, 迫使,把……强加于

That giant company tried to enforce this contract with us.

那家大公司企图把这份合同强加在我们头上。

Vocabulary Building

soft environment 软环境	absorb foreign capital 吸引外资
advanced technology 先进技术	modern management 现代化管理
market economy 市场经济	intellectual property right 知识产权
illegal piracy 非法盗版	service industry 服务业
high-tech industry 高新企业	technology-intensive project 技术密集型项目
world-known corporations 世界知名企业	
district headquarters 地区总部	
research and development centers 研发中心	
administrative environment 管理环境	
medium-sized enterprises 中等规模企业	
foreign-funded enterprises 外资企业	

Word Formation：Verb Suffixes

Verb Suffixes	Meaning	Added to	Examples	Illustrative Examples
-fy, -ify	make or become	nouns, adjectives	beautify, simplify, purify, intensify, rarefy, uglify, clarify, satisfy, codify, classify, electrify, gasify, glorify	This salt has been purified for use in medicine.
-ize, -ise	make or become	nouns, adjectives	computerize, globalize, modernize, industrialize, popularize, familiarize, centralize, economize, normalize, mechanise, revolutionize	A famous dancer popularized the new hairstyle.
-en	make or become	nouns, adjectives	quicken, ripen, deafen, widen, shorten, weaken, brighten, darken, deepen, richen, harden, strengthen, lengthen, youthen, heighten	Excessive smoking will shorten people's life.

-ish	make or cause	verbs	nourish, flourish, vanish, diminish, abolish, impoverish, famish, embellish	His illness diminished his strength.

Post-reading Activities

I. True or False Questions.

1. According to the passage, China's policy direction of absorption of foreign investment should be further improved in a variety of fields.

2. Only improving the political and legal environment for foreign investment seems quite urgent for China now.

3. It is implied that improper collecting fees from foreign companies as well as improper inspection and fine of them does exist in China now.

4. Service industries in China seem a big attraction for foreign investors.

5. With more foreign businesses investing in high-tech industry, most Chinese enterprises will inevitably face greater challenges, which will pose greater difficulty for their own technology development.

6. Domestic small and medium-sized enterprises in China still have a lot to do in technology development.

II. Fill in the blanks with the words or phrases given in the box. Change the forms if necessary.

explore	adopt	pose another focus for	enforce	speed up	open up
take actions against		render service to	in accordance with		apart from

1. Most government officials agreed to _____ tougher approaches to the international terrorists.

2. As more and more border cities _____ to neighbors in the southern region, most southwestern provinces of China leaped greatly in their import and export trade.

3. The Workers' Union has to _____ the possible upcoming employment cut.

4. The sharply dropped oil price _____ the western countries and their allies.

5. _____ the boss's orders, the secretary cancelled the meeting this afternoon.

6. _____ being too large for me, the color of that jacket doesn't suit me, either.

7. It is reported that ABC Company has attempted to _____ a contract with their supplier.

8. All the shopping centers in this community _____ nursing _____ those shoppers with trotters.

9. Production of the new model must _____.

10. We have to _____ several solutions to that problem.

Ⅲ. **Complete the sentences with the proper forms of the words given in parentheses.**

1. Man is born with a strong curiosity to _____ (explore) both the outer world and the brain, the inner universe.

2. His complete _____ (absorb) in his work makes us feel a little ashamed of our hasty working attitude.

3. He believes everything with childish _____ (simplify).

4. Our sales manager has _____ (approve) of our new working plan.

5. The _____ (adopt) of that advanced machine has given a big boost to our production efficiency.

6. Efforts to _____ (standard) English spellings have not been completely successful.

7. I am learning English now, but I still can't speak it _____ (proper).

8. It is _____ (legal) to break into someone's house with arms.

9. She was born with artistic _____ (tendency).

10. Every group member should learn how to _____ (cooperation) well with his or her other workmates if they want to pass this demanding test.

Ⅳ. **Dictation.**

Exercises

Ⅰ. **Structures**: Noun Clause（名词性从句）

名词性从句通常是指在一个句子中起名词或名词短语作用的从句。名词性从句根据其在句子中的作用不同可分为主语从句、宾语从句、表语从句和同位语从句四种。名词性从句由关联词引导。

Noun clause usually refers to a clause which functions as a noun or a noun phrase in a subject-predicate structure.

Subject Clause（主语从句）: Subject clause is usually used as the subject in complex sentence, and is mainly introduced by connectives(关联词) of the following four groups:

Connectives: that/whether/if/as if/as though

Connective pronouns: who/whom/whose/what/which/whoever/whatever/whichever

Interrogative adverbs: when/where/why/how

How-phrases: how many/how long/how far

1. That she will succeed is certain.

2. What he needs is more experience.

3. It is estimated that a round-trip to Mars would take more than a year.

4. How the prisoner escaped is a mystery.

5. How long this battery can last is not known yet.

Object Clause (宾语从句): Object clause generally serves as object after transitive verbs or prepositions.

1. I don't think (that) he is right.

2. He wonders if the letter was miscarried.

3. He was not conscious of what an important discovery he had made.

4. We are not sure whether we can persuade him out of smoking.

5. I shall see to it that he is taken good care of when you are absent.

Predicative Clause (表语从句): Predicative clause is used as predicative after link verbs: be, look, seem, and remain. Besides that, some fixed structures like "the reason is that..." or "it is because...".

1. It seems that it is going to rain.

2. The question remains whether we can win the majority of the people.

3. That is why Jack got scolded.

4. The reason why he was dismissed is that he was careless and irresponsible.

Appositive Clause (同位语从句): Appositive clause is usually placed after abstract nouns to illustrate its meaning, such as fact, news, idea, thought, truth, demand, proposal, suggestion.

1. The news that we are invited to the conference is very encouraging.

2. Einstein came to the conclusion that the maximum speed possible in the universe is that of light.

3. Is there any certainty that she will win the match?

4. The rumor that he was arrested was unfounded.

After examining the above four types of noun clause examples, please finish the exercises with an appropriate connective.

1. _____ she is still alive is sheer(纯粹的) luck.

2. The assumption is _____ things will improve.

3. The difficulty lies in _____ we haven't found some good materials.

4. _____ will chair the meeting has not yet been decided.

5. Tell us _____ of you will go to the exhibition.

6. That is _____ we used to live.

7. _____ did that should admit it frankly.

8. The news _____ he was resigning his position proved to be incorrect.

9. There is a possibility _____ he has lied to us.

10. Whether we can succeed depends on _____ we cooperate.

Ⅱ. Vocabulary

1. The _____ (dramatically) changes in the past 15 years left a deep impression upon the visitors.

2. My niece felt uncomfortable when she was _____（在去学校的路上）to her school.

3. We can extend your loan so _____ and no _____ (far)（到此为止,不能再拖）.

4. They were suffering from losing their youngest daughter. _____（与此同时）, another bad news came and the whole family broke down completely.

5. All the Asian countries agreed to _____（结成同盟）to fight against the Japanese troops.

6. Jennifer thought that was a nice piece of work, _____（除了）a few slight faults.

7. Most college graduates feel it lucky to _____（有机会）to do their share for the coming Olympic Games in Beijing in the year of 2008.

8. The general manager declared that they would _____（重点放在）the development of new products.

9. By far, the Starbucks has _____（建立）more than 150 branch services in Eastern China.

10. The only chance for our basketball team to _____（胜出）lies in whether they can beat their last opponent.

Ⅲ. Translation

1. 刚刚毕业的大学毕业生应该多多积累实际工作经验。(build up)

2. 一年级的新生需要快速扩大他们的词汇量。(expand)

3. 通过引进先进的设备,这种产品的生产时间被大大缩短了。(shorten)

4. 对中小企业来说,成功的第一步首先是寻找一个合适的合作伙伴。(the first step)

5. 在所有的细节确定之前,不要急于签合同。(settle)

6. 我们应当采取措施来帮助这些失学的孩子。(take measures to)

7. 提高生产效率对这家工厂来说已刻不容缓。(urgent)

8. 所有在考场上的作弊行为都是不允许的。(prohibit)

9. 近十年来,这个村子的经济取得了长足的进步。(leap)

10. 他们回避那个话题是不想让你感到难堪。(in order to)

IV. Cloze

Some people argue that the pressure on international sportsmen and sportswomen kill the essence of sport——the pursuit of personal excellence. Children kick a football __1__ for fun. When they get __2__ and play for local school teams, they become competitive but they still enjoy playing. The individual representing his country cannot __3__ to think about enjoying himself; he has to think only about winning. He is responsible for a (n) __4__ nation's hopes, dreams and reputation.

A good example is the Football World Cup. Football is the world's most important sport. Winning the World Cup is __5__ the summit of international sporting success. __6__ "Argentina" to someone and the chances are __7__ he'll think of football. In a __8__, winning the World Cup "put Argentina on the map".

Sports fans and supporters get quite __9__ about the World Cup. People in England felt that their country was __10__ important after they won in 1966. Last year __11__ of Scots sold their cars, and even their houses, and spent all their money traveling to Argentina, where the finals were played.

So, am I arguing that international competition __12__ the idea of sport? Certainly not! Does the Argentinean really believe that because __13__ of their men proved the most skillful at football, their nation is in __14__ way better than all others? Not really. But it's nice to know that you won, and that in one at __15__ your country is the best.

1. A. around   B. about   C. away   D. aside

2. A. elderly   B. older   C. elder   D. younger

3. A. pay   B. know   C. afford   D. like

4. A. whole   B. entire   C. complete   D. total

5. A. perhaps   B. 100%   C. usually   D. mostly

6. A. Speak   B. Talk   C. Express   D. Mention

7. A. what   B. that   C. which   D. where

8. A. meaning   B. extent   C. sense   D. conclusion

9. A. sensible   B. interested   C. reasonable   D. irrational

10. A. somewhat   B. somehow   C. somewhere   D. sometime

11. A. thousands   B. thousand   C. hundred   D. millions

12. A. preserves   B. kills   C. defeat   D. lose

13. A. 11   B. 12   C. 13   D. 14

14. A. certain   B. every   C. all   D. their

15. A. most   B. worst   C. best   D. least

V. Reading Comprehension

The History of Volkswagen

Ferdinand Porsche started work on the "people's car" with money he received from the German government in 1934. First of all he traveled to America to learn about car production. Then in 1938 he returned to Germany, founded Volkswagen Gmbh and started production with his new American machinery in Wolfsburg, Lower Saxony.

Commercial production stopped during the war and the factory and its 9,000 workers fell into British hands in 1945. After the war the British helped the local economy by ordering 20,000 cars but decided not to take over the company as they did not think it had a future. Instead, Heinrich Nordhoff took over as Managing Director and the Volkswagen success story began.

Within five years annual production went from 20,000 to 230,000 cars and the company founded its first South American subsidiary, Volkswagen do Brazil S. A. In 1949 the first exports to the USA arrived in New York, where they were described as "beetle-like" and the VW Beetle legend was born. Thirty-two years later the 20 million Beetle rolled off a Volkswagen de Mexico production line. In 1960 Volkswagen became a public limited company valued at DM 600m.

The company continued its globalization by setting up its own production facilities in Australia (1957), Nigeria (1973) and Japan (1990) while expanding into the USA (1976) and Spain (1986) by buying car manufacturers. The company also set up a joint venture in China (1982). Political events at the end of 1989 gave VW the opportunity to move into central Europe, where it soon began production in the former East Germany and expanded into the Czech Republic.

Today Volkswagen AG is Europe's largest car-maker with 242,770 employees and a turnover of $ 65 b. With new versions of the two world's most successful cars, the Beetle and Golf, the future for VW locks every bit as bright as its past.

1. During the war the company _____.

    A. stopped producing cars completely

    B. stopped producing cars for sale to the public

    C. continued producing cars as before

    D. moved to England

2. Porsche produced the first Volkswagen car _____.

    A. ten months after he received government money

    B. three years after he received government money

    C. four years after he received government money

    D. four months after he received government money

3. The company opened a Chinese joint venture in _____.

    A. 1947   B. 1982   C. 1994   D. 1990

4. The company exported the first Beetle to USA in _____.

    A. 1949   B. 1957   C. 1976   D. 1990

5. The British did not take over the company because _____.

    A. they did not think it would survive

    B. they did not have enough money

    C. Heinrich Nordhoff had already bought it

    D. they had their own car companies

6. Between 1945 and 1950 production increased _____.

    A. every year by 20,000

    B. from 20,000 to 230,000

    C. by 20,000 to 230,000

    D. by 10%

VI. Writing

(I) Writing Basics: Unity and Coherence

Unity

Paragraph unity is usually achieved through the "leadership" of the paragraph— the topic sentence. The topic sentence is the central theme, summarizing the main idea to be expressed in the paragraph. All the supporting sentences in the paragraph should focus on the single major thought—the controlling idea. In the following paragraph, all the details are chosen and developed around the controlling idea "lazy".

We Americans are incredibly lazy. Instead of cooking a simple, nourishing meal, we pop a frozen dinner into the oven. Instead of studying a daily newspaper, we are contented with the capsule summaries on the network now. Worst of all, instead of walking even a few blocks to the local convenience store, we jump into our cars. This dependence on the automobile, even for short trips, has robbed us of a valuable experience—walking.

Coherence

Coherence can be achieved by arranging all the supporting sentences in a clear and logic order. This means arranging materials in a meaningful sequence consistent with the logic and our thought patterns.

Commonly used logical arrangements include temporal order, spatial order, climatic order, casual analysis, comparison and contrast, and process analysis. Frequently we combine various methods in developing a paragraph.

Besides that, useful connectives and transitional phrases, such as first, second, thirdly, can also make one sentence run smoothly to another, so that readers can follow the writer easily.

My day yesterday was a mess. We got off to a bad start because I had forgotten to buy coffee. My tan belt broke when I was on my way to work. When I finally got to work, I found the interesting project I'd been working on was canceled and I spent the whole day doing boring filing. My husband forgot I didn't have a car, so he failed to pick me up after work. Because I was upset, I burned the steak I had splurged on. The baby sitter was sick so we couldn't go to the movies we were looking forward to. Feeling there was nothing else to do, I flung myself on my bed—which immediately collapsed. I hope I don't have such a frustrating day soon again.

(Ⅱ) Writing Assignment

You are supposed to write a composition on the topic **Advantages and Disadvantages of the ATM**? Write about 100 to 120 words and base your composition on the following outline.

1. The ATM has both advantages and disadvantages.
2. The advantages of the ATM.
3. The disadvantages of the ATM.
4. My point of view about the ATM.

Ⅶ. Presentation(Speaking)

Work in pairs and talk about what kind of music you like best. You and your partner may have different tastes. Find out more details about the music you prefer most by referring either to music magazines or to music channels online. Write down the information you have found and give a presentation next time.

You may refer to the following terms or expressions:

classic music   pop(popular music)   jazz   rock'n' roll   rap(说唱乐)
blues   light music   folk music alternative(另类音乐)   country music
I like classic music very much, as I think it can...
I am fond of popular music, partly because...
Rock'n' roll is not my cup of tea(我不喜欢摇滚乐), and I just can't stand the noise and the big crowd.

Sometimes light music can make me feel relaxed and even refreshed after a whole day's tiring work.

Enjoy Your Time

Good Excuse

Police officers hear plenty of excuses from people caught parking at places reserved only for handicapped persons. Once, a policeman tried to stop a man from doing so. When the man was questioned whether he knew the parking regulations, he answered affirmatively. Then the policeman further questioned why he was parking his car there. "Oh, I injured my leg last week. The doctor said I would become disabled if I didn't get proper treatment. Now I am experiencing what I'll feel like to be a disabled person."

Unit 8

Business and Culture

Learning Objectives

In this unit you will ◆understand the importance of culture in international business;
◆learn how to communicate across cultures;
◆review the usage of "as".

Pre-reading Activities

New Words: aesthetics   dynamics   abstract

Ⅰ. **Listen to the following short passage twice and fill in the blanks with the words you've heard.**

There are three ways in which people become ___1___ of new cultures: through studying the language and talking to people who speak it; through studying of the history of the ___2___ , government, religion and aesthetics of a society; and by examining the dynamics of culture itself—the ways in which people of a culture communicate with each other.

The study of language is ___3___ to ___4___ learning and communication; we have to learn to understand what is being said and to make ourselves ___5___ .

Studying the social ___6___ , history, religion and abstract ___7___ of a culture is helpful to understanding the culture, but it ___8___ a student with only an abstract understanding of a culture. It will do very little to ___9___ interaction of family members, forms of address and dating and __10__ customs—very important aspects of any culture.

Ⅱ. **What should we pay attention to and what should we avoid when doing business cross-culturally? Choose from the list below. Discuss with your classmates and tell why.**

Social Values ☐   Ways of Making Decisions ☐

Cultural Context ☐   Social Customs ☐

Using an Interpreter ☐   Cultural Biases ☐

Flexibility and Patience ☐   Language Barrier ☐

Text A

Culture and International Business

Culture is one of the most challenging elements of the international market place. It is defined as an integrated system of learned behavior patterns that are characteristic of the members of any given society. It includes everything that a group thinks, says, does, and makes—its customs, language, material artifacts, and shared systems of attitudes and feelings. The definition, therefore, includes a wide variety of elements from the materialistic to the spiritual. Culture is inherently conservative, resisting change and fostering continuity. Every person is enculturated into a particular culture, learning the "right way" of doing things. Problems may arise when a person enculturec in one culture has to adjust to another one. The process of acculturation—adjusting and adapting to a specific culture other than one's own—is one of the keys to success in international operations.

The ever-increasing level of world trade, opening of new markets, and intensifying competition have allowed—and sometimes forced—business to expand their operations. The challenge for managers is to handle the different values, attitudes, and behavior that govern human interaction. First, managers must ensure smooth interaction of the business with its different constituents, and second, they must assist others to implement programs within and across markets. It is no longer feasible to think of markets and operations in terms of domestic and international. Because the separation is no longer distinguishable, the necessity of culturally sensitive management and personnel is the most important.

As firms expand their operations across borders, they acquire new customers and new partners in new environments. Two distinct tasks become necessary: first, to understand cultural differences and the ways they show themselves and, second, to determine similarities across cultures and exploit them in strategy formulation. Success in new markets is very much a function of cultural adaptability: patience, flexibility, and appreciation of others' beliefs. Recognition of different approaches may lead to establishing best practice; that is, a new way of doing things applicable throughout the firm. Ideally, this means that successful ideas can be transferred across borders for efficiency and adjusted to local conditions for effectiveness. Take the case of Nestle. In one of his regular trips to company headquarters in Switzerland, the general manager of Nestle Thailand was briefed on a summer coffee promotion from the Greek subsidiary, a cold coffee concoction called the Nescafe Shake. The Thai Group swiftly adopted and adapted the idea. It designed plastic containers to mix the drink and invented a dance, the Shake, to popularize the activity.

Cultural competence must be recognized as a key management skill. Cultural incompetence, or inflexibility, can easily risk millions of dollars through wasted negotiations; lost purchases, sales, and contracts; and poor customer relations. Furthermore, the internal efficiency of a multinational corporation may be weakened if managers and workers are not "on the same wave-length". The tendency for U. S. managers is to be open and informal, but in some cultural settings that may be inappropriate. Cultural risk is just as real as political risk in the international business arena.

The most complicated problems in dealing with the cultural environment stem from the fact that one cannot learn culture—one has to live it. How to deal with cultural diversity in the business world? Some people think that business is business the world around. In some cases, globalization is a fact of life; however, cultural differences are still far from converging.

Some others propose that companies must tailor business approaches to individual cultures. Setting up polices and procedures in each country has been compared to an organ transplant; the critical question centers around acceptance or rejection. The major challenge to the international manager is to make sure that rejection is not a result of cultural myopia or even blindness.

Words & Expressions

1. element/'elimənt/*n.* a part; a component 要素,元素
2. behavior pattern 行为模式
3. characteristic/ˌkæriktə'ristik/*adj.* typical of a person or thing 特有的
4. artifact/'ɑːtiˌfækt/*n.* an object that is made by a person 手工艺品
5. definition/ˌdefi'niʃən/*n.* a statement that explains the meaning of a word or phrase 定义 define *vt.* 下定义 defined *adj.* 定义的,清晰的 definable *adj.* 可定义的,可限定的
6. materialistic/məˌtiəriə'listik/*adj.* of materialism 物质的,唯物主义的
7. inherently/in'hiərəntli/*adv.* existing as a natural or basic part of something 固有地,生来就有地
8. conservative/kən'səːvətiv/*adj.* tending not to like or trust change 保守的,传统的
9. foster/'fɔstə/*v.* to encourage the development or growth of (ideas or feelings) 鼓励,促进
10. enculturate/in'kʌltʃəreit/*v.* make one's behavior or thoughts adjust to a culture 使行为或思想等适应某种文化 enculturated *adj.* 适应某种文化的
11. particular/pə'tikjulə/*adj.* special or single 特定的,特别的
12. acculturation/əˌkʌltʃə'reiʃən/*n.* 文化适应,文化改观
13. intensify/in'tensifai/*v.* (cause sth to) become more intense or intensive 加剧,加强 intensification *n.* 增强,强烈化
14. interaction/ˌintə'ækʃən/*n.* effect on each other; cooperation 相互影响,配合
15. constituent/kən'stitʃuənt/*n.* one of the parts that a substance or combination is made of 构成成分
16. assist/ə'sist/*v.* to help 帮助,协助
17. implement/'implimənt/*vt.* to put a plan or system into operation 实施,贯彻 implemental *adj.* 作为手段的,起作用的
18. feasible/'fizəbl/*adj.* able to be made, done or achieved; possible or reasonable 可行的,可能的 feasibility *n.* 可行性
19. exploit/ik'sploit/*v.* to use for advantage 剥削,利用
20. formulation/ˌfɔːmju'leiʃən/*n.* action of formulating 公式化,形式化
21. transfer/træns'fəː/*v.* hand over 传递
22. brief/briːf/*v.* to give instruction or information 向……简单介绍情况

23. concoction/kən'kɔkʃən/ *n.* concocting 调制
24. on the same wave-length 步伐统一, 合得来
25. arena/ə'ri:nə/ *n.* place or scene of activity or conflict 竞技场, 表演场
26. stem/stem/ *v.* to originate; to develop or grow (from) 源于, 由……造成
27. diversity/dai'və:siti/ *n.* state of being varied; variety 多样性 diversify *vt.* 使变化; 使……多样化
28. be far from　be a long way from 决不; 绝非
29. converge/kən'və:dʒ/ *v.* to move towards the same point and meet there 会合, 趋于会合
30. tailor to　to prepare for a special purpose 使适应
31. transplant/træns'plɑ:nt/ *v.* remove(a growing plant) with its roots and replant it elsewhere 移植 transplantation *n.* 移植, 移民
32. rejection/ri'dʒekʃən/ *n.* refusing to accept; disagreement 拒绝, 不接受, 不同意
33. myopia/mai'əupiə/ *n.* inability to see distant things clearly 近视

Notes

1. This text is selected and adapted from *International Business* by Michael R. Czinkota etc.
2. acculturation: Culture change resulting from contact between cultures, a process of external culture change.
3. value: It is a term that expresses the concept of worth in general, and it is thought to be connected with reasons for certain practices, policies, or actions.
4. cultural competence: The capacity of individuals to incorporate ethnic/cultural considerations into all aspects of their work relative to substance abuse prevention and reduction. Cultural competence is maximized with implementer/client involvement in all phases of the implementation process, as well as in the interpretation of outcomes.

Word Study

1. foster

   v. ① to take care of (a child) as if it were your own 养育, 收养, 照料

   Would you consider fostering (children) if you couldn't have children of your own?

   如果你不能生孩子, 会不会考虑收养孩子呢?

   ② to encourage the development or growth of (ideas or feelings) 鼓励, 促进, 培养

   I'm trying to foster an interest in classical music in my children.

   我试图培养孩子们对古典音乐的兴趣。

   They were discussing the best way to foster democracy in some countries.

   他们在讨论一些国家推动民主的最好方式。

   adj. 收养的, 领养孤儿的

   The children lived in different foster homes.

   这些孩子住在不同的领养家庭里。

2. intensify *v.* (cause sth to) become more intense or intensive 加强, 变尖锐

   China is to intensify pollution control in next five years.

   中国将在随后的五年里加强污染控制。

   The price wars are intensifying.

   价格战争在加剧。

   Debates on working mothers intensify.

   对有工作妇女的争论加剧了。

3. assist *v.*

   ① (fml) to help 帮助, 协助

   We assisted the firefighters in putting out a fire.

   我们协助消防员灭火。

   The Consultative Group to Assist the Poor (CGAP 扶贫顾问组) is a group of 33 public and private development agencies working together to expand access to financial services for the poor.

   扶贫顾问组由 33 家公立和私立发展机构组成, 为了扩大对穷人财政服务的渠道而共同工作。

   ②【BrE】协助警方破案

   As a citizen, we have the responsibility to assist the police whenever necessary.

作为公民，我们有义务在必要时协助警方破案。

4. implement *v.* to put (a plan or system) into operation 实施，贯彻

The changes to the national health system will be implemented next year.

国家健康体系的改变将在明年实施。

Government will review the proposals to implement Article 23 of the *Basic Law*.

政府将重新考虑实施《基本法》第 23 条的提议。

5. transfer

v. ① move from one place to another 搬，调动

The office was transferred from New York to Chicago.

办公地点已从纽约移到了芝加哥。

That football player is hoping to transfer to another team soon.

那位足球运动员希望赶快转到另一个球队去。

② hand over the possession of (properly, etc.) 转让(财产)

The millionaire transferred his property to the young man.

那位百万富翁将自己的财产转让给了那个年轻人。

No information under this contract shall be transferred to a third party.

本合同规定的信息资料不得转让给第三方。

n. ① the process of moving from one place to another 转移；迁移；转让

The company is responsible for developing a Transfer Services.

该公司负责提供转接业务。

New technology will speed up the transfer of information.

新技术将加速信息的传播。

② changing to a different vehicle, route, etc. during a journey 换乘

Some transfer passengers missed their flights from Toronto because of the delay in Tokyo.

一些中转旅客由于在东京的耽误而错过了来自多伦多的航班。

Post-reading Activities

I. Comprehension Questions.

1. What is culture according to the text?

2. What is one of the keys to success in international operations?

3. How can a manager cope with the challenges from cultural diversity?

4. What are the results of ignoring cultural differences?

5. What are the different opinions toward cultural diversity?

II. Fill in the blanks with the words or phrases given in the box. Change the forms if necessary.

integrate	conservative	ensure	interaction	intensify
assist	exploit	subsidiary	diversity	feasible

1. Following the plane crash, the airline is taking further steps to _____ public safety on its aircraft.

2. It is reported that fighting around the capital has _____ in the last few hours.

3. The company needs more financial _____ from the government.

4. The new director of the television station wants to _____ its programs.

5. The town's modern architecture is very well _____ with the old.

6. We are studying the _____ of building a new shopping center outside town.

7. He's such a _____ dresser—he always looks as if he's wearing his father's clothes.

8. There's not enough _____ between the management and the workers.

9. Their main reason for not buying the car was that it was too big— _____ reasons were the style and quality.

10. We should make sure that we _____ our resources as fully as possible.

III. Fill in the blanks with suitable words or phrases to complete the summary of the text.

The increase of the world trade forces companies to __1__ overseas markets. That means the managers have to __2__ people with different culture backgrounds. They have to understand __3__ and the ways they __4__ and to determine __5__ across cultures. __6__ of the difference may lead to establishing the best practice. __7__ should be recognized as an important management skill.

IV. Translate the following sentences into Chinese.

1. 他们在讨论促进一些国家繁荣的最佳办法。(foster)

2. 上次的会议有没有产生什么问题？(arise)

3. 我似乎无法与他相处，我们根本合不来。(on the same wave-length)

4. 国际贸易绝非易事。(far from)

5. 我们可以依你个人的需要，供应大量货物。(tailor...to)

Text B

Learning to Communicate across Cultures

Every culture that has ever existed has proclaimed itself the one, true species of humanity. One of the most blatant illustrations of this can be seen in the fact that words exist in every language to describe the foreigner as someone who is different and strange. The efforts of people to preserve their "pure" culture from foreign influence through physical destruction (such as conquering or extermination), geographical isolation or economic or religious exploitation provide further illustrations. If one examines the history of cultural interaction in the world, it soon becomes obvious that people prefer mirror images of themselves.

As the famous anthropologist Edward Hall has said, "Culture is communication." In order to study and understand a culture, we must examine its communicative style: how members of a culture interact.

There are several things to look at when looking at communicative style:

First, we should observe who talks to whom in a culture. This phenomenon can tell us a great deal about social relationships. How, for example, do the young address the old? When do men address women? Are children allowed to address their parents at any time, or are there times when they are expected to be "seen and not heard"?

A second social custom to look at is when and how personal issues are discussed. To understand the importance of this, think of the following topics: marriage, personal income and sex. Then think of when, in your culture, you can "bring up" these topics; how long must you know a person, for example, before you can ask him or her if he or she is married? How much money he or she earns? The "rules" governing discussion of these topics are quite strict in each culture; and they are very different in different cultures.

A third phenomenon to examine in a study of cultural communication is where people talk. What kinds of conversation take place in the kitchen, in the bedroom, or in the living room? What topics are discussed in bars or cafes, only in the home, inside, outside, or only in a psychiatrist's office?

A fourth important aspect of communication is the set of rules that govern conversation. In order to communicate effectively, visitor must know and understand such things as (1) what is considered a "dangerous" topic; (2) what emotions are generally not expressed in public; and (3) who can and cannot be criticized in polite conversation (for example, religious or political authorities, or the old).

Nonverbal cues and codes are a fifth, very important aspect of cultural communication. An understanding of the meaning of body language (gestures, physical contact, etc.) is crucial to cultural understanding. Understanding what is communicated nonverbally through dress, touch, intonation and silence is equally important.

In summary, if we are going to attempt successful communication in another culture, we must resist the cultural isolationism and chauvinistic tendencies that have inhabited intercultural communication in the past. We must learn to study and understand other cultures through the study of language, abstract values, and—most importantly through study of communicative style.

Words & Expressions

1. proclaim/prə'kleim/*v.* announce publicly or officially 宣布,声明
2. true species of humanity 人类唯一真正的文化
   humanity/hjuː'mæniti/*n.* human beings 人类
3. blatant/'bleitənt/*adj.* obvious or intentional 极明显的,公然的
4. illustration/ˌiləs'treiʃən/*n.* illustrating or being illustrated 举例说明,图解
   illustrate *vt.* 举例解释
5. preserve/pri'zəːv/*v.* to keep something in order to prevent it from being damaged 保留,保护
6. pure culture 纯正文化
7. physical destruction 肉体的毁灭
8. conquer/'kɔŋkə/*v.* to take control or possession by force 征服,击败
9. extermination/iksˌtəːmi'neiʃən/*n.* being destroyed completely 消灭
10. geographical isolation 地区隔离
11. exploitation/ˌeksplɔi'teiʃən/*n.* using unfairly for your own advantage 剥削
    economic and religious exploitation 经济与宗教剥削
12. mirror image 镜像
13. anthropologist/ˌænθrə'pɔlədʒist/*n.* people who study scientifically human beings 人类学家
14. address/ə'dres/*v.* use in speaking or writing to sb 称呼
15. personal issue 个人问题
16. psychiatrist/sai'kaiətrist/*n.* specialist in psychiatry 精神病医生

17. cue/kjuː/*n.* a word or action 对白和动作
18. code/kəud/*n.* a system of words, letters or signs 代号，代码
19. body language 体态语言
20. intonation/ˌintəu'neiʃən/*n.* the sound changes produced by the rise and fall of the voice when speaking 语调
21. cultural isolationism 文化隔离
22. chauvinistic/ˌʃəuvi'nistik/*adj.* 沙文主义的
    chauvinistic tendency 沙文主义倾向
23. inhabit/in'hæbit/*v.* occupy 占据，阻碍
24. abstract/'æbstrækt/*adj.* existing in thought or as an idea but not having a physical or practical existence 抽象的

Notes

1. This text is selected and adapted from *A Tree*, *A Rock*, *A Cloud* by Dean Barnlund.
2. social relationship：Content of social action among mutually related individuals such as friendship, erotic relationship, and exchange.
3. address：The manner of speaking to another individual.
4. body language：The gestures, poses, movements, and expressions that a person uses to communicate.
5. chauvinism：Extreme and unreasoning partisanship on behalf of a group to which one belongs, especially when the partisanship includes malice and hatred towards a rival group. The term is derived from Nicolas Chauvin, a soldier under Napoleon Bonaparte, due to his fanatical zeal for his Emperor.

Word Study

1. proclaim *v.*

   ① (fml) to announce publicly or officially 宣布，声明
   That was the famous speech in which he proclaimed that slavery(奴隶制)was dead. 在那次著名的演讲中他宣布奴隶制已经灭亡。
   ② make something clear 表明，显示
   Wearing scarves(头巾) and hats which proclaimed their allegiance(忠心), the football fans flooded into the bar.
   足球迷们头戴以示忠心的头巾和帽子，涌入酒吧。

2. preserve

v. ① keep or maintain 保护

Children should preserve their eyesight.

孩子们应该保护视力。

The brave soldier has preserved many people's lives.

勇敢的士兵保住了许多人的生命。

② keep sth safe or alive for the future 保存

People have preserved some of Lu Xun's manuscripts.

人们保存着鲁迅的一些手稿。

Koreans like to preserve food with salt and spices.

韩国人喜欢用盐和调味品腌制食品。

③ maintain 保持

It is very difficult to preserve one's self-respect in that job.

那样的工作很难让人保持自尊。

n. ① jam strawberry preserve 草莓酱

② an activity that is only suitable or allowed for a particular group of people 爱好,专长

She regards negotiating prices with customers as her special preserve.

她将与顾客讨价还价作为自己的特长。

3. conquer *v.*

① take possession of sth by force 以武力占领,征服

The Normans conquered England in 1066.

诺曼人于 1066 年占领英格兰。

The young man's ambition is to conquer the world in the future.

年轻人的理想是将来征服世界。

② gain the admiration, love, etc. of (somebody/something) 赢得某人某事物的赞誉,爱慕等

She has conquered the hearts of many men.

她征服了许多男人的心。

③ defeat 击败

France has conquered the main rivals(对手) in the first round of the competition.

法国队在第一轮比赛中击败了主要对手。

4. address

n. details of where a person lives or works 住址

Tell me if you change your address.

如果你换住址要告诉我。

v. ① write the name and address 写名字或地址

The letter was wrongly addressed to my parents' home.

这封信地址写错发到我父母家了。

② make a speech 正式地讲话

The president is to address to the audience.

总统将向观众讲话。

③ to use in speaking or writing to sb 称呼

The little boy addressed the old man "grandpa".

小男孩称老人为"爷爷"。

5. issue

n.. ① supply and distribution of items for use or sale 出版,分发

The students want to have the latest issue of a new edition of the dictionary.

学生们想要最新出版的新版字典。

② important topic for discussion 重要议题,问题

The Senate raised a new issue in the meeting.

议员在会议上提出了新问题。

v. ① supply or distribute sth to sb for use 发放给某人使用

The government issues clothing and food to the people from the flooding area.

政府向洪水灾区的人们发放衣物及食品。

② publish or put into circulation 出版,发行

The publisher refused to issue the young man's novel.

出版社拒绝出版那个年轻人的小说。

Vocabulary Building

collectivism 集体主义	individualism 个人主义
reserved 保守的	outgoing 外向的
cultural clash 文化冲突	cultural shock 文化冲击
cultural desert 文化沙漠	body language 身体语言
cultural sensitivity 文化敏感性	cultural bias 文化偏见
language barrier 语言障碍	social value 社会价值观
cultural context/background 文化背景	cultural concept 文化观念
customary belief 习惯性信仰	cultural diversity 文化多元化
business culture 企业文化	

Word Formation：Adjective Suffixes and Adverb Suffixes（形容词与副词后缀）

Adjective Suffixes	Meaning	Added to	Examples	Illustrative Sentences
-ful	full of, having or giving	nouns	useful, successful, hopeful	The meeting was highly successful.
-less	without, not giving	nouns	childless, speechless, careless	That famous businessman made a careless mistake.
-ly, -like	having the qualities of	nouns	manly, worldly, statesmanlike, childlike	He speaks with a childlike directness.
-y	like, full of, covered with, etc.	nouns	silky, meaty, hairy	Advertisements claim that using hand cream keeps your hands smooth and silky.
-ish	belonging to, having the character of, etc.	nouns	Swedish, foolish, selfish, boyish	His face brightened up in a boyish smile.
-some	producing, likely to	nouns	burdensome, troublesome	Will the extra tasks be too burdensome / troublesome for you?
-worthy	deserving of or suitable for	nouns	trustworthy, seaworthy	Television should be a trustworthy source of information from which the public can find out what's going on.
-arian	believing in, practising	nouns	humanitarian, vegetarian, authoritarian（专制的）	His manner is extremely authoritarian.

-al, -ial, -ic, -ical	of or concerning	nouns	musical, editorial, heroic, historic, economical	The publication of this book is the great cultural event of the year.
-ive, -ous	having a tendency to or the quality of	nouns	attractive, expensive, dangerous, mountainous	Big houses are expensive to maintain.
-able, -ible	having or showing the quality of	nouns	comfortable, horrible	Since I've put on weight I don't feel comfortable in my clothes.
-free	without	nouns	carefree, duty-free	Duty-free goods are luxury goods bought in special shops in airports.
-ed	having...	nouns	walled, pointed, open-mouthed, simple-minded	The boy stared at the elephant in open-mouthed wonder.
-ish	somewhat	adjectives	youngish, reddish, tallish	The visitor is a youngish man wearing a pair of glasses.
-able, -ible	that may or must be, tending to	verbs	eatable, readable, changeable, divisible	Matter is infinitely divisible.
-ant, -ent	that has, shows or does	verbs	significant, different, insistent	The sales department has made a significant contribution to the company's performance this year.

Adverb Suffixes	Meaning	Added to	Examples	Illustrative Sentences
-ly	in a … manner	adjectives	happily, easily, surprisingly	Ever since the illness I get tired very easily.
-ward(s)	manner and direction of movement	adverbs, nouns	onward(s), backward (s), homeward(s), westward(s)	With the day coming to an end, they started to walk homewards.
-wise	in the manner of, as far as… is concerned	nouns	clockwise, otherwise, weather-wise, education-wise	He told the children to start moving clockwise around the room.

Post-reading Activities

Ⅰ. **True or False Questions.**

1. Every culture has proclaimed itself the true species of humanity through physical destruction.

2. When you meet a man from the United States for the first time, you can ask how much money he earns.

3. When communicating cross-culturally, you'd better avoid some political issues.

4. If we are going to communicate in another culture, we must insist that our culture is the best one in the world.

5. In different places, people usually discuss different topics.

Ⅱ. **Fill in the blanks with the words or phrases given in the box. Change the forms if necessary.**

exist	proclaim	illustration	destruction	interaction
phenomenon	govern	emotion	criticize	attempt

1. The lecturer _____ his point with a diagram on the blackboard.

2. Most of the old part of the city _____ during the war.

3. They are _____ a very difficult climb.

4. The play has been well received by the _____.

5. Many people question the _____ of God.

6. My doctor said the problem was more _____ than physical.

7. It's interesting at parties to see how people _____ socially.

8. That was the famous speech in which he _____ that slavery was dead.

9. The _____ is trying its best to improve life level.

10. There's evidence to suggest that child-abuse(虐待儿童) is not just a recent _____.

Ⅲ. **Dictation.**

Exercises

Ⅰ. Structures：The Usage of "As"

通常放在句首，引导原因状语从句	*As* Chile is a long, narrow country, the temperature varies considerably from north to south.
引导非限定性定语从句时,表示熟知的事实	*As* is known to us all, smoking does harm to our health.
与 as,such,same,so 等连用,引导定语从句	It is not such a good job as he has promised us.
在形容词、副词或名词后引导关系从句,相当于 although	*Child as he is*, he knows how to operate this complicated machine.
与 if 连用,表示似乎	He treats me *as if I were* a stranger.
其他搭配：as/so long as, as soon as, as well as, as...as..., as far as, as for(至于某事物), as to sth(提到某事物)	I will call you *as soon as* I arrive in America.

Fill in the blanks with the words or phrases given in the box.

as well as, as soon as, as long as, as if, as...as..., as far as, as for, as to, as

1. You can go out, _____ you promise to be back before 10 o'clock.
2. I have the same trouble _____ you.
3. _____ correcting our homework, the physics teacher always makes us do it ourselves.
4. _____ the hotel, it was very uncomfortable and miles away from the sea.
5. _____ I know, he is keen on business.
6. I'll give you an answer _____ I've finished reading your report.

7. Hard _____ he tried, he has to face the reality of failure.

8. He grows flowers _____ vegetables.

9. He behaved _____ nothing had happened.

10. This dress is twice _____ expensive _____ that one.

II. Vocabulary

Fill in the blanks with the words or phrases given in the box. Change the forms if necessary.

other than	assist to do	in terms of	adjust to	be crucial to
stem from	make sure	in summary	be aware of	preserve...from

1. _____ you _____ the price of shoes like those?

2. I can't _____ living on my own.

3. The calm pilot _____ the passengers _____ danger.

4. And so I would say, _____, that the performance has been a great success.

5. _____ you lock the door behind you when you go out.

6. Consider it _____ an investment.

7. Two men _____ the police _____ find out the criminal.

8. You will have time to visit _____ places _____ those on the itinerary.

9. Their argument _____ a misunderstanding.

10. Getting this contract _____ the future of our company.

III. Word Formation

Fill in the blank with the proper form of the word given in the parentheses.

1. Company needs more financial _____ (assist) from the government.

2. We are studying the _____ (feasible) of building a new shopping center outside town.

3. The play has been well received by the _____ (criticize).

4. Many people question the _____ (exist) of God.

5. The lecturer _____ (illustration) his point with a diagram on the blackboard.

6. The _____ (govern) is trying its best to improve life level.

7. My doctor said the problem was more _____ (emotion) than physical.

8. The new director of the television station wants to _____ (diversity) its programs.

9. A high wall _____ (isolation) the house from the rest of the village.

10. The company has appointed a new marketing director to broaden its _____

(strategy) expertise.

Ⅳ. Translation

translate the following sentences into English.

1. 国际市场充满形形色色的挑战。(a variety of)

2. 保守的人们通常抵制变化。(conservative, resist)

3. 全球化的进程加大了各国之间的竞争。(intensify)

4. 该公司成功的关键在于是否能适应市场变化。(key to success, adjust to)

5. 对我们公司来说,在美国开发新的市场是可行的。(feasible)

6. 文化的多样性使得不同文化背景的人交流起来有困难。(cultural diversity, cultural background)

7. 近年来,各国之间和不同文化之间的交流势在必行。(interact)

8. 人们可以通过观察一种文化中的人际交往方式来了解新的文化。(be aware of, communicate)

9. 学习语言对跨文化学习与交流是至关重要的一个方面。(be crucial to, intercultural)

10. 西方家庭成员之间的称呼方式与中国家庭不同。(forms of address)

Ⅴ. Cloze

Mr. White is a sales __1__ of a Canadian electronics company. He __2__ for the company for years, and has built up some loyal __3__ who have helped him a lot. Among those clients there is a Mr. Wang from Beijing, China. It __4__ that White was asked by the company to test the Chinese market for the electronic products. The first idea that came to his mind was that he should go and see Mr. Wang.

In their __5__ talks before, White learned from Mr. Wang that it would be better for a visitor to bring some gifts when he wants to visit someone in China. In order to give a better __6__ on his first visit, White decided that he should bring a special gift to Mr. Wang—a new model of electronic clock. He was very glad of his idea and even felt __7__ of it. But, to his __8__, Mr. Wang looked __9__ when he saw the clock (though it was a new model). He simply refused to __10__ it with no explanation for his __11__. White felt embarrassed and puzzled. Later on, he found a/an __12__ to ask Mr. Nelson, a "China Hand" for help.

"You've made a silly mistake," said Mr. Nelson.

"Why silly?" asked White, all the more __13__.

"In Chinese pronunciation, the equivalent of clock (zhong) __14__ the word for death (also pronounced as "zhong"). Therefore, when one brings a clock (no matter what kind of clock it is) to another, it sends some disinformation to the receiver. That was the reason for Mr. Wang's refusal."

White was greatly surprised by Mr. Nelson's explanation. However, he was very
___15___ for his help. At the same time, he also told himself "take it as a lesson and try
to learn more about the Chinese culture."

1. A. girl   B. representative   C. secretary   D. clerk
2. A. worked   B. works   C. is working   D. has worked
3. A. customs   B. people   C. clients   D. friends
4. A. happening   B. happens   C. has happened   D. happened
5. A. casual   B. usual   C. extra   D. daily
6. A. expression   B. impression
   C. thought   D. appearance
7. A. sad   B. disappointed   C. proud   D. excited
8. A. surprise   B. sadness   C. joy   D. amusement
9. A. pleased   B. satisfied   C. worried   D. offended
10. A. receive   B. borrow   C. accept   D. buy
11. A. acceptance   B. purchase
    C. worry   D. refusal
12. A. way   B. opportunity   C. time   D. clock
13. A. puzzled   B. happy   C. understanding   D. clear
14. A. is   B. has   C. matches   D. similes
15. A. surprised   B. grateful   C. acceptable   D. hateful

Ⅵ. Reading Comprehension

Arabs consider it extremely bad manners to start talking business immediately. Even the busiest government official or executive always takes extra time to be polite and offer refreshments. No matter how busy you are you should make time for this hospitality.

The "conference visit" is a way of doing business throughout the Arab world. Frequently, you will have to discuss your business in the presence of strangers, who may or may not have anything to do with your business. Do not be surprised if your meeting is interrupted several times by people who come into the room unannounced, whisper, or speak softly to the person with whom you are talking, and leave. Act as though you do not hear, and never show displeasure at being interrupted.

Making decisions quickly is not an Arab custom. There is vagueness in doing business in the Middle East which will puzzle a newcomer. Give yourself lots of time and ask lots of questions.

Patience is an important quality. You may have to wait two or three days to see high-level government officials as they are very busy. Give yourself enough time.

Personal relationships are very important. They are the key to doing business in Arab countries. Try to identify the decision-maker regarding your product or service immediately and get to know him on a friendly basis. Do your homework. Be prepared to discuss details of your product or proposal. Be ready to answer technical questions.

Familiarize yourself with the Moslem and national holidays. Avoid a visit during Ramadan, the Moslem month of fasting. Most Arab countries have a six-day workweek from Saturday to Thursday. When matched with the Monday to Friday practice in most Western countries, it leaves only three and a half workdays shared. Remember this in planning your appointments. Moslems do not eat pork. Some are strict about the religion's prohibition against alcoholic beverages. If you are not sure, wait for your host to suggest the proper thing to drink.

When an Arab says yes, he may mean "maybe". When he says maybe, he probably means "no". You will seldom get a direct "no" from an Arab because it is considered impolite. Also, he does not want to close his options. Instead of "no", he will say "inhasllah" which means, "if god is willing". On the other hand, "yes" does not necessarily mean "yes". A smile and a slow nod might seem like an agreement, but in fact, your host is being polite. An Arab considers it impolite to disagree with a guest.

1. The main purpose of this article is to explain _____.
   A. why you need extra time when you visit Arab countries
   B. how to be polite when doing business in the Arab countries
   C. why Arab officials are so busy
   D. why Arab officials are angry
2. In Paragraph 4, "give yourself enough time" refers to "_____".
   A. having patience   B. being a busy official
   C. being important   D. being flexible
3. Paragraph 5 discusses, in general _____.
   A. personal relationships   B. decision makers
   C. technical questions   D. personal questions
4. According to Paragraph 6, what is Ramadan?
   A. The six-day workweek.
   B. A good month to visit Arab countries.
   C. The Moslem month of fasting.

D. The month for them to have a rest.

5. In general, Paragraph 7 explains why _____.

A. "yes" may mean "maybe"

B. an Arab may give you a vague answer

C. you need lots of time to do business

D. an Arab refuses to answer your questions

6. Why are so many sentences in this article in the imperative(command)?

A. Because the author is giving your instructions.

B. Because the author likes these customs very much.

C. Because the author thinks you have already known about these customs.

D. Because the author is trying to convince you.

Ⅶ. Writing

(Ⅰ) Writing Basics: A Good Paragraph: Focus and Completeness

A paragraph is not complete if it is not properly ended. A carelessly ended paragraph leaves the reader unsatisfied despite an effective topic sentence and adequate supporting sentences.

Sometimes a paragraph discusses several points or several aspects of an idea. We can arrange them in climatic order and save the most important or the most striking for the conclusion. It will bring the paragraph to a smooth end. In this case, there is no need to bother writing an extra concluding sentence.

In the following paragraph, the writer discusses the popularity of the Walkman in terms of its size and price. The writer stresses the pleasure that Walkman users get by putting it at the end. It serves the purpose of concluding the paragraph.

New technology has made possible the development of miniature cassette recorders. The Sony Walkman, for instance, is small enough to fit into a pocket or handbag. It has become the constant companion of millions of Americans who walk, shop, jog, and commute to the music of their choice. The wide availability of Walkman and its moderate price have made it so popular that it can be found in many public places. The muffled sound of music, a smiling face, and tapping feel reveal the Walkman's presence. There is no use shouting hello or goodbye at Walkman users because they won't hear you. They are in a musical world of their own.

(Ⅱ) Writing Assignment

You are supposed to write a composition on the topic **How to Communicate across Cultures.** Write about 100 to 120 words and base your composition on the following outline.

1. With the increase of globalization, people have more chances to communicate cross-culturally.

2. People especially businessmen should be aware of the cultural differences and learn to respect others' cultures and some ways to communicate across cultures successfully.

3. Some suggested ways: they should study the language; study the history of different aspects; and examine their communicative style.

VIII. Presentation(Speaking)

Study the following minicase with your partner and try to find out the cultural conflict between the Americans and the Japanese relating to business standards. Can you think of more similar rules?

Minicase

Watanabe: Jones appeared surprised... maybe insulted.

Sato: Why?

Watanabe: I broke the rule of American business behavior.

Sato: What did you do?

Watanabe: I knocked on Jones' door, lightly and quickly... and entered his office.

Sato: What was the problem?

Watanabe: He appeared very shocked that I walked into his office without his secretary's approval or announcement.

Sato: Where was his secretary?

Watanabe: She wasn't at her desk.

Sato: Why did you need her permission to enter his office?

Watanabe: It seems as if a closed door and walls are serious items in American corporations—they mean "stay out" unless formally invited in.

Sato: How did you find out? Did Jones tell you that?

Watanabe: No. He just acted rather annoyed. I could tell by the tone of his voice, the way he shuffled his papers with abruptness... that he was angry.

Enjoy Your Time

God is a Girl

by Groove Coverage

Remembering me,
All over the world,
To those who are free,
Forgotten as the past
God is a girl,
Do you believe it,
God is a girl,
Do you believe it,
God is a girl,
Do you believe it,
God is a girl,
Do you believe it,
She wants to shine,
She is so driven,
She wants you to be
A girl like me
Illuminating us,
That we truly trust
A beautiful sunrise eternally

Discover and see
She's known as a girl
The mind shall be key
Cause history will last
Wherever you are,
Can you receive it?
Whatever you say,
Can you receive it?
However you live,
Can you receive it?
She's only a girl,
Can you receive it?
Forever in time,
She's always mine cleanly and free,
A part of the future,
There is a sky,
Someone is out there
There is a rainbow for you and me

Examination Two (Unit 5 – Unit 8)

I . Make a guess of the underlined word or phrase in the following statements and tick off the best choice that has the closest meaning. ($1 \times 15 = 15$ **points**)

1. She abandoned her husband and children and went off with another man.

   A. forgived   B. left for ever   C. stopped doing D. changed

2. The experiment is at a critical stage—we will know the result soon.

   A. most important   B. necessary

   C. negative   D. enough

3. Every country has its capital, which is its chief city and usually its seat of government.

   A. the furniture for people to sit on B. sit down

   C. base or centre   D. experience

4. Surprisingly, new problems arise every day.

   A. happen   B. stand up   C. fight for   D. cause by

5. The farm yielded the largest wheat harvest in its history last year.

   A. gave up   B. obeyed

   C. produced or supplied   D. waited for

6. The patient scanned the doctor's face for any sign of hope.

   A. looked through very quickly   B. passed across

   C. obtained   D. looked at carefully

7. You may think we have been making a profit, but in fact the reverse is the case.

   A. change for the worse   B. opposite or contrary

   C. underside or back   D. exchange

8. He has an edge on the other students because he studies harder.

   A. sharp

   B. advantage over

   C. outside limit or boundary of a solid

   D. reduce or soften

9. The musician's execution of the music was perfect, but he played without feeling.

   A. performance   B. carrying out

C. killing as an punishment   D. skill

10. I do not feel <u>bound</u> to give you everything you want.

    A. certain to do sth

    B. ready to do

    C. obliged by law or duty to do sth

    D. closely connected

11. They prefer to <u>associate</u> with friends of their own age.

    A. connect ideas in one's mind

    B. act together with or deal with sb

    C. join together

    D. agree with

12. Most people believe that language is <u>peculiar</u> to human beings.

    A. strange

    B. unwell

    C. belonging only to somebody/something

    D. special

13. They have always had to do with relatively small profit <u>margins</u>.

    A. blank space on a page

    B. edge or border

    C. amount of space

    D. difference between cost price and selling price

14. We must <u>substitute</u> a new chair for the broken one.

    A. take the place of   B. change

    C. put away   D. throw away

15. The unexpected win against Germany <u>boosted</u> the Chinese football team's morale(士气).

    A. helped or encouraged   B. reduced

    C. expected   D. discouraged

Ⅱ. **Complete the following statements by ticking off the best choice.** (1 × 15 = 15 points)

16. No one was _____ for the damage of the broken window, because it was broken by the storm.

    A. accounted   B. considered

    C. excused   D. responsible

17. The poor boy soon became _____ to the hard work and bad food.

A. accustomed   B. due

C. inferior   D. familiar

18. The stock exchange is _____ to rumors of war.

     A. resistant   B. sensitive   C. common   D. hopeful

19. _____ your proposal, I would like to make one suggestion.

     A. In one's opinion   B. With regard to

     C. Without   D. With great respects

20. During war, all men between 18 and 45 _____ should serve in the army.

     A. in person   B. as a rule

     C. without exception   D. in general

21. The manager admitted that the company was going down, but he said it was not his _____.

     A. mistake   B. shortcoming

     C. fault   D. defect

22. Unless the workers' demands are _____, there will be a strike soon.

     A. met   B. given   C. permitted   D. replied

23. When the class was over, we went back to our _____ dormitories.

     A. complacent   B. respectable

     C. respective   D. respectful

24. I got this Walkman _____; it was very cheap.

     A. for sale   B. on sale

     C. on purpose   D. on average

25. Give me your telephone number _____ I need your help.

     A. in case   B. so that

     C. unless   D. whether

26. _____ is known to the world, Mark Twain is a great American writer.

     A. That   B. Which   C. As   D. It

27. Mr. Johnson preferred _____ heavier work to do.

     A. to be given   B. to be giving

     C. to have given   D. having given

28. He hoped the firm would _____ him to the Paris branch.

     A. exchange   B. transmit

     C. remove   D. transfer

29. I am looking for a job in the city but haven't found my _____ yet.

     A. best   B. ideal   C. perfect   D. suitable

30. After the Arab states won independence, great emphasis was laid on expanding education, with girls as well as boys _____ to go to school.

    A. to be encouraged   B. being encouraged

    C. been encouraged   D. be encouraged

Ⅲ. Fill in the blanks with the words or phrases given in the box. Change the forms if necessary. (1 × 10 = 10 **points**)

superior	facilitate	give... an insight into	depend on	in the eyes of
involve	render service to	feasible	attempt	intensify

31. The government has _____ its anti-smoking campaign.

32. Some boys _____ to leave for camping but were stopped by their parents.

33. This western restaurant is _____ to the one we went to last week.

34. My English teacher's instruction _____ me _____ the way we learn English well.

35. That plan, although not very _____, has been approved by the committee last week.

36. Everyday they wanted to _____ their children in every activities they did.

37. The new underground railway will _____ the journey to all parts of the city.

38. _____ the public, foreign movies are one of the best means for them to know other cultures well.

39. Don't _____ your parents so much, you should build up your own confidence about how to do things well.

40. As this supermarket _____ better _____ the consumers, more and more residents in the neighborhood prefer to go shopping here.

Ⅳ. Cloze (1 × 15 = 15 **points**)

Nowadays people are talking more and more about the advantages and disadvantages of China's joining WTO. Opinions differ greatly. Some hold that China will definitely gain more by paying a great deal __41__ taxes on her imports. __42__ think that China will certainly __43__ more since many of her domestic products cannot compete __44__ foreign imports either in quality or in price.

In my opinion, China's joining WTO is a matter of great __45__. __46__, when China enters WTO, her position, __47__ a big socialist power, in international economic affairs will be acknowledged, and her influence on the development of world economy and trade will become increasingly __48__. Economically, __49__ foreign foods, with their better quality and ___50___ price, may ___51___ a large part of her domestic market, China can make more profits by considerably increasing the amount of goods ___52___ to foreign countries. ___53___, the broad masses of Chinese consumers will benefit a great deal from purchasing foreign products. Finally, China's joining WTO will certainly have a ___54___ effect on her future economic development.

Taking all things into ___55___, there will be more advantages for China when she joins WTO.

41. A. more   B. many   C. less   D. least
42. A. Some else   B. Other   C. Another   D. Others
43. A. gain   B. take   C. lose   D. benefit
44. A. with   B. against   C. to   D. along
45. A. meaning   B. significance C. influence   D. effect
46. A. Politically   B. Economically C. Possibly   D. Interestingly
47. A. like   B. as   C. being   D. taken as
48. A. greater   B. less   C. great   D. little
49. A. through   B. because   C. though   D. as
50. A. cheaper   B. expensive   C. cheap   D. more expensive
51. A. dominate   B. occupy   C. challenge   D. steal
52. A. imported   B. exported
    C. to be imported   D. to be exported
53. A. After that   B. Anyhow   C. Moreover   D. All in all
54. A. positive   B. negative   C. affirmative   D. objective
55. A. plan   B. anticipation C. effect   D. consideration

V. Reading Comprehension(2 × 10 = 20 **points**)

(A)

You can use your Business Telecard International at any card phone in the UK. Here is some information about making international phone calls.

You can now phone almost any country in the world, although in some cases you can only call major cities. When you cannot make direct dialing calls, you can ask the international operator to help you. This is more expensive and takes more time, but it may be helpful if you want to speak to a particular person and no one else; in this case you should ask for a "person-to-person" call. Even more expensive is a reverse charge call where the person who receives the call pays.

If the international line is busy, you can reserve a call; explain the number you want and the operator will call you back when the line is free.

You can save money by calling outside office hours, eg. early in the morning, late at night, and on Sundays. Remember that the time may be different in the country you are calling. International time is based on GMT (Greenwich Mean Time); London is on GMT and Moscow, for example, is 3 hours ahead. There is one problem; change to DST(Daylight Saving Time) for the Summer. In the UK, clocks are put forward one hour in Spring and put back in Autumn, and so London is actually one hour ahead of GMT in the summer. If you are unsure about the time, the operator will help you.

You can use your Business Telecard International for domestic calls as well, but there will be an additional charge over the standard rate.

56. What is the most expensive type of call?
    A. Reverse charge call.   B. Through the operator.
    C. Direct call.   D. Trunk call.

57. What can you do if the international line is engaged?
    A. Call back outside office hours.
    B. Make a "person-to-person" call.
    C. Book a call.
    D. Redial after several minutes later.

58. When is cheaper to make an international call?
    A. 12 a.m.   B. 6 p.m.   C. 11 p.m.   D. 19 p.m.

59. How many hours in Moscow ahead of London during the summer?
    A. 2.   B. 4.   C. 6.   D. 8.

60. If you use your Telecard to make a local call you must _____.
    A. pay salary   B. pay extra
    C. use a card phone   D. use it on public phones

(B)

When a consumer finds that an item she or he bought is faulty or in some other way does not live up to the manufacturer's claim for it, the first step is to present the warranty(保单), or any other records which might help, at the store of purchase. In most cases, this action will produce results. However, if it does not, there are various means the consumer may use to gain satisfaction.

A simple and common method used by many consumers is to complain directly to the store manager. In general, the "higher up" the consumer takes his or her complaint, the faster he or she can expect it to be settled. In such case, it is usually settled in the consumer's favor.

Consumers should complain in person whenever possible, but if they cannot get to the place of purchase, it is acceptable to phone or write the complaint in a letter.

Complaining is usually most effective when it is done politely but firmly, and especially when the consumer can demonstrate what is wrong with the item in question. If this cannot be done, the consumer will succeed best by presenting specific information as to what is wrong, rather than by making general statements. For example, "The left speaker does not work at all and the sound coming out of the right one is unclear" is better than "This stereo(立体声音响) does not work".

The store manager may advise the consumer to write to the manufacturer. If so, the consumer should do this, stating the complaint as politely and as firmly as possible. But if a polite complaint does not achieve the desired result, the consumer can go a step further. She or he can threaten to take the seller to court or report the seller to a private or public organization responsible for protecting consumers' rights.

61. When a consumer finds that his purchase has a fault in it, the first thing he should do is to _____.

    A. complain personally to the manager

    B. threaten to take the matter to court

    C. write a firm letter of complaint to the store of purchase

    D. show some written proof of the purchase to the store

62. If a consumer wants a quick settlement of his problem, it's better to complain to _____.

    A. a shop assistant   B. the store manager

    C. the manufacturer   D. a public organization

63. The most effective complaint can be made by _____.

    A. showing the faulty item to the manufacturer

    B. explaining exactly what is wrong with the item

    C. saying firmly that the item is of poor quality

    D. asking politely to change the item

64. The phrase "live up to" (Para 1, Line 2) in the context means"_____".

    A. meet the standard of   B. realize the purpose of

    C. fulfill the demands of   D. keep the promise of

65. The passage tells us _____.

    A. how to settle a consumer's complaint about a faulty item

    B. how to make an effective complaint about a faulty item

    C. how to avoid buying a faulty item

D. how to deal with complaints from customers

VI. Translate the following Chinese sentences into English. （2 × 5 = 10 **points**）

66. 对中国企业来说,缺乏日益提高创新的技术就意味着付出更高的代价。

67. 小组式面试既给了应试者认识更多面试者的机会,又可以使他亲眼目睹该公司员工如何协同工作。

68. 如今没有哪个小企业能承受因忽略合资方式而带来的损失。

69. 在国际贸易舞台,文化沟通和适应能力被视为一项关键的经营策略。

70. 最好的合作关系是建立在双方共赢基础之上的。

VII. Write a short passage of no less than 100 **words according to the sentences given below.** （15 **points**）

The E-mail

E-mail is an entirely new way of communication by means of computer and Internet service.

_____

_____

Compared with the old letter forms, E-mail has lots of advantages. _____

_____

_____

With the rapid development of the Internet service, E-mail is becoming increasingly popular among all age groups. _____

_____

_____

Appendix I Vocabulary

absorb *vt.*

accentuate *v.*

accompany *vt.*

acculturation *n.*

address *v.*

administration *n.*

adopt *vt.*

advent *n.*

affect *v.*

alliance *n.*

analyze *v.*

annual *adj.*

anticipate *vt.*

applicable *adj.*

appreciate *v.*

approval *n.*

arena *n.*

article *n.*

aspect *n.*

assembly *n.*

assign *vt.*

associate *adj.*

audit *v.*

automatically *adv.*

barrier *n.*

bilingual *adj.*

blatant *adj.*

body language

border *n.*

brief *v.*

bunch *n.*

abstract *adj.*

accession *n.*

accomplishment *n.*

accuracy *n.*

adjust *v.*

administrative *adj.*

advanced *adj.*

advertising *n.* & *adj.*

affordable *adj.*

alter *v.*

animator *n.*

anthropologist *n.*

appliance *n.*

applicant *n.*

appreciate *v.*

aptitude *n.*

arrogant *adj.*

artifact *n.*

assemble *v.*

assess *v.*

assist *v.*

assure *v.*

authority *n.*

available *adj.*

behavior pattern

biomedical *adj.*

board *n.*

boost *vt.* & *n.*

brand *n.*

built-in *adj.*

capture *v.*

category *n.*

center *n.*

certified *adj.*

character *n.*

clarity *n.*

coach *v.*

colleague *n.*

comedy *n.*

commission *n.*

community *n.*

competent *adj.*

complementary *adj.*

complicated *adj.*

conduct *v.*

conquer *v.*

constituent *n.*

contact *n.*

contrast *n.*

converge *v.*

co-ordination *n.*

corporation *n.*

CPA（Certified Public Accountant）*n.*

critical *adj.*

cultivate *vt.*

cultural isolationism

currency *n.*

curve *n.*

defective *adj.*

deliver *v.*

device *n.*

discretion *n.*

distort *vt.*

distributor *n.*

division *n.*

domestic *adj.*

cell phone *n.*

centralize *vt.*

characteristic *adj.*

chauvinistic *adj.*

clash *vt.*

code *n.*

combination *n.*

comic *n.* & *adj.*

commitment *n.*

compete *vi.*

complement *n.*

complexity *n.*

concoction *n.*

confident *adj.*

conservative *adj.*

consume *v.*

contract *n.* & *v.*

conventional *adj.*

cooperation *n.*

corporate *adj.*

costly *adj.*

credibility *n.*

cue *n.*

current *adj.*

decade *n.*

definition *n.*

demonstrate *v.*

digital *adj.*

disperse *v.*

distribution *n.*

diversity *n.*

domain *n.*

domestic market

dominance *n.*

dramatically *adv.*

dynamic *adj.*

electrical and mechanical engineering

eliminate *v.*

enable *v.*

enculturate *v.*

enhance *vt.*

enterprise *n.*

equipment *n.*

establish *v.*

estimate *v.*

evolve *v.*

expansion *n.*

expertise *n.*

exploitation *n.*

extermination *n.*

extraordinary *adj.*

facilitate *v.*

feasible *adj.*

finance *n. & v.*

forge *n. & vt.*

formulate *vt.*

foster *v.*

framework *n.*

geographical isolation

gimmick *n.*

grapevine *n.*

headquarters *n.*

heritage *n.*

hike *n.*

ideally *adv.*

ignore *vt.*

illustration *n.*

impenetrable *adj.*

doom *n.*

duration *n.*

efficient *adj.*

element *n.*

emotion *n.*

encounter *v.*

enforce *vt.*

ensure *v.*

entiltle *vt.*

erect *adj.*

establishment *n.*

evaluate *v.*

exceed *v.*

experiment *v.*

exploit *v.*

explore *vt.*

external *adj.*

extreme *n.*

factor *n.*

feature *n.*

focused *adj.*

format *n.*

formulation *n.*

fraction *n.*

geographic *adj.*

giant *n.*

global *adj.*

headline *n.*

healthcare *n.*

high-tech *n.*

horizontal *adj.*

identify *v.*

illegal *adj.*

image *n.*

implement *v.*

impression *n.*   improper *adj.*

incompatible *adj.*   incorporate *v.*

incorporation *n.*   indicate *v.*

individual *n.*   inefficiency *n.*

informality *n.*   inhabit *v.*

inherent *adj.*   inherently *adv.*

inheritor *n.*   innovation *n.*

input *n.*   integrated *adj.*

intellectual property   intensify *v.*

interact *vi.*   interaction *v.*

internal *adj.*   interpersonal *adj.*

intonation *n.*   inventory *n.*

investment *n.*   involve *vt.*

isolationism *n.*   issue *n.*

jet lag   job seeker

joint venture   junk *n.*

Korean *adj.*   lack *v.*

latitude *n.*   launch *v.*

leap *n.*   legal *adj.*

lengthy *adj.*   lifestyle *n.*

literate *adj.*   logistics *n.*

low-end *adj.*   maintain *vt.*

managerial *adj.*   manufacture *v.*

margin *n.*   mass *adj.*

materialistic *adj.*   maximum *n.*

medium-sized *adj.*   mirror image

misconception *n.*   mobile *adj.*

mood *n.*   motivation *n.*

multi-channeled *adj.*   multinational *adj.*

multiple *adj.*   mutual *adj.*

myopia *n.*   neglect *vt.*

negotiate *v.*   negotiation *n.*

nimble *adj.*   objective *n.*

open-ended *adj.*   opening-up *n.*

operation *n.*   opportunity *n.*

originally *adv.*

panel *n.*

particular *adj.*

partnership *n.*

patent *n.*

personality *n.*

physical destruction

piracy *n.*

pixel *n.*

portable *adj.*

practice *n.*

prediction *n.*

preserve *v.*

proceed *v.*

proclaim *n.*

productivity *n.*

profitability *n.*

promotion *n.*

psychiatrist *n.*

psychologist *n.*

pursue *v.*

qualified *adj.*

raw material

recruit *n.*

refrigerator *n.*

release *n.*

reliable *adj.*

remote *adj.*

representative *n.*

resource *n.*

responsibility *n.*

resume *n.*

revenue *n.*

sacrifice *v.*

screen *v.*

outlet *n.*

participation *n.*

partner *n.*

passion *n.*

penetration *n.*

persuasive *adj.*

pilot *adj.*

pitch *v.* & *n.*

plant *n.*

potential *n.* & *adj.*

predict *v.*

presentation *n.*

primary *adj.*

process *n.*

producer *n.*

professional *n.*

promote *v.*

provincial *adj.*

psychological *adj.*

pure culture

qualification *n.*

quantity *n.*

recharge *v.*

reduce *v.*

rejection *n.*

reliability *n.*

rely *v.*

repeatedly *adv.*

resolution *n.*

respective *adj.*

responsive *adj.*

retail *n.*

revolutionize *v.*

Saudi Arabian

segment *n.*

selective *adj.*

self-development *n.*

semester *n.*

series *n.*

ship *v.*

sign *v.*

significant *n.*

similarity *n.*

simplify *vt.*

sledgehammer *n.*

slide *n.*

slot *n.*

sound *adj.*

specification *n.*

standardize *vt.*

static *adj.*

stem *v.*

stockholder *n.*

strategic *adj.*

subdivide *v.*

subordinate *adj.* & *v.*

subsidiary *adj.*

substantial *adj.*

substitute *v.*

superior *adj.*

supervisor *n.*

surpass *v.*

surround *n.*

survey *n.*

switch job

synchronize *v.*

target audience

technique *n.*

technology-intensive *adj.*

tendency *n.*

the executive committee

time-consuming *adj.*

trait *n.*

transaction *n.*

transfer *v.*

transmission *n.*

transplant *v.*

trillion *n.*

true species of humanity

turnover *n.*

unbearable *adj.*

universal *adj.*

unravel *vt.*

vacant *adj.*

valid *adj.*

value-added *adj.*

variation *n.*

variety *n.*

vary *v.*

versatile *adj.*

viewpoint *n.*

welfare *n.*

win-win *adj.*

wrestle *v.*

Appendix II Useful Expressions

a host of	apply to
at first glance	be concerned about
be concerned with	be far from
be relevant to	be supposed to do
carry out	come up with
communicate with	define . . . as . . .
differentiate . . . from	get in touch with
give birth to	in addition
in bad shape	in high demand
in terms of	interact with
keep pace with	lack of
map out	on the same wave-length
pay off	play/take a role/part in . . .
prohibit. . . from. . .	provide . . . with . . .
put emphasis on sth	put. . . into action
refer to	regardless of
resort to	see to. . .
set upon	specialize in
stay abreast of	tailor to
take on	take. . . action
up to	

Appendix Ⅲ Word Study

absorb *vt.*

adjust *v.*

advertising *n.* & *adj.*

anticipate *vt.*

assemble *v.*

assist *v.*

assure *v.*

boost *vt.*

come *v.*

conquer *v.*

contact *n.* & *vt.*

deliver *v.*

distribute *v.*

enforce *vt.*

establish *v.*

evolve *v.*

facilitate *v.*

finance *v.* & *n.*

foster *v.* & *adj.*

incorporate *v.*

intensify *v.*

involve *vt.*

lack *v.* & *n.*

maintain *vt.*

neglect *vt.* & *n.*

persuasive *adj.*

pose *v.*

preserve *v.* & *n.*

address *n.*

adopt *vt.*

affect *vt.*

appreciate *vt.*

assess *vt.*

associate *v.* & *n.*

audit *v.*

capture *v.*

conduct *v.*

consume *v.*

contract *n.* & *v.*

demonstrate *v.*

distribution *n.*

ensure *vt.*

estimate *v.* & *n.*

experiment *n.* & *v.*

feature *n.* & *v.*

formulate *vt.*

implement *v.*

indicate *v.*

interact *vi.*

issue *n.* & *v.*

launch *v.* & *n.*

manufacture *v.* & *n.*

negotiate *v.*

pilot *n.* , *v.* & *adj.*

predict *v.*

process *n.* & *v.*

proclaim *v.*

pursue *v.*

release *v.*

sacrifice *v.* & *n.*

simplify *vt.*

substitute *v.* & *n.*

vary *v.*

promote *v.*

reduce *v.*

respective *adj.*

sign *n.*

specialize *v.*

transfer *v.*